AFRICAN MARKET WOMEN

African Market Women
Seven Life Stories from Ghana

GRACIA CLARK

Indiana University Press
Bloomington and Indianapolis

This book is a publication of

Indiana University Press
601 North Morton Street
Bloomington, IN 47404-3797 USA

www.iupress.indiana.edu

Telephone orders	800-842-6796
Fax orders	812-855-7931
Orders by e-mail	iuporder@indiana.edu

⊗ The paper used in this publication meets the minimum requirements of the American
National Standard for Information Sciences—Permanence of Paper for Printed Library
Materials, ANSI Z39.48-1992.

Manufactured in the United States of America

Library of Congress Cataloging-in-Publication Data

Clark, Gracia.
      African market women : seven life stories from Ghana / Gracia Clark.
          p.   cm.
      Includes bibliographical references and index.
      ISBN 978-0-253-35417-4 (cloth : alk. paper) — ISBN 978-0-253-22154-4
(pbk. : alk. paper)
      1. Women, Ashanti—Ghana—Kumasi—Social conditions. 2. Women,
Ashanti—Ghana—Kumasi—Economic conditions. 3. Women, Akan—Ghana—
Kumasi—Social conditions. 4. Women, Akan—Ghana—Kumasi—Economic
conditions. 5. Women merchants—Ghana—Kumasi. 6. Market towns—
Ghana—Kumasi. 7. Kumasi (Ghana)—Social conditions. 8. Kumasi (Ghana)—
Economic conditions. 9. Kumasi (Ghana)—Politics and government. I. Title.
      DT507.C53   2009
      305.48'8963385—dc22
                                                                    2009025620

2   3   4   5   15   14   13   12   11

To Kumasi Central Market
Edwa Keseε paa ne no!
Nananom, yεda mo ase oo!

CONTENTS

Acknowledgments   vii

Introduction: Trading Lives   1

1. ABENAA ADIIYA
   Portrait: An Adventurer on the Road   30
   Story: Patience and Pleading   32

2. MAAME KESEWAA
   Portrait: A Quiet Saver   63
   Story: Someone Has Set Herself a Goal   65

3. MADAME ATAA
   Portrait: A Good Citizen   83
   Story: A Man Would Marry You Properly   84

4. AMMA POKUAA
   Portrait: A Market Daughter   113
   Story: All of Them Depend upon Me   115

5. AUNTIE AFRIYIE
   Portrait: A Shrewd Dealer   129
   Story: If You Have Wisdom, You Can Do Many Jobs   131

6. SISTER BURONYA
   Portrait: An International Observer   164
   Story: If I Had Money, I Would Go   165

7. MAAME NKRUMAH
   Portrait: A Grateful Sister   187
   Story: She Has Cared for Me and My Children   189

Conclusion: Little by Little   218

Appendix   247
Glossary   251
Notes   255
References   259
Index   263

ACKNOWLEDGMENTS

My thanks go out to hundreds of traders who have shared their lives with me over the years. In my own life, I thank Carmen Paz, my lifelong companion, who kept my life whole. My father, Kenneth Courtright Clark, taught me to delight in people, and my mother, Eleanor McKenna Clark, taught me to respect toughness.

These narratives were first recorded thanks to funding from a U.S. Fulbright Africa Regional Research Fellowship and a Social Science Research Commission grant. The Indiana University Office of the Vice President for Research funded subsequent summer followup research, and an IU sabbatical leave was critical for completing the first manuscript. The support and patience of a series of department chairs helped me survive the writing.

My partners in transcribing and translating all of the tapes were Mr. A. K. Yeboah (a retired Twi teacher at Prempeh College, Kumasi), Mr. Edward Asiedu (the choir director at Bantama Presbyterian Church), and Mrs. Mary Appiah (of the Kumasi Presbyterian Women's Fellowship). Mrs. Appiah also contributed greatly to the interview process with her contacts and life experience in Kumasi Central Market. Ms. Boadiccea Prempeh of the CEDEP Women's Forum (Kumasi) also provided valuable encouragement and advice.

My esteemed colleagues Beverly Stoeltje and Jean Allman were always ready with helpful comments, and they closely read parts of an earlier version. The late Susan Geiger also provided a rigorous and positive role model for life history work with African women. Rudith King (KNUST, Kumasi), the next-generation scholar of Kumasi Central Market, motivates me to continue my work. At Indiana University Press, editor Dee Mortensen and copyeditor Shoshanna Green were the ideal collaborators: enthusiastic, critical, and respectful.

AFRICAN MARKET WOMEN

INTRODUCTION

Trading Lives

The dramatic ups and downs of Ghana's economy over the last fifty years of the twentieth century have given the seven women traders who tell their stories here an indelible experience of the processes of global economic change. With an extraordinary vantage point as traders in one of West Africa's largest marketplaces, these ordinary women have become economic experts the hard way. They have had to assess the dangers and opportunities facing them on a daily and yearly basis in order to stay in business and provide for their families. Unlike Wall Street investment experts, who gamble with other people's money, they have had to bet with their own meager capital and credit. Some have read those processes well and prospered, while others have endured bankruptcy and despair. These stories reveal what they think has brought good and bad times to themselves and their community.

Since 1978, I have followed this dizzying roller coaster ride as closely as possible from the sidelines. A series of ethnographic projects relating to Kumasi Central Market brought me to share their living and working environment for periods ranging from two months to two years. The privilege of working with them has brought companionship and built my career as an anthropologist in academic and development work. As a white, college-educated foreigner I could never be like their other friends, but some of our relationships did build mutual affection and mutual responsibility.

My focus has shifted over those thirty years. I began by concentrating on their regional marketplace system, the networks that linked them to rural producers, their credit practices, and their commodity-based associations. I explored their strategies for combining family and work responsibilities and the effects of government price controls and several acute shortages—of food, gasoline, and foreign exchange. Meanwhile, Ghana's faithful implementation of neoliberal structural adjustment programs (SAPs) made it a much-publicized positive example for the World Bank, and then an instructive illustration of those programs' shortcomings (World Bank and United Nations Development Programme 1989; Clark and Manuh 1991).

As a group, these Kumasi Central Market women lived through a period that saw one socioeconomic transformation after another. The oldest among them heard stories of the precolonial trade networks that linked Kumasi to Europe and North Africa, and themselves experienced the adjustments to British colonial occupation in 1896. The next decades brought rapid urbanization, railways, road transport, and the shortages of two world wars. The youngest among the group grew up around the time Ghana gained its independence in 1957, proud to be the first African colony to shake off foreign rule.

Fierce rivalries between political parties exploded during the elections of the late 1950s and early 1960s, bringing violence right into Kumasi Central Market. A series of regime changes then shifted national economic policy between African socialism and free market capitalism, after which the country had more than a decade of military rule until electoral democracy was firmly reestablished after 1992. The rapid reversals in official regulations affecting markets (notably price controls and foreign exchange restrictions) repeatedly challenged traders to adapt their strategies to new conditions. Chronic inflation often doubled prices each year, lending drama and meaning to the long price lists that punctuate several of the stories told here. The same cloth that cost three hundred cedis in the 1970s would cost thirty thousand in the 1990s. Even after public policy stabilized in 1985, fluctuations in world price levels for cocoa and petroleum continued to rock the economic environment.

The pivotal mediating role played by Kumasi Central Market means that its supply, patronage, and price levels can serve as a gauge of economic conditions across a wide region. Most of the consumer goods destined for the 800,000 residents of Kumasi, Ghana's second largest city, pass through it. The forested Ashanti Region surrounding Kumasi enjoys generous endowments of gold, cocoa, and timber—still Ghana's three major exports. Kumasi Central Market also redistributes goods between ecological zones in a much broader catchment area, reaching from coastal ports through tropical forest to the dry savannah region (see map 1). Its traders cross national boundaries, to and from cities and rural farming areas in neighboring Burkina Faso, Togo, and Côte d'Ivoire.

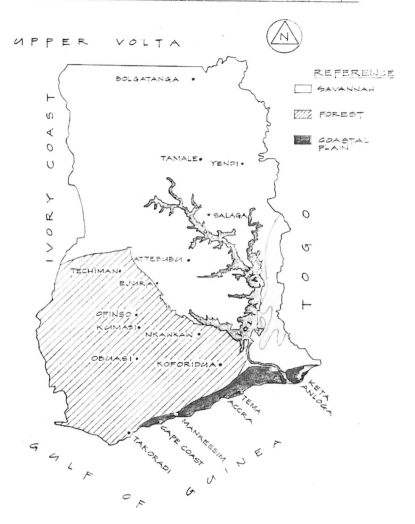

GHANA: VEGETATION ZONES WITH SOME IMPORTANT MARKETS

UPPER VOLTA

BOLGATANGA •

IVORY COAST

REFERENCE
☐ SAVANNAH
▨ FOREST
▰ COASTAL PLAIN

TAMALE • YENDI •

SALAGA •

ATTEBUBU •

TECHIMAN •

EJURA •

OFINSO •

KUMASI •

NKAWKAW •

OBUASI •

KOFORIDUA •

KETA ANLOGA

TEMA

ACCRA

MANKESSIM

CAPE COAST

TAKORADI •

GULF OF

TOGO

Map 1

KUMASI: CENTRAL MARKET AND SMALLER MARKETS · 1967

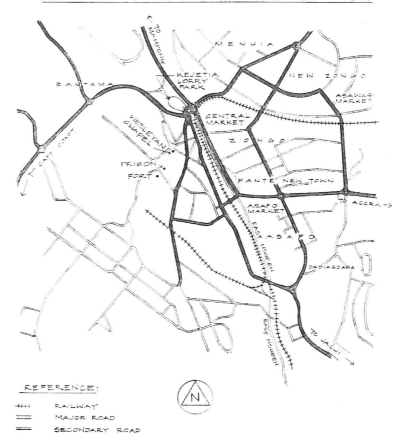

REFERENCE:

+++ RAILWAY
= MAJOR ROAD
= SECONDARY ROAD

Map 2

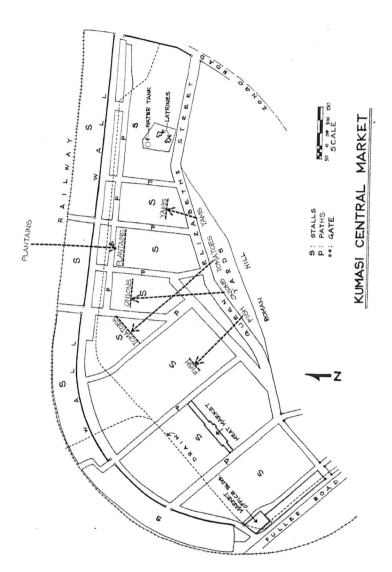

KUMASI CENTRAL MARKET

S : STALLS
P : PATHS
== : GATE

SCALE

Map 3

Within the city of Kumasi, the Central Market sits just between the northernmost terminus of Ghana's railway line and the central crossroads of the national highways (see map 2). Across the road is the Kejetia lorry park, which sends passenger buses and freight trucks to every corner of Ghana and beyond. Ringing the lines of retail stalls are a set of whole-sale yards for locally produced foodstuffs that coordinate large volumes of supplies for institutional buyers and smaller towns throughout the market's hinterland (see map 3). An estimated twenty thousand traders offer goods for resale and personal consumption to countless buyers in Kumasi Central Market six days a week (King 1999).

Women traders based in this market are well respected in the local community; in 1979, 70 percent of them were from the locally domi-nant Asante ethnic group. Asante is one of the thriving Akan cultures, whose matrilineal organization gives women authority and support within their birth families, regardless of their marital status. Gender ideals push both men and women to work in their own behalf, for an income they control (Clark 1999). Commercial activity was thoroughly integrated into Akan chiefship, lineage, and marital relations during the centuries-long history of international trade in the region. Marketplace trade is today associated with women across southern Ghana, although 30 percent of the traders in this market in 1979 were men. In Kumasi, as in other cities of southern Ghana, around 80 percent of the female population of working age is employed in trading.

Conforming to cultural and statistical norms unfortunately did not insulate these hardworking Akan mothers from public hostility and scapegoating in the twentieth century, generated by the economic trau-mas their communities endured. Plummeting terms of trade, meaning higher prices for imports and lower prices for exports, were combined with chronically high inflation rates that frequently topped 100 percent, doubling prices each year and pushing real incomes down to about 10 percent of 1960 levels. Escalating public rhetoric displaced blame onto market women, portraying them as useless parasites and "bloodthirsty human vampire bats" (*Daily Graphic* 1979). Such ideology had real material consequences: violent raids and demolitions by soldiers on the national level,[1] and quarrels over relative incomes and contributions to family expenses, on the most intimate level.

Another lightning rod for hostility was the fierce loyalty traders had to their commodity associations, which organize suppliers, wholesalers and retailers of the same commodity in a given location. Association leaders help traders resolve disputes and represent themselves to others in ways that support rather than prevent energetic competition for profits and business growth. When official attacks on traders peaked during times of stringent enforcement of price controls, all such commodity associations were treated as conspiracies to hoard goods and drive up prices, and their leaders were targeted as criminal bosses.

Ghana's SAP spared traders further physical attacks after 1985, but continued to discriminate against them. They were specifically disqualified from small business loans under Ghana's pioneering Programme of Action to Mitigate the Social Costs of Adjustment, soon replicated across Africa. Food riots and other populist reactions against the removal of price controls or subsidies erupted in more and more countries that had accepted SAPs. The World Bank began to modify its Washington Consensus to take into account this type of political backlash, but without changing its basic top-down dynamic.

Alternatives to conventional development approaches began to emerge, often calling for incorporating indigenous perspectives and priorities into the goals and implementation methods of international and national development efforts (G. Sen 1985; Escobar 1994). I could not furnish indigenous ideas directly, as a First World academic, but the market traders I knew definitely could. Their input was not being imagined, let alone included, in the design of either free market or communalist models of participation. It seemed that I could honor my relationship with them most effectively by promoting more respect for their indigenous economic knowledge.

Learning through Relationships

The enquiring relationship is especially central to ethnographic fieldwork, since intentional personal interaction, the core of participant observation, is an intrinsic part of all the various modes of interviewing that ethnographers use. Theories of situated knowledge assert that all knowledge is relational, and the underlying standpoints of the participants necessarily influence the generation of any knowledge, whether or not this influence is explicitly acknowledged (Haraway 1988; Wolf 1996). Ethnographers tend to attend more meticulously than scholars in other disciplines to the concrete particulars of the relationship, and contemporary ethnographers accept that readers need to know the relational basis of a research project in order to interpret its results accurately.

Life history interviews commonly create an intense relationship between the narrator and the recorder, because of their length and depth and because of the intimate topics that may be included. They both require and create a considerable degree of trust and commitment on both sides, which the critical reader needs to verify. Published life narratives therefore show a degree of reflexivity above the average for academic work in other genres. Geiger pioneered these insights in relation to oral history work in an influential article, and her own later book models an exemplary balance (Geiger 1986, 1997).

A continuing debate over the appropriate level of reflexivity considers it on ethical, political, and aesthetic grounds. The challenge is to present enough of the work's relational context (including the intellectual and personal history of the recorder) to allow it to be rigorously scrutinized, without displacing the narrator from center stage and further marginalizing that voice (Wolf 1996). With this concern in mind, this book places the more reflexive passages in this introduction and the shorter introductions to each narrator's story, but presents the seven stories largely without editorial interruption.

Like many other life history projects, this one began after I had already completed earlier ethnographic work that had brought me to Kumasi several times for a total of nearly five years. By 1994, when I began recording these stories, I had already been working in and around the market for fifteen years. My thesis research (1978–80) relied heavily on participant observation, sitting beside market traders while they were in the market and discussing the decisions and events we had both seen. To round out my sense of traders' lives and work, I followed them to their Kumasi homes to see how they organized their domestic lives, and I lived alongside several traders in a multifamily house near the market. I accompanied a smaller number of traders out to their buying locations, riding on rickety buses and trucks to remote farming villages, small-town markets, factories, flour mills, and coastal ports. The interviews done then used both more and less structured methods, including a survey of Kumasi Central Market and oral histories of most commodity groups. Searches of national and royal archives garnered documents covering some of the same time periods as these life stories.

Consulting for several development agencies in the 1980s brought me to consider Ghana's agricultural marketing from the farmer's viewpoint again, though without the same opportunity for extended co-residence. On return visits to Kumasi, I updated my sense of traders' priorities and concerns, along with their trading conditions. They sometimes requested me to present their ideas to policymakers, though I made clear that my influence was very limited. The personal contacts and background information I had accumulated in all this previous research turned out to be vital when I recruited life story narrators in 1994 and interpreted their stories. In addition, my familiarity with conventional development rhetoric might help me translate their stories into language with more leverage in current policy debates. My relationship with traders and my relationship with multinational agencies thus opened a channel for making these women's insights available to a wider public.

Narrative Traditions

I knew that market traders thought hard about the economic processes they saw in daily life, but my first efforts at collecting their ideas were frustrating. For example, they often complained that life had become very hard in Ghana, but when I asked directly what made times so hard, they replied with formulas like "God only knows." I had to think hard myself about how they were comfortable presenting complex ideas in order to avoid distorting their intended meanings. Meanwhile, gathering materials with which to teach my growing repertoire of Africa-related courses brought to my attention valuable scholarship on Asante narrative traditions and on life histories in general.

When Asante people want to debate important community decisions or teach moral and philosophical values, they turn to one or more of the forms of narrative in which they have been trained since childhood (Obeng and Stoeltje 2002). Every time children go on an errand or adults pay a visit, they are asked on arrival to present their *ɔkwansu*, the story of their trip. This narrative should not be interrupted. It starts with the circumstances that led up to their making the journey and ends with their arrival. Relatives and neighbors judge a child's maturity and intelligence by the coherence of the *ɔkwansu*. The story also sets the stage for any subsequent request by describing the circumstances which created the need for it. Ideally, it should alert listeners to the intended request before it is voiced explicitly, so that they can be ready with a response or an alternative solution.

The world-renowned Ananse stories (*Anansesɛm*) also convey moral and pragmatic wisdom in narrative form. They feature Ananse the spider and his family and neighbors, a familiar cast of anthropomorphic animal characters whose misadventures still amuse and instruct both children and adults. Other folktales (often also involving specific animals as characters) narrate the events that have been condensed into Asante proverbs. I have heard Kumasi children showing off to each other by demonstrating how many proverbs they know and can explain by telling the associated stories. Knowledge of these stories and proverbs still constitutes real social capital for Asante.

The most eloquent and sophisticated orators, in venues such as the Asante royal palace and its court hearings, argue by referring to proverbs that support their interpretation of the case or issue at hand (Yankah 1995; Stoeltje 2000). The ability to correctly interpret and deploy esoteric proverbs qualifies court elders to participate in these high-level debates. More ignorant bystanders cannot understand these references, and so cannot even report the proceedings in detail.

The ideal style in all these genres is not didactic but indirect, with listeners expected to draw the appropriate conclusion themselves. Telling an adult directly the moral of a story or proverb insults his intelligence and experience. For example, when my Twi teacher, Mr. A. K. Yeboah, suggested we had covered enough grammar to benefit more from working on a story, he presented one as a story about why chickens have no ears and why they steal corn. During a famine, a mother hen bargained hard with a fox for corn to feed her chicks. After selling him their ears one by one, she decided they had paid enough to be entitled to any corn they could find. Only later did I realize the story he had selected was precisely relevant to my research on growing poverty and inequality under free market policies, and to economists' theories of entitlement (A. Sen 1981; Clark and Manuh 1991). The women whose stories are included in this book gave more explicit explanations than usual, perhaps in response to my own ignorance and that of the imagined audience overseas. But for the most part we are still left to figure out their meaning for ourselves, inevitably adapting it to our own circumstances and level of understanding.

Life histories worked well in my classes to engage the interest of novice students and to convey complex relationships clearly, memorably, and convincingly. This suggested that this narrative-based methodology might also be well suited to my two goals of identifying local economic agendas and presenting them persuasively. Feminist scholars have deployed life stories with great effect to foreground submerged voices and make scholarly materials more accessible and engaging (Personal Narratives Group 1989; Patai 1991; Behar 1993). Power differentials between narrator and researcher still infuse the knowledge generated, but their effects in a one-on-one interaction can be more explicitly perceived and addressed. Negotiations with individual narrators could legitimately accommodate diverse perspectives, including my own, on a more equal footing.

By the 1990s, changing political conditions in Ghana also enabled me to focus more strongly on individuals. In the 1970s and 1980s, market women repeatedly faced confiscations, demolitions, beatings, and other expressions of hostility; their commercial practices, formerly accepted, were now not only made illegal, but judged so retroactively. While I had collected many personal stories, portraying recognizable individuals in my first book had seemed too risky (Clark 1994). Such attacks had gradually subsided after 1985, when a structural adjustment program had been adopted. Commercial deregulation had remained in place for ten years by 1994, making potential narrators more confident about the idea of publishing their life histories.

Life history interviews are relatively undirected, so I hoped to find clues to each narrator's conceptual framework by paying close attention to what topics she considered important enough to address, and what other issues brought them to mind. The significance to narrators of various aspects of economic change can be gauged by how often they are mentioned in descriptions of good and bad times, and in what context. Passages explaining narrators' personal choices give a revealing perspective on their moral priorities. This is true even if the narrators do not depict their decisionmaking processes strictly accurately, since denials and exaggerations still represent what they believe their audiences will find plausible and defensible. Gender takes its place alongside ethnicity, class, community, and many other identities as each narrator weaves them together. Since they are not thrust into the discourse by an outside researcher, as would be done by a questionnaire, the importance of these identities becomes subject to dialogue and empirical analysis, not just theoretical assertion.

Interviewing Strategies

To learn as much as possible from the structure and rhetoric used in these narratives, I needed to intervene as little as possible. This mandate paradoxically required me to consciously arrange the interviews so as to encourage the participants to speak at length and to follow their thoughts to a natural finish. Their bustling market stalls and crowded homes meant frequent interruptions that made continuous narratives impossible. The interactive pattern of my earlier research, when I had spent most of my time in the market and fitted in my questions around their work routines, had to be replaced by more formal interview sessions at my house. I even chose to live in a bungalow with a large yard, to provide a quiet environment for tape recording. It felt very different from my previous room in a multistory house, whose courtyard had introduced me to the dynamics of shared kitchens and bathrooms and hosted instructive incidents of conflict and mutual aid.

Market women could not easily pry themselves away for an hour or two from their many responsibilities for trading, housework, and family ceremonies. Some weeks I spent more time nagging traders for appointments than interviewing them. Bringing them to my living room reminded me uncomfortably of colonial "verandah ethnography," as did the crumbling colonial relic where I lived, too far from the market to walk there. The traders, on the other hand, often remarked that they appreciated the chance to sit quietly with their Fanta and cookies and tell stories, all too rare an interlude in their busy urban lives. One close friend promptly fell asleep each time, as soon as she settled down on the sofa. Several also remarked that these genteel surroundings were much more appropriate to my mature status as a university teacher than was the bustle of the market, as was the car I bought to bring them home.

My initial determinedly nondirective interviewing, however, made a number of them uncomfortable. By the more participative norms of Asante storytelling and ordinary conversation, my unusual passivity and frequent silences counted as deviant. In a few of the first interviews, the narrators felt compelled to check whether I was distracted, bored, or even annoyed, because of my strange lack of comment. To minimize this disruptive effect, I developed a repertoire of sounds, noncommittal but positive, that did not observably push them either to change the subject or to pursue it. I learned to interject such sounds frequently to encourage the speakers to continue.

It took longer to dislodge my assumption that my personal agenda must not be disclosed before the interview, for fear of inadvertently suggesting topics and formats that would obscure those of the narrator. When explaining the project to potential narrators, I took care to be vague about what I hoped to learn. Evidently some Platonic ideal of the truly transparent narrative still lurked in my mental shadows long after I had stopped endorsing it intellectually. The traders knew better and insisted I explain my actual intentions. Those narrators I had already worked with for years understood my underlying interests, probably better than I did, and our prior shared experiences likely were already shaping their choice of topics. The other half of the narrators, who had just met me, had done so through the traders who did know me or through my research assistant, Mrs. Mary Appiah, who had long worked in the market. These contacts usually vouched for my character by describing my past habits and my present intentions. My attempts at concealment only left more room for these second-hand reports and for unspoken speculation.

After a few months, I developed a more honest opening routine that included a compressed version of my underlying goals in undertaking life history work. Since they had seen so much economic change in their lives, I said, their life histories would contain some valuable information about how times had become so hard and what might make them better. This new approach acknowledged that I had arranged the recording sessions for a purpose, and I was asking them to help me accomplish that purpose. It provided a plausible reason why I wanted to know what they thought was important and did not have a list of topics or a favored format in mind. After this opening, I answered their questions as directly as I could. This approach also placed my project explanation, like the culturally expected *ɔkwansu,* as the normal opening stage of a personal request. They felt in a better position to decide what they wanted to say, because they could interpret my attempts to communicate rather than my attempts to avoid communicating.

The interviewing procedures that resulted from this tacit negotiation process apparently worked well enough that the narrators could in practice address the topics they felt were most important. Their life stories patently did not follow a standard format, such as a chronological pattern, that I may have inadvertently suggested. Striking variations between the stories, along with some narrators' persistence on topics that made me uncomfortable, reassured me that they had kept control of their own narratives.

One good example are the highly moralistic passages bemoaning teen pregnancy, found in the stories by Maame Nkrumah, Madame Ataa, and Amma Pokuaa. These certainly put me off at first, probably because they reminded me of moralistic discourses in the United States on the same subject, but they were clearly important to these women. As my initial reaction wore off, I perceived the instructive differences between these stories and the U.S. versions. While these narrators did strongly condemn the girls' precocious sexual activity, sexual morality was not their primary concern. They spent far more time bemoaning the economic consequences of premature parenthood than any lasting stigma or shame. Paying close attention thus opened a window onto the very intimate intertwining of sex and gender with economic issues of family survival in Asante cultural values. These passages may have harked back to the homily given at the ceremony marking an Asante girl's first menstruation by an exemplary woman sponsor, a rare and prestigious occasion for direct moral exhortation.

My recording the interviews seemed not to intimidate most of those who agreed to participate, and seemed to inspire or liberate some of them. Those whom I knew well from the market could assess the limits of my linguistic skills quite accurately. Now they could let loose, freely using more colloquial or allusive language, because they knew I could get the difficult passages explained to me later by the transcription assistants. As my skills improved under the welcome challenge of the interview sessions, perhaps they felt more confident that I could understand more complex constructions.

The interviews had some autonomy as a performance event, and also as a cottage industry that made and processed tapes. At this time cassette tapes were familiar to Kumasi residents; relatives overseas frequently mailed them tapes they had recorded, full of greetings, stories, and pleas for help. The interview was not a private moment between the narrator and me, but was also mediated by my research assistants and the imagined reader overseas.

Not all narrators were equally comfortable, and those I knew best were not necessarily the most at ease in this new context. I had known one trader for years in the market, where she was a flamboyant extrovert fond of verbal play, and I expected a vivid tale when she agreed to tell me her story. Her terse, mumbled remarks frustrated both of us, but expanded only slightly when I even tried direct questions on basic life stages such as childhood and motherhood. Nor were all the speakers equally expressive or skilled storytellers. One trader I knew only slightly slipped easily into an eloquent, elegant style she must surely have practiced in other contexts. The narratives selected for full-length publication here are longer and more expressive than most, and they also address some common themes more substantially than others did.

Shared Themes

The two most conspicuous concerns in these stories are family advancement and business expansion. Each goal is considered the primary reason to strive for the other, but also appears as the chief obstacle to achieving the other. Children's school fees, clothes, and medical expenses threaten to drain trading capital, but well-educated, healthy, and loyal children remain the best long-term economic security. The stories portray vividly the constant competition between these two mandates for market women's time and money. But they also describe the triumphs possible when both agendas reinforce each other. The phrase "little by little," a constant refrain, signals the unremitting effort needed to pull ahead while maintaining the balance between them.

Reliable family relationships create favorable conditions for business growth, and vice versa. Success in both spheres entails building long-term relations with both the partners we choose and those we do not choose, as our relatives and business colleagues. Competition is expected and individual wealth applauded at home as in the market, but only when fellow family members and colleagues also benefit. Elders must be consulted and mutual survival supported. For example, early pregnancy is denounced for landing economic burdens not just on the girl herself,

but also on her mother (Clark 2001b). Receiving goods on credit likewise ranks as exploitation when only the borrower profits, but otherwise
as a concession to the customer. Lack of respect for people is the central
vice shared by antisocial activities in both spheres.

The time-honored goal of building a house supplies another popular theme that unites affective and economic motivations. Building a
house is a good investment and also keeps the builder's name alive in the
family, often literally by inscribing it above the front door. More than
one storyteller remarks that those who now build houses or have more
capital had relatives who contributed directly or indirectly to their capital. Inheritances and remittances from abroad laid many house foundations, but on a smaller scale reliable child support was still a major asset.
Finding a good husband and sending a child or sibling abroad were other
major concerns.

The stories about marriage are rich in detail about their motives and
aspirations. The narrators may endorse idealized models for marriage, but
their own marital careers and those of close relatives demonstrate many
alternatives to the recommended pattern. They describe various routes
to finding a partner (including arranged marriages), reasons for choos-
ing and leaving partners, and the consequences of divorce and widow-
hood. On the other hand, a few narrators barely mentioned their own
marriages.

Relations with peers in the market also carry a heavy emotional and
economic weight, analogous to that of kinship. Traders commonly refer
to their colleagues (who are also their main competitors) as **sisters**,[2] and
to their adult subordinates as children. They speak of their commodity
group leader as a mother looking after her children. Customer relations can also be highly charged with feelings of loyalty and betrayal.
Managing credit relationships took skills not every trader could muster, generating sagas of debt catastrophe as well as tales of rescue and
benevolence.

Given the global reputation for success of Ghana's SAP, it was interesting that none of these women mentioned it by name. Instead, they spoke
about its prominent features: currency devaluation, deregulation of trade,
massive civil service layoffs, and higher fees for public services to balance
the budget. The sharpest change they noted was the abrupt suspension

of price controls in 1983. These controls had targeted trade in cloth and imports since independence but had become broader and more strictly enforced over the decades. The stories here describe repeated raids and evasions, but also how the narrators suffered from the rising black market prices over the same period and the rapid currency devaluation that followed. Price controls were anathema to free market neoliberals in the World Bank, who made their immediate cancellation a primary condition of the rescue package, along with credit restraint, higher service fees, and public-sector retrenchment. The capital and income crunch that resulted forced as many commodity changes and reduced the scale of business of as many traders as had the former years of price control raids.

Two new subjects, religion and emigration, appear obsessively in several accounts as expressions of despair over local economic prospects. Sending at least one child overseas was a goal shared by many parents (and many children who hoped to go), and the subject of endless strategizing and risk-taking. Salvation can easily seem more assured than access to the elusive visa giving access to that other world overseas. Christian beliefs have become a major preoccupation in more and more Ghanaian lives (Meyer 1999). End-time cosmologies based on the Book of Revelation provide a coherent explanation for the sorry state of the country and come with a readily available solution—the second coming of Jesus. Fervent believers are assured a favorable outcome for themselves, and active prayer at least maintains their sense of agency when mounting frustrations about commercial constraints render it apparently useless to strive for worldly success. From the outside it is easy to ridicule both these obsessions as unrealistic; my job here is to present how realistic they felt to the women who spoke of them with such conviction.

My choice of life history methodology would seem to move the task of self-representation automatically to center stage, but individuals responded very differently to this invitation to focus on themselves. The narrators position themselves differently within their stories as leaders, observers, participants, or victims. This sets up interesting comparisons between their analyses of the problems of society at large and their complaints about their own problems. Even when the two contradict each other, both reflect beliefs about the usual causation of positive or negative outcomes.

Editing Choices

A successful transition from oral to written narrative requires some editing, if only because the fragmentary sentences and repetitions that add emphasis to an oral presentation will distract a reader. The wide range of variation among these narratives reflects not only their narrators' different personalities, but also their different ideas about the appropriate tone to take in storytelling. The enthusiastic self-promotion of Auntie Afriyie balances the more impersonal approach Madame Ataa takes to describing community life as she saw it. Maame Kesewaa sometimes turns self-deprecating, reflecting "if only I had known," while at other times she gleefully explains that she did know exactly what to do.

I had to carefully weigh the impact of my editing decisions on the accuracy and accessibility of the published narratives, for fear of negating the very reasons life stories are so effective. I have edited these interviews with the lightest hand I felt was consistent with general readability, to allow readers to learn from the expressive choices the narrators made.

Some speakers seem more concerned than others to tell an entertaining or gripping tale. Their topical and stylistic choices reflect Asante verbal aesthetics and local humor. Sister Buronya and Maame Kesewaa took an ironic tone that skewered the foibles of relatives and colleagues as effectively as an *Anansesɛm*. Asante comedic traditions also include the concert party (a kind of traveling musical theater), standup comedians at the Cultural Center in Kumasi, and Twi sitcoms on national public television (Cole 2001). Madame Ataa used sharp sarcasm to express her cynical views of popular concepts of progress or modernization. Amma Pokuaa and Abenaa Adiiya turned to melodrama or pathos to underline their misfortunes, in highly emotional accounts that hit even harder than the dramatic events they lived through.

The structure of these narratives tells its own story about how these speakers imagine the reader learning their intended lesson. Several stories return repeatedly to their central themes over the length of the narrative, even seeming disorganized or disjointed. By arranging these themes in different ways in successive sequences, they gradually and indirectly guide the reader to draw complex connections between them. Since an Asante narrator expects the listener to figure out such connections without direct prompting, the cumulative momentum of this pattern of argumentation makes sense and complements the didactic statements placed at intervals within it. This iterative rhetorical path creates a spiral logic that mimics and provokes the lived intellectual process.

When I first returned to Kumasi after recording these stories, I brought back transcripts and translations and invited the narrators to participate in the editing process by commenting on the Twi transcripts, which were read aloud to them. It soon became clear that they were only interested in confirming the accuracy of the transcripts. Only the two youngest narrators asked to delete one incident each, which they thought might offend family members. I accepted this apparent indifference with more grace as I began to realize how thoroughly they had already edited their oral presentations to their own satisfaction. As mature Asante women, they constantly practice placing implicit messages in oral narratives in many important contexts, and they took responsibility for saying what was appropriate to the audience the first time. At the same time, their stance challenged me to take responsibility for my own work, by defining the transformation from an oral to a written medium as my job. Their trust in my honest intentions and my competence to implement them remains a cherished compliment, although my pleasure at it is tempered with enough realism about my abilities and character that I hope the inevitable limitations will not be felt as a betrayal.

The degree to which questions from myself and my interview assistant appear in the edited narratives reflects a compromise. Including them can break the momentum of the argument and distract attention away from the narrator herself, but deleting all dialogue can obscure significant power dynamics of narration, recording, and translation. In some published cases a dialogic presentation succeeds brilliantly, allowing a more multilayered interpretation of the subject matter to emerge (Mbilinyi 1989). In another, erasing these dialogues fed controversy over who initiated topics and controlled their sequence, and who possibly distorted major issues (Menchú 1984). I decided upon a middle path, preserving the dialogic content at moments of contestation over its direction or over the meaning of particular episodes. At these points, the other speakers' words appear in italics, attributed to my interview assistant Mrs. Mary Appiah (noted as MA) or myself (noted as GC).

Most of the time, when the narrative flows smoothly without them, our questions are edited out.

Translation Issues

In this volume, as in so many others, the imperfect filter of language translation is also a necessary step to reach a wider audience. A literal translation would not be accurate in effect, because its awkwardness would misrepresent the fluency of the original speech. One that distanced the reader by sounding too exotic or discouraged readers because it was difficult to follow would defeat the purpose of bringing traders' insights more powerfully into focus. I have tried to strike a balance between transmitting an accurate impression of their narrative skill and transmitting accurately the insights inscribed in their Twi word usages and turns of phrase.

Capturing the nuances of form and expression was only possible through the efforts of the reliable and gifted research assistants I was able to hire to transcribe and translate the taped interviews. Mrs. Mary Appiah, who also assisted in conducting the interviews, and Mr. K. Asiedu acquired their Twi literacy in the schools of the Presbyterian Church of Ghana. Mr. A. K. Yeboah had studied Twi to the college level and taught Twi for many years at Asanteman Secondary School before retiring to work as a consultant teacher. Younger applicants for the work had computer skills but could not match their fluency and accuracy in written Twi. They patiently wrote the original Twi interviews out in longhand and then translated that transcript into formal English word for word. They showed incredible patience in deciphering barely audible passages in consultation with each other.

To better capture the vivid forcefulness of the original oral performances, I consulted their Twi and English versions to produce a more colloquial English translation that flows with some of the smoothness and naturalness of the original Twi. This leaves me completely responsible for the final wording, rather than my three translators. In the appendix, readers can evaluate the editing process by comparing parallel passages from all three versions. The tapes, transcripts, and translations remain available on request for future linguists to analyze.

The raw transcripts of these interviews were dotted with bursts of repetition of phrases or whole sentences, either in immediate succession or after a short interval, that were clearly a deliberate rhetorical device. Sometimes the effect seemed musical or rhythmical, like a refrain. In many cases I abbreviated these chains of repetition because they lose their intended effect in written form. In Twi, they also harmonize with other repetitive structures within the language. Reduplication is a prominent grammatical feature of Akan languages, used to express continuation over time and to replace English adverbs like "very." English (written or oral) uses repetition much more sparingly, so preserving this feature intact made the speakers sound defensive or confused. I have therefore retained it sparingly, when the emphasis seemed most critical.

Another judgment call concerned the frequent interjections of phrases that refer to the listener. Because they add so much interactive flavor to the narratives, I was reluctant to remove all instances of "you see?" (*wahu?*) and "do you understand?" (*woate asɛɛ?*). Instead, I left them in Twi, in order to signal how commonplace such usage is in Twi. Another very common phase, "it means" (*kyerɛ sɛ*), can be interjected much like the English phrase "I mean," but that carries an unfortunate connotation of witlessness in the United States. One narrator used it so often that leaving at least one in each line made her seem ridiculous. In this case I decided to omit most of the interjections and translate only those that formed part of a normal sentence. Conversely, simply translating the interjection "Father!" (*Agya!*) into English conveyed little of its wide range of meanings. These include something like the stereotypical Italian *Mamma mia,* but with many other gradations of appeal or surprise.

The narrators themselves sprinkled some English words into their Twi speech, notably "time" and "civilization." Kumasi residents are notorious for using relatively many English words, especially kin terms like "papa," "maame" (the local spelling of the loan word "mama"), "sister," and "auntie." Words that were originally in English are shown in **boldface**, to distinguish them from translations from Twi. Also, Ghanaians give some English words a markedly different meaning or connotation than they have in the U.S. The Twi equivalents cover a wider range of collateral relatives; for example, *ɛna* refers correctly to both one's mother and her sisters. In practice, the English terms are used much more casually as fictive kin terms for acquaintances of appropriate age and gender, though they are also widely used for immediate relatives. Any adult man or woman can be politely called Papa or Maame, and one's own mother might be usually called Auntie. By contrast, the Twi term *ɛna* is rarely used loosely, but only for those in the appropriate relationship. English words with distinctive usages appear in the glossary together with Twi words, for easy reference.

Both English and Twi terms related to development concepts will receive special attention, including the noun *anibue* ("eye-opening" or "enlightenment") and the verbs *kɔ so* and *kɔ w'anim* ("to move on or get ahead," hence "progress"). The colonial transplant "civilization," like other English loan words, carries different meanings and connotations to the localized ear and the novice reader, and thus requires discreet annotation to prevent misunderstanding (Chernoff 2004). Signs of the opposite process, degeneration, were often condemned as *basabasa*. In translation of such terms here, I have looked for an English word with a similar meaning in the specific context, while noting the original Twi used.

The same warning applies to the events and comparisons within the narratives. A life history can appear deceptively unmediated and self-explanatory, but readers actually interpret it in relation to their pre-existing knowledge. It draws its listener in through an identification with the narrator that creates complicity and starts to build an imagined community (Behar 1993). By the same process, the "false intimacy" of the genre intensifies the danger of appropriation and exoticization by glossing over any power differences existing between narrator, recorder, and other mediators (Ong 1988). The harmful stereotypes of African women widely promulgated in textbooks and public media make such interpretations less likely to be accurate, although they may seem to be clear and obvious because they are based on past experience. To disarm these learned assumptions and allow a life history to have full impact on a more general public, the background information that follows needs to address the most common misconceptions directly, while outlining the basic framework of economic, cultural, and political institutions.

Historical Context

Life histories preserve and highlight the uniqueness of individual perspectives and personal agency, as these interact with the wider sweep of historical events and social structures. They can empower narrators without the literacy or time to write an autobiography, by inserting their life experiences and insights into scholarly and political discussions that do not otherwise respect them. First-person stories are used in many arenas to compel a reluctant audience of policymakers, voters, or the like to listen. Their nonconfrontational appeal can sidestep stereotypes and platitudes, making them especially useful in addressing sensitive topics like race and poverty. They can condense the complex combination of many social forces into a coherent, digestible story, just as people need to combine many disparate strands in living their daily lives.

Simply by showcasing the agency of African women, these stories contradict one of the most pervasive stereotypes about them, that they are passive victims. These market women are shrewd, determined fighters; many need to scramble to feed their families each day, and the more successful keep scrambling to get as far ahead as they can. Despite their best efforts, some fail; personal tragedies and crushing economic pressures conspire to defeat them. They need not be passive to be victims of the tall odds stacked against them as Africans, as women, and as members of the world's poor majority.

Another stereotype assumes that European conquest brought in commerce: that it was foreign to African communities, whose communalist traditional cultures had no experience of producing for sale or trading for individual profit. On the contrary, West Africa as a region has participated in international trade since before Roman times, as an anchor of the trans-Sahara caravan routes linking it to the Mediterranean world (Hopkins 1973). Akan peoples lived on the southern edge of these savannah networks, providing gold, kola, and slaves that reached Europe through North Africa throughout the Middle Ages. By 1490, the Portuguese were making regular trading voyages along the West African coast to Elmina, in present-day Ghana, and this route served as Columbus's training run before he set out for the New World (van Dantzig 1980). Dutch and English traders soon joined them, in companies whose trading profits went to fund the birth of the capitalist world economy in Europe.

Early Arab and European traders' accounts record how Akan cultural and political institutions grew up taking this commercial involvement for granted (Marees [1602] 1987). Local chiefs were expected to attract trade to their towns and negotiated favorable intermediary roles for local citizens. Neighbors who earned riches through trade were acclaimed, not rejected, although their political influence was carefully controlled. Coastal chiefs awarded wealthy traders special titles, but also tapped their wealth and connections for political ends.

Asante was a relatively young inland Akan political unit, founded around 1680 to control major trade routes linking the savannah cara-van towns to the coast (McCaskie 2000). It organized within the deep forest territory already known for gold and kola (Hopkins 1973). The *Asantehene* and *Asantehemma,* its male and female chiefs, regulated mar-ket access, collected taxes at borders, gave out loans to prominent trad-ers, and traded directly through designated court officials (Wilks 1975). Far from being unprepared for the experience of globalization, Asante tend to be more sophisticated about its dynamics and contradictions than many U.S. citizens are.

A more subtle but persistent stereotype holds that African women have traditionally produced only for family use, leaving cash crops and the handling of money to the male head of household. In Asante, both men and women historically planted crops intended for sale and grew food for home consumption. The Asante lineage assumes that every adult member has an independent cash income, for example when it collects per capita assessments for shared expenses like funerals and court cases. Women start paying their shares when they have children, while men wait until they marry. Women pay half the assessment men do, to allow for the money and time they spend on their children. Less formal contributions, also monetary, mark the relationships between husband and wife or between young adults and their elderly parents and other relatives.

In this matrilineal system, children belong to the mother's lineage whether or not she marries or divorces, and so they represent her major contribution to it. A ceremony at each girl's first menstruation, called the *bragɔrɔ,* formally introduced her to her ancestors and her commu-nity and legitimated her fertility (Sarpong 1977). Since puberty arrived later before the twentieth century, usually after age sixteen, she was then ready to marry. Today the ceremony is usually abbreviated or omitted, but for the eldest narrators included here it was the high point of their young lives. Younger women still rely heavily on their maternal uncles and brothers, while hoping to bear girls to continue their lineage name. Under Asante matrilineal rules, the boys will inherit property from their maternal uncles rather than their fathers (Rattray 1923).

The lineage's pressure to have children can be intense. One woman from an old and wealthy Kumasi lineage told me her grandmother had offered to sign over all her property to her if she would drop out of secondary school and start having children immediately. She was the only granddaughter in the senior branch of their lineage (descendants of the eldest sister), so all its reproductive hopes rested on her performance. As a young woman she had insisted on completing university, but agreed to marry and have children while she did so, with abundant home help from the lineage.

Romanticization of matriliny and dual-sex systems in West Africa by some feminists also distorts a clear understanding of gender dynamics in Asante (Afonja 1986). Male and female chiefs share power at each level of the hierarchy, but male elders pack the councils of elders and the powerful court bureaucracy (Wilks 1975). Matriliny gives women important safeguards, but senior men can dominate decision making within the lineage to women's disadvantage. Women get preferential access to lineage land to raise food for their children, but brothers are favored over their sisters for access to land for cocoa plantations and capital for business investment (Mikell 1989). Within marriage, husbands get deference and domestic services in return for giving wives a monetary allowance for their own meals, called chop money. Mothers' primary financial responsibility for feeding their children legitimizes their right and duty to work, but it also siphons off most of their income, since rising food prices constitute the largest budget item for the average household.

Asante culture also offers exceptions to many generalizations or assumptions about the nuclear family household. The fundamental and permanent pair in the Asante kinship system is a brother and sister, not a husband and wife. In the classic idealized village setting, both spouses continue living in their family houses as they did before marriage (Rattray 1923). The wife cooks for her husband at her home, then bathes and packs his dinner into an attractive dish before taking it to him and spending the night with him. As children arrive they live with their mother and her own mother and siblings, but they also run in and out of their father's house at will. Young boys grow up with two or more male role models available—their fathers, their maternal uncles, and their older brothers. Men should and do contribute to the support of their children, but they have more permanent responsibility for their sisters' children, who will eventually revere them as ancestors.

For many decades, Christian education and Western romantic imagery have promoted companionate marriage and the dominance of the husband and father in the Asante home, with some success. These lifestyles carry more prestige, but resistance to them remains strong because of lineage loyalties. Even when people migrate to large cities like Kumasi and rent rooms, this duolocal residence pattern persists. About 70 percent of the traders I surveyed in 1979 were married, but only two-thirds of those lived with their husbands (Clark 1994). The desire for individual independence is also powerful, and frequent examples of formal and informal polygyny feed women's reluctance to commit to joint marital property (Mikell 1989).

Joint bank accounts seem unbelievably exotic and dangerous to Asante women, and likewise West African women traders' autonomy has fascinated European visitors for centuries because it contradicts European gender norms about public and private spheres and male rights in marriage. Throughout the forest and coastal zones of West Africa, whether communities are patrilineal or matrilineal, they recognize the right of married women to earn and control an independent income and their right to trade in public places. Pieter de Marees carefully noted that Elmina men and women sold different commodities, ending with a rosy pastoral image:

> These women are very eager traders; they are so industrious in their trade that they come here every day, walking five, some of them even six miles to the place where they do their trade, laden like Asses; she carries her child tied to her back and in addition a heavy load of fruits or millet on her head. Laden in this way they come to market and in turn buy Fish to carry home. . . . These women go together in three or four pairs and are very merry and happy on the way; for they usually sing as they walk, and greatly enjoy themselves on the road. (Marees [1602] 1987, 64)

Three centuries later, a British colonial observer found Accra market women more unsettling, perhaps because European ideals of domesticity had changed by then.

> Strong as buffaloes, large-boned, strident, gaily dressed in patterned clothes with little jackets, either plump and soft as marshmallows or else lean as old leather, their faces look imperious and uncom-

pliant, like the faces of cattle-dealers in English country towns.
(Huxley 1954, 79)

Hewing to another stereotype, that African cultures are "traditional"
and unchanging, analysts like Little (1973) assumed that women pre-
dominated in West African market trade because they always had. Asante
history, however, displays a complex division of labor by gender, one that
adjusted to other labor force constraints and opportunities. Akan men
and women have both been active farmers and traders, with men pre-
dominating in long-distance trade before colonial conquest. Afterward,
British firms took over the more lucrative higher levels of import and
export trade. Planting cocoa for export then lured Akan men out of trading in the 1910s and 1920s by offering them larger incomes. Asante men
could ask for lineage land and count on wives to feed their children while
the cocoa matured. Lacking these structural supports, Asante women
rarely established large cocoa farms (Okali 1983; Mikell 1989).

Market trading promised women immediate income, and markets
were expanding rapidly during the same period. In southern Ghanaian
cities like Accra and Kumasi, census figures soon reported about 80 percent of the adult female population engaged in trade. By 1979, market
trade had become so thoroughly identified with women that men and
women both told me men were constitutionally incapable of trading
(Clark 1994). This male stereotype thrived despite its constant contradiction by living memory and by the presence of successful men traders
from non-Asante ethnic groups.

Northern immigrants conspicuously continued to trade, men dominating important savannah commodities like cattle and kola. Like women,
they lacked access to cocoa land and the educational qualifications
demanded for formal private-sector and government jobs. In Kumasi,
fights broke out in 1937 and 1946 between Asante women yam traders
and Gao men (from Mali) who wanted control of wholesaling (Kwanteng
1946). Expulsion orders and confiscations targeted foreign traders from
Nigeria, Burkina Faso, and Lebanon, who were mostly men. Falling real
wages in the formal economy destabilized the precarious financial balance
in many Akan families and fed gendered tensions. Violent price control
raids during the 1970s and 1980s derived considerable public support
from these intra-household resentments. As the century turned, more

young Asante men could not find more appropriate waged work and began to filter back into the marketplace for good (Mikell 1997; Overå 2007).

The backlash against traders could be traced to the discrepancy between local norms of appropriately gendered economic roles and their actual performance. Even Kumasi residents, most of whose mothers and sisters were traders, found it patently unfair that illiterate traders could make higher incomes than better-educated managers and civil servants. Neither category of employee had existed before colonial rule, but their legitimated economic privilege had become "our tradition." Men's shameful inability to fulfill their economic responsibilities due to lower incomes was blamed on selfish and grasping women traders. Men should work in clean stores, sell in large quantities, and make more money. Women must remain poor and powerless to be considered virtuous, conforming to an image of self-sacrificing mothers as barefoot farmers and hand-to-mouth vendors. All too many women lived in these stereotypical conditions and were desperate to escape them. The few prosperous women wholesalers or group leaders made convenient scapegoats for high prices and catastrophic unemployment (Robertson 1983).

An Encouraging Word

The knowledge contained within these stories can be harvested at many levels. They contain a great deal of valuable information about historical events, trading practices, and family relationships in earlier decades of the twentieth century. These seven women's lives stretch over considerable distances with respect to geography, class, and other variables. Many of these social locations have never been the focus of scholarly research or public records. That makes these stories a good corrective to the speculative generalizations, based on Western assumptions, that often guide public policy.

The fears and aspirations of these seven traders are not rooted in ignorance but in their considerable experience of some of the same historical and economic forces that affect the lives of people in many parts of the world. Subject to the limitations of retrospective accounts, they show how Asante people felt about the increasing pace of socioeconomic change, which destabilized many distinct social categories. They include tales of success and disaster, of wealth and destitution, from moralizers and cynics. The narrators' choice of topics and the order in which they address them also convey messages about their conceptual frameworks, how they relate one aspect of life to another. Their stories will resonate with many readers wrestling with similar dilemmas in their own daily lives.

Because these traders share identities of nationality, ethnicity, occupation, gender, and approximate age, one tends to expect them to share a basically uniform perspective on major issues. But such expectations of homogeneity collapse quickly upon reading the stories, because their variation of tone, content, and intention is impossible to miss. Their individual perspectives emerge vividly through their contrasting styles and incidents. Different kinds of family resources and personal histories ensure that each trader has experienced the dramatic boom and bust cycles of the last fifty years in her own particular way. Privileging this individuality plays to the special strengths of life stories, which is the depth of their interpretive insight rather than their typicality. These complicating factors are rooted in multiple cross-cutting identities that enact social cleavages but also constitute connections across each of them. Individual stories can be read to follow those bridges, treating the multiplicity of voices not as confusing static but as additional resonances generating broader and deeper meanings.

The Asante style of narrative exposition leaves it primarily up to the listener to get the point. That means it assumes and requires a degree of active agency on the part of the audience. I decided to respect local genre conventions enough to allow readers to construct their own interpretations by not thrusting my own conclusions forward. While these choices ask for additional effort, they bring compensatory pleasure in exploring the unique personality and thinking style of each narrator. For those who rise to the challenge, their active engagement will reward them with a more flexible range of insights that should be more timely and relevant to their own immediate concerns.

CHAPTER 1

Abenaa Adiiya

Portrait: An Adventurer on the Road

Our work, it's like a lottery. If God helps you, then you go out and you win.

Abenaa Adiiya was a short, robust, businesslike woman in early middle age. She cheerfully kept up a grueling weekly schedule of predawn departures on buying trips, maintaining several distinct travel patterns in different seasons. In social conversation, as in this narrative, she mainly talked about profits and losses on particular routes, with a rueful laugh for the stories of bad luck. The relatively high capital required for her tomato wholesaling business put her into the top level of traders in perishable foodstuffs, but this financial capacity was stretched at times. She considered herself tough and was proud of it, with confidence in her own strength and judgment.

Her square, closed face and stocky build rarely showed much sentiment. Her eyes became wistful only when she talked off the record about her early, unwilling marriage. When I asked her to record her life history, she was also matter-of-fact. "Let's do it right now, I'm ready," she answered. By the time we reached my house, she had her piece to say worked out, short and direct. It was hard to get her to elaborate. "Didn't you understand it? I said it all," she responded. She had no qualms about having her name and picture used: why, she asked?

Yet she would do anything for those she loved. She never begrudged taking time off for her relatives' illnesses or funerals. She was brusque with the several small grandchildren who lived with her, yet she admitted they live with her partly because otherwise she would live alone. She fiercely vowed to educate them, since she had missed that chance with her children. Her regrets and ambitions for her children and grandchildren are expressed in terms of the core material aspiration for many Asante: to build a house to leave them. Her dim view of current economic prospects for herself and her country can be measured by her single-minded aim to get them out of Ghana, in order to have a chance at achieving this basic security.

I had stayed with her in Bolgatanga, in the far Upper Region, for several weeks in 1979, so we knew each other well and even shared a few secrets. On Sundays, I often found her at home resting after attending an early church service in the neighborhood. In her old clothes, she liked to watch old U.S. and Chinese children's serials on television. When I later came in my car, she would often suggest going to visit someone—the retired leader of her tomato buying group in Bolgatanga, or her elderly unmarried aunt in the suburbs. If she had a weekday off, she would get dressed and go down to the wholesale yard to discuss prices with her colleagues.

Her story is full of business details; she revels in prices and credit strategies. Gradually, I understood how this steady stream of transactions inscribes her life's events, emotions, and wisdom, just as it enabled her to realize them over the course of her life. Her pride as a young wife, her ambivalence about modernization and city life, even her faith in God are all documented and inflected by the prices and profits of the day. The perishability of her tomatoes makes her very aware of risk, and she discusses the various hazards of supply volatility, unreliable transport, and credit default.

She talks more about government policies than many traders, and considers them influential on market conditions. At that time, the official annual budget still set the sale price of gasoline and the buying price of cocoa despite international pressure to deregulate. She understands that increased competition from new traders lowers her income, but does not blame the massive public-sector layoffs under the SAP. Instead, she blames population growth, the result of more children being born and surviving. Before all, she finds comfort in the thought that her fortunes and misfortunes are ultimately part of God's plan.

The year she reviewed her transcripts, this confidence was severely shaken. The theft of her whole trading capital, while she rested at the end of a delivery run, had left her stunned and financially unable to continue traveling as before. Even buying a secondhand freezer to sell ice water and popsicles was beyond her means. Then a fire in the market destroyed the major remaining family asset, her aunt's stall. After trading in tomatoes all her life, she was now scrambling to imagine what kind of work she could still do to support herself, let alone to reach the goals she had set for her family.

Story: Patience and Pleading

At first, the world was good, and as for me, I know what I know, in my own mind. What I mean is, the **Bible** says that this is not true, and if things are good now, times will come that are bad. First of all, I know that my mind tells me that the **Bible** said that when the world is coming to an end, conditions will be hard. That's how I know that very time has come.

When you first came, and you and I used to play around, about **four years** ago—

*MA: About **ten years**.*

About **ten years** ago—

*GC: It was about **fourteen years** ago.*

Well, at that time **fourteen years** ago, when you and I were going to Bolga, how much did the car even charge us? Five hundred cedis. We boarded the State **Transport** bus, and it was five hundred. Today, the fare to Bolga is six thousand cedis. I mean, the world is going up [kɔ so]. Everything is going up and finally, too, the people are too many. If we are too many, then problems will set in with everything. At first, in trading, the people who were trading were not many, only a few people. The **more** we get, the more everyone struggles to get into trading. Nowadays, for example, look at this handbag I am holding now. If I were selling it and not many people came around, I could not raise the price very high. *Wahu?* If you come by, and Akua comes by, and someone else also comes by, I know that someone will surely buy it, and this lets the price go up.

OK, it is partly due to the **petrol**, too. I mean, what makes things get expensive is petrol. At **first**, when I was **starting** to travel, the car charged me 2500 cedis. Then they raised the price of petrol, and when they raised the price, they raised the fare to 3000. Just the other day it went up again, and now they charge 3500. That's why I know very well that if they **change** the **budget** and raise the petrol price again, they will raise the fare again to 4000. These days, the very high prices of things are really due to petrol. I mean, if they raise the price of petrol, it affects everything. I mean, people have to take a car. If you sell things, you need to take a car, you see? That's why foodstuffs and everything, cloth or clothing, everything is so expensive. Everything really depends on petrol, really. That's why I say the rising price of petrol has caused all of the problems in Ghana today. A person cannot pick up this chair and, with your own strength, walk with it for half a mile. You cannot carry this **table**. Whatever happens, you have to take a car. *Wahu?*

A few days ago I went to buy yams at Ejura. When we **first** went to buy, for every hundred yams the car charged two thousand cedis. Today, if you go to buy a hundred, they charge five thousand. Just like that, they raised it three thousand cedis. That's why, if at **first** I sold the yams for two hundred each, now I cannot sell them for two hundred. I have to sell them for about three hundred each. So as for the hard times, really it is because they are raising the price of petrol so very fast. Petrol makes everything hard. Today food is also hard. All of it ends up with this petrol business.

In the old days, as a poor person, if you had even five hundred cedis to take to market, you could eat. Today, take me and these children of mine. Now, even if I haven't bought much I have spent eight hundred cedis, only for the staples, before you have gone to look for meat. And **sister**, the work you do, if you work for one day, how much will you earn? How much will you get? That's why, as for me, the thing I know is that it all, mostly, is because of petrol. Petrol has made the prices of things get very, very high, and as soon as they raise it, it affects everything. **OK**.

I mean, they say they have raised the price of cocoa, and then the prices of things have got very expensive. As for cocoa, I don't have any myself; you don't have any. None at all, none of my relatives have ever planted any cocoa at all. But if they raise the price of cocoa, and the prices of all other goods go up, it affects all of us. So, the things that have changed in this world, they are due to cocoa and petrol, the two of them. That's what is on my mind. If she has anything to ask about it, she can ask so that I can explain.

GC: When you were young, was it this hard?

No, not at all. At the **time** I was a child, when I grew up enough to be buying cloth, I paid three hundred cedis. I bought cloth for three hundred. I gave birth, we named my child, they gave me six hundred. With the six hundred, my mother bought three cloths for three hundred each. Even the really expensive cloth she bought was four hundred cedis. *Wahu?* But today, if you wear European cloth, if you are buying it and you don't have fifty or fifty-five thousand cedis, you won't be buying any. Fifty-five or sixty, you see? In the past, that kind of cloth we bought for five hundred cedis. Today, funeral cloth is ten thousand, and plain funeral cloth used to be cheap, but today it is ten. So between the old days and these days, there is no comparison.

When I had just married, at **first** [*repeats this three times*] my hus-band gave me five shillings. Five shillings a day I took to do the market-ing. Only five shillings, and I did a lot of shopping. Later, when he had brought his nephew to live with us, so that his nephew could learn car repair, then he was giving me six shillings. That six shillings, it was really something! I mean, times changed and he gave me ten shillings, and finally he was giving me twelve. I mean, with that twelve shillings I was quite a rich woman. I was only a young girl, and I had senior Magazine workers to look after.[1] I was really wealthy. But **sister**, the way I am liv-ing now, when I go to market, I can take three or four thousand, and it is not enough for my shopping. So I mean, in time, everything is going up. As **time** passes, everything goes up.

People are also getting too many. At **first**, people were not so many at all, like today.

GC: Why were people not as many as today?

OK, like at **first**, when you had given birth, I mean, like, today we are giving birth **more**, in the end. My mother was an only child, now she has had seven children. Now, I also, my own flesh and blood, they are ten. Myself I had three, and my children had five. It adds up to how many? Isn't it eight? We are growing. I mean, people are really too many. So, because we are so many, everything will go up. *Wahu?*

Comparing today to before, then a lot of people did not try to come live in a big town, also. Today, all the children who finish school in a village say, "I am going to Kumasi, I am going to Accra." Instead, if a child finished then, he would not decide to go anywhere. He would stay right there with his mother. Today too, everyone wants to come to a big town so he can be modern.[2] And when modernization gets really too much, things will also get expensive. Right now, modernization is rising fast. People are too modern.

MA: Now, preacher, tell about your own life.

As for my own life, oh, as for my own life, **sister**, it is also hard. Only because of God, I mean, right now, I have this work I am doing. **OK**, my husband is a driver, if he goes on the road, but recently he has just stayed home. For about **two years**, he has had no work.

GC: He doesn't have a car?

No, he has no car. I mean, because it's all on me, I get so tired. If I go and earn something, and I come back, little by little, we make it by ourselves, little by little. So if he does earn something, if he is someone who works for someone, it isn't like the one who works for himself. So right now, he goes and comes and if he earns two thousand and, *agya,* if he gives it to me, I take it. The day that he doesn't earn anything, too, I just hang on.

So it's just like that with me, in this work that I do, that's the thing that doesn't let me get ahead, you see. I mean, the food money is too much. The people living with me now, we are eleven. As a nursing mother[3] in Kumasi for these eleven people, if I get up in the morning and I say, "Little children, I am giving out your money," if I take out 1500 cedis, none will be left over. So every day, I give out 1500 to these children, before I go looking for what we will eat at noon, what they will eat at noon. When those of us who go to school come back, what we will eat then. This is before we ourselves eat, in the evening. So if I do say so myself, I am putting all this together, and I mean, each day we use about five thousand cedis.

So look at an average woman, it's because of the work. **OK**, the work that I do, it goes like this. Our work, it's like a lottery. If God helps you, then you go out and you win. I mean, let's say I am going to buy this. The day after tomorrow, when I go, I don't know at what price I am going to buy it. You arrive there, and if the farmer says he is going to charge one hundred pounds, if you can afford it, you buy.[4] If you cannot, then you come back. When I go out, too, I don't know what price I am going to get. So I go and then I bargain, so that I say I will take three hundred for it, if I have bought it at two hundred there. If I say I will take three hundred cedis, and if they want it and they **feel** like buying and it looks good to them, then they buy it. If it isn't a good deal, they don't buy. *Wahu?* So it can happen that you go once, and you might lose two hundred thousand cedis. Recently, I went to Bolga for a year, and my loss was four hundred thousand. Because of this, there are some days that you lose money, and the loss exceeds your profits. It is that kind of work; the losses are big. The profits can't cover your debt. In fact, I mean, the losses don't usually come very often, but when they come, they are big.

So sometimes, it gets me in big trouble. Sometimes, I mean, all the trading capital that I have, look how I use up that money! **OK**, as a woman, I don't have any **capital** that amounts to anything in my hands. You see? It happens some days that the money can shrink until finally, doing my work becomes difficult. I worry and worry, until maybe, if you are someone I love, then maybe I come to you, maybe "**Sister**, give me a loan, maybe, for fifty," and if it is there, then you give it to me. So if, Akua, if you give it to me, maybe one hundred, and I put them together, I travel for a little while. When I **feel** that [the earnings] can buy back the loan, then I pay it off. So it happens that sometimes there are problems in life. It also happens sometimes that, by the grace of God, it is all right.

GC: So what about the places that you go to get things, and the places that you take them? You were saying that you take them here and you take them there.

Yes, some days, I mean, there are some goods at Akumadan, at Afrantuo, at Tanoso, at Kumawu, eh, at Saboronoom, or at Tuabodom.[5] So if in the evening like this, I am going, if today, like I was going tonight, and I went to Anwonaga, and if I went to stand there, *wahu?* Those who do it, some go Sundays, some go Mondays, some go Tuesdays, so I go and those of us who go Sunday, today, are coming back. So if I see them I ask, "**Sister**, where did you go today?" Maybe she says, "I went to Derma." "Maybe, what was the price there?" She says, maybe, this much. So you go on, and maybe Akua has come. "Akua, where have you gone?" She says, maybe, "I went to Saboronoom." "Maybe, what was the price?" She says, "Nine thousand." So I go asking around, and if I see where the price is low, I mean, I go there, and I go buy some.

MA: Will you go there today?

Yes, I will go there tomorrow. I will go tonight, I will buy them tomorrow.

GC: But the ones who always travel, will they tell the truth?

Yes, oh, those of us who trade like that, if you meet them, they will tell you the truth. She will tell you. I mean, if we meet, where I stand like that, the two of us are standing there. The thing is, if we are going to buy, me and my **sister**, maybe I will go stand there first, and I bargain. And if I am leaving, then I leave a message that if she comes, maybe she should say that I had bargained for sixpence or threepence, so she shouldn't come and bargain a new price. Some other day, she will go first, and she goes to bargain. When I come, she leaves a message that they should tell Abenaa that I have bargained, so when she comes, she shouldn't bargain again.

So some days, you go around and God is good to you, and you will earn something on top. Another day, you won't get anything, and you will take a loss. Some days you will earn five hundred cedis; there will be another day that you earn a thousand. One day you will earn two thousand; that day God has been really good to you. At the markets we go to, the day that you get two thousand, it means that the day you went, there was a shortage. The profits we normally get are one thousand and five hundred, one thousand or five hundred.

MA: For each box?

Yes. One thousand or five hundred. So the day that you go and make two thousand in profit, that day there was a real shortage. God has been good to you, to let you make money.

MA: So Takoradi and where else do you sell them?

Ah, **OK**, if I start, I start from here, I arrive at Fosu. At Fosu, the people there always buy some. I leave Fosu and I stop at Cape Coast, and they unload some. When we finish unloading some at Cape Coast, on the road I stop at a town called Beposo, and they also unload some. If they take some at Beposo, we pass Beposo and the goods run out. If they don't run out at Beposo, we also arrive at Efiakuma. They take some at Efiakuma, then I arrive at Ntweaban and they take some, and then I arrive at Takoradi and they are finished. It happens some days that I unload so much on the road, I don't even make it to Takoradi before I turn back. So on a day that the trading goes well, some days I haven't gone far at all before it runs out. So wherever I arrive and sell out, I turn around.

How we do it is, when we go on ahead, they do not pay us off. What money I brought last week is for tomorrow Monday. So what I am going to buy and go with, I mean, I am going to buy it tomorrow Monday, I will arrive there Tuesday morning. So what I took along last week Tuesday, when I go, then I will collect the money for it, and this week's will remain there. So each time, we trade by the week. When you go, you will not find a person who will give you the money right away. Every week you take the new goods along, and you collect for the old ones.

So all the **time**, the work requires money. You have to have money to do it. If you don't have money in hand, you will be in trouble every **time**. I mean, those farmers, they don't give us credit. As for the farmer, if you buy and there is even one hundred cedis left, and he says he won't let you take them, if he doesn't want to. "I'm not giving them to you," he says. If he won't let you take them, he will take them back and keep them. But as for us, we give credit for a week, and then we get our money.

MA: So, when you say that you give credit for a week, if one day you go and the goods are really scarce, do you take cash payment?

Well, you and they are **customers**. You and they work together that way, so she should take it. But if someone also sees someone passing, and they don't know them, then the money that is for you, they take it to buy for cash. Some people, if you go, and you haven't got anything to give her, she will tell you frankly, "I am taking the money to go and look for some to buy." She won't give it to you. Fantis,[6] that's how they do it. If you go and you haven't got some goods to give her, she will tell you, "If I give you the money, I won't get anything to buy, so I am taking your money to go look for some to buy." I mean, she's been your customer, and we traded with them! So it was, all the **time**.

GC: So what did you do to find your customers? Did you just meet them?

OK, it happened like this. At **first**, you and I were selling them here in Kumasi, and I didn't go there. But after a while, finally, I saw that if I stayed in this market they weren't buying enough. Maybe I can say it like this: my problem was, if I went and stayed there, not even one box would be sold out. With one box like that, I wouldn't earn even one thousand cedis. So staying here like that would eventually bring disgrace.

At that time, a friend of mine traveled there, and she and I talked about her taking me with her. Then she said, "Oh, I will take you along." Each day we talked, and she said, "I will take you along." Each day I said it, and still she didn't take me along. Then one day I said, "I will go myself." By myself I bought some and loaded them on the **train**. I loaded them on the **train**, and I had a conversation with someone. I told her I was going to Takoradi, but I didn't know the place. But she said, "Oh, when we arrive, I will show you." We arrived and we all took a car and went to town. So when we went, she took me to one of the women. "I beg you, one of my friends is unloading these goods, sell them for her." And the woman sold the goods for me. She sold them for me and I was a stranger, so that same day she collected my money to give me. I spent three days. She told me I should spend three days. It took three days for her to collect the money to give me. She collected it and she asked me what day I would be coming back with more. And I asked her, "What day should I bring them?" And she fixed me a day that I should bring them.

So at **first**, I took them on the **train** like that. I bought them, then I took a car, then I took the **train**. After a while, the **train** was often breaking down, and tomatoes get spoiled overnight. The **train** was also very hot inside. So if we pack them inside, maybe when we get underway, they are spoiled. It can't go on. So I thought carefully, and I said, "If it is like that, I will stop." And finally, by that time, I had saved up a little money, enough to take a car. Right now, I have an Urvan [a minivan]. I take an Urvan to go every day. So after a while, if I go like that, really, I get on little by little. So I left the **train** and took to the road.

If it is hard to get tomatoes, and you are traveling, someone will follow after you. She may say, "Unload some and let me buy them." You and she bargain and set the price, and she buys. If she bought, then you ask her, "What day should I come here, and you will buy some?" You ask her that because you are looking for a **customer**. So you ask her what day. I say, "I go on Tuesdays and Thursdays. I buy them Monday and I unload them Tuesday, I buy them Thursday and I unload them Friday. And I tell you that Thursdays I come here." So then she says that the day that you will arrive there, she will be there.

So let's say I might unload about twice, and maybe someone else doesn't have any to buy. She will ask the first woman, "Where did you get some to buy?" She says, "A **sister** brings some by here," and she also will join in. *Wahu?* Then others also ask, "Where did you get some goods to buy?" Someone else has asked whether some **sister** brings them, and intends to buy some. Finally, you will see when they have become many. They are very many now. Look, it can happen that even someone, when you stop, they can buy all that you have.

That's what makes us get customers. I mean, if you go, and it is hard to get some, then they stand in the road to look for some to buy. So they stop you, and they do business with you, and people watch how you talk, your character, and how you act. If you treat people well, they will join you. So every time, it's like, if you haven't come, if the car has not even come, they stand there waiting for you, until the time you come. A few days ago, my car broke down until about two o'clock. But they kept asking the cars that were coming, "Have you seen Auntie Abenaa's car?" They said, "I saw that the car had broken down." They kept on waiting. When I went, they were still standing there waiting for me, saying, "We heard that your car broke down." So they waited until two, and when I went, they unloaded from me.

GC: If you got to Takoradi and your tomatoes were finished and you turned back, wouldn't your customers there be angry?

You have to try and let everyone get some. If one person has not got any, you must talk sweetly to her, you tell her something. *Wahu?* Recently, I went there like that, and someone did not get any. Those who had not come early, I told them, "I went to the countryside, and I didn't get enough goods to buy, so my goods were few. So I beg your pardon, please have patience, and Tuesday everyone will get some." So if you talk nicely to the person, it makes her calm down. If you look and you see that the goods don't amount to much, then for two people, maybe you say, "Take this one, and divide it, and let everyone have a little." If you take three people and you plead for them to all understand how to work so that today, because I did not get many goods, maybe the three of them should take one box and share it little by little, and when I come Tuesday or Friday, everyone will get one. If you talk with them like that, they will get to understand, and they share it. So trading with them is nothing but pleading and patience. If you have patience, you really can trade with them all the **time**. But they take a lot of our money. Right now, as I am standing here, if I figure it out, it will add up to more than three hundred thousand cedis.

*GC: If you go and she has not paid you for **last week**'s goods, would you give her more of these, to add to it?*

OK, she might be someone, among those who buy, that someone might take some from her to sell in the village. Maybe, you will look and the money is not all there. She will tell you the real truth. If someone respects herself, then you know that she is not like that. So she will say, "Auntie Abenaa, I beg of you, what they took away from me, they have not brought the money. So I do not have enough, so go and come back Thursday." Someone like that, when you come, she will give it to you. But another person, too, has made up her mind that she will be dishonest. As for her, even if she takes some, you won't see her again. *Wahu?* Maybe, if she takes some, you won't see her again.

But these people, what there is about them is that they themselves don't have the money to work with. So whatever they buy, they buy on credit. So if you and a Fanti are doing business and, for example, her child gets sick, you know that if your money is with her, it is gone. If the husband gets sick, your money is gone. Anything that happens to her, I mean, she won't let your money sit there untouched when she is having real problems. So if you go, she will tell you, "This person bought some, but if I didn't have your money what would I do? So I have taken it until the end of the month." Well, after a month, sometimes even a year, she hasn't paid you. I figure that the money I have out there is more than three hundred thousand cedis. And right now, the money that I have with me is very little. All the money has gone into these debts.

A few days ago, an old lady who is working with me, and we really work together, her child, a beautiful young woman, got sick. So she has bought some tomatoes. She also works with her children, so when I go they can take four or five boxes. If they unload some, if I go in four days, they will unload more. So for the boxes that she had taken when her child got sick, now she owes me fifty thousand. She took it to look after the child, and it didn't do any good, and the child died. So now, even to ask her about the money is difficult; it would be hard for me to ask for the money. Only a few days ago, I told her, "Mother, what about the money?" She said that she herself knows about it, so I should have patience, she will pay me, and she went home. *Wahu?*

GC: So tomorrow, if she hasn't paid, will she come to buy more?

She will buy. These people, it is their nature that if you are trading with them, and she is buying, and she goes into debt, if you haven't given her any more, she won't pay for it. I mean, she doesn't have any money put aside. So if she gets into debt, you have to give her more, and she will use it to pay off the debt.

MA: She sells it, and she pays the debt.

And working with it, she pays off the debt gradually. So, even if she owes you money, you have to give her something to sell. One woman will have a good brain in her head. She worries about her debt, and so whatever she gets, she will bring it to you. Someone else has made up her mind that as for her, nothing bothers her. Well, if you give her this one shipment, and you see that it is no good, you have to stop. You need to collect your money, but you don't get it. So you don't add anything to it, and you leave behind the old debt. And someone else can come and buy, and you never see her again.

*MA: But a **new customer** like that, can you give her time on it, without anyone holding security?*

Yes, even a **new customer**. I mean, if she has just now come, later she will be old. You will see that she follows someone and has come with her. "Me and this **sister** have come, so if you don't trust me, ask this **sister**." *Wahu?* Then this **sister** will take it and worry about it so, when she even sees her, she will run away. That's their way. Trading with Fanti people is all patience. If you don't have patience, you can't work with them.

GC: In the business that you do, between you and them, who gets more of the profit?

OK, sometimes their profit is more than ours, because they sell it retail. So there are some days that she even buys some to take away and there is none in the market. *Wahu?* Just a few days ago, I bought some goods here. I bought them, and I went to sell them to them at seven thousand cedis. One woman told me frankly that the goods she bought for seven thousand, she retailed for sixteen thousand. I mean, she took them away and there were none in the market, so the profit was hers. So she goes and she remembers, she tells me, "Auntie Abenaa!" I went back and she had gone to buy something with the money. She says, "Auntie Abenaa, as for you, you are my mother," and because of how I treat her, she won't be calling me "my own nursing mother."[7] That is how the Fanti are. She says, "This is my nursing mother." "If I tell you the story, as I live, the goods earned me sixteen thousand. So I went to buy cloth to remember your name." When she went, there was none in the market. So some days, they make a really good profit, more even than we who ride in the car.

Some days, too, when you go, you may not have earned much. Then when she retails it, she has also lost money on it, and maybe you have at least got your one thousand. If you look into it, they usually get more than us who sit in the car. God might be good to her when she goes, but only if it is really scarce, and the market goes well. Another person might have just bought some and she gives it to someone else for a markup. If someone can buy when someone else hasn't got any, maybe the other person says, "Give it to me, and I will give you one thousand," so she turns around to give it to her.

GC: When you were selling in Kumasi, were they doing that?

Yes, it is all over Kumasi here. It is there. In Kumasi, well, those lorry-chasers are there, who cry out, "It's mine." To buy it, one person might not be able to get up early, but someone else could get up early and bathe in cold water. Buying it, she puts it aside. When the one who comes later arrives she wants some, and she says, "Maybe add one thousand or two thousand on top for me and take it." If you want it, you will take it. It is everywhere here in Kumasi.

MA: You are in the market here, and are there rules among you that this one is for her, this is hers, this is hers?

Well, it is the truth. We set aside some for them.

GC: Then explain it, to let us understand.

These tomatoes, for example, if you take some away, we take out some to give to the queen mother.

MA: Which queen mother? The market queen or the Asantehemma?[8]

We take out some to give the *Asantehemma,* and we take out some to give the market queen. Those for the *Asantehemma,* they usually take them on *Akwasidae,* when it is getting toward that day, on the Saturday before the *Akwasidae* comes on a Sunday morning. That is, it isn't something that they take every day. The *Akwasidae* is about every month or **forty days**.[9] *Akwasidae,* it seems to me that it is every **forty days**. So every **forty days**, they take out one to give to the *Asantehemma.* I mean, the market queens do it; every kind of goods in the market has its queen. Plantain has its queen.

MA: Those for the Asantehemma, do they take some from everyone's goods? And how much do they take? Or does the person come and say?

Those for the *Asantehemma,* I was saying that each kind of goods has its queen. So each market queen, the pepper queen goes to take out a little pepper, and the garden egg queen goes to take out some garden eggs. Then the plantain queen goes to get hers. I mean, they know everyone. Every queen takes out what belongs to her.

MA: Yes, you say that the onion queen has to.

GC: Yes, she has to take out some onions to go there.

Ah yes, when it is getting near the *Akwasidae,* but truly, we don't take it out every day. I mean, what we give on Saturday, the eve of *Akwasidae* morning, the goods for the *Asantehemma,* it goes to the palace. Theirs, they don't take it every day. But our own queens, for instance, tomatoes, pepper, and garden eggs are together, and plantain has its queen; cassava also has its queen. So if some tomatoes come in, if I bring in one box myself, we will take out two to give to the tomato queen. The Gao[10] who carries it to put there, we don't give him money. He will also take out some tomatoes. And the one who stands up to sell for me, we also don't give him money. He also takes out some. That's how the picking out is done.

GC: Do they do like this in Takoradi, too?

Yes, in Takoradi we take some out, but in Takoradi we don't take out a lot, like here. As for Takoradi, the one who writes it down takes two, and the one who unloads it from inside the car onto the ground also takes two, and another one also, the one who, when you have finished buying, he carries everything to put in your car, he also takes two. That is exactly what they take out of each box.

GC: Does the queen take any?

Aha, the queen. You take some out for the queen. You take some out for the queen. But we don't take out as many as in Kumasi. Here, they take out a lot. Here, from one box we will take out five or six. There, they take out two by two. So in Takoradi, we don't take out many, not like here.

*MA: So when your work is taking you back and forth like that, do you pay **income tax**, or a **license** fee, or something like that?*

Yes, they charge us **tax**. When we go to Bolga [Bolgatanga], we pay **tax**. If we go all the way to Bolga, they charge us up there. Plus we pay the car ticket and everything else. On one of our boxes, some places in the countryside there, you can go some places where they collect one hundred cedis each, and some other places they collect two hundred.

GC: So before, when you worked in Kumasi, selling in the market, where did you buy the tomatoes, in the village or the market?

In the market.

GC: Right now, what is hard about the work?

OK, as for Kumasi, at **first** I was not sitting in the car. I stayed in one place. Aha, at **first**, I only came from Kuro foforɔ mu[11] to the market and I didn't go anywhere.

GC: Really? When you were a young woman?

Yes, when I was a young woman and I had never given birth. I did it before I had all the children. My mother's sister was doing it then, and I hadn't grown up yet. I stayed right in it, so when I did it I was then a young woman.

GC: Did you go on the road?

Aha, when I was a young woman, if someone brought some in, then I would also buy some and retail it. But I didn't go on the road. It's what I was doing when you met me in the market. I was not traveling, except only to Bolga, where I was going then. As for Bolga, at the end of the year I would go there. When I came back, I wouldn't go anywhere else besides Bolga. Even that work, in Bolga, belonged to my mother's sister. When she got old, and she could not go herself, she turned it over to me. So every New Year arrived and I went off to buy, and then I came back. So when that season had passed, I didn't go anywhere else.

GC: You didn't go to Kumawu, like today?

At **first** I didn't travel, but now I go everywhere. Even tomorrow, I might go to Kumawu.

GC: Excuse me, but what made you decide that you would go on the road, you would go to Bolga? Because when you were a child you were following after your mother. What gave you the idea "I will go to Bolga"?

The Bolga business belonged to my mother. Yes, my mother was going herself. But later, she got old and she couldn't go, and she gave it to me so that I should go. Because if I go myself and I am an elder, then I give it to my child, so we should go together.

GC: So when you were a young girl, you stayed in the market here and your mother went on the road?

Yes, then I was in the market and my mother went on the road.

*GC: So when you were a child and stayed in the market, was it because your mother traded **tomatoes** that you wanted to do **tomatoes**? Didn't you like to do anything else?*

No, I didn't sell anything else. It happened that even those children that finished school, my mother didn't allow any of them to get any job. Now I regret it, but it is long past. That time was not like today. You see, the world was so cheap then that if you went and earned even five hundred cedis, you had got real money. At one time, I even went traveling to Nigeria, but when I went, I saw how the **accidents** were happening on the road. I said, "I will go back to doing that same work, because, when I go, I will get enough to eat." That made me stop.

*MA: So the **tomato** business didn't allow you to send your children to **secondary school**?*

Oho, as for my children, they did not try hard there, so none of them learned anything. So when everyone finished, they said, "As for me, I won't continue further."

*MA: When you began selling **tomatoes**, what good work might have been there, in addition to the **tomatoes**, so that you earned money to get ahead more than in the **tomatoes**?*

OK, as for that, I didn't think about any work in addition. I mean, that was what was in my mind, so I didn't consider any other kind of work. The work that I might have tried to do was when going to Nigeria was popular, and I decided to go. But I went for about six months, and the road **accidents** were happening so much that I said, "No, if I don't die, I don't know what I will earn, so I will stop and do my same old work." That's why, *agya,* I haven't really considered any other kind of work. I mean, that was the real work.

GC: Does it seem to you that the tomato trade makes more money than anything else?

That is what my strength can do. Whatever happens, I can do it. There is no other business that my money can do. As I am sitting here now, if I get a chance, I would stop, but I can't get a lot of money that I could take to go on the road. *Wahu?* Now I **feel** if I stop this and do another kind of work, it would be good for me. This work I am doing now, I can't take it and get property. It is just for buying something to eat, what you can use to buy food. It's not a business that I can use to build up any property. When I look carefully at it, if I had capital that was a little heavy, then I would also stop it. I might go on the road, as people are doing. But I don't have it, I don't have the strength for that, so I am just holding on here like this.

*GC: Is there anyone that you started out with in the **tomato** business, and now she has been able to build up some property, or are they all the same?*

Someone who started out with me? **OK**, my younger **sister** is an example. I started out before her, but now she has built her house, like I am not able to do.

*GC: Did she do it with the **tomato** business?*

The fact is this, I don't know if she did some extra work or not; I can't tell. As for the tomatoes, among those of us who sell them, I really haven't seen any of us who have done that, even our elders. I mean, it isn't the kind of money that piles up. I have said that the costs are more than the profit. So it isn't money that piles up so that you can do anything with it, if you don't have another extra business. Because it's work for a nursing mother, you just get something every day to buy food to eat. That is the nature of the work. It's not a business to bring in piles of money, like if I go once I get about two hundred thousand cedis and I put it aside, or I even get one hundred [thousand]. It doesn't come in like that.

MA: So, like you were saying, maybe if your husband's work is good, and you are not paying for food money.

If it is like that, and the man is doing that, then as a woman, you might make even ten pounds. Since you haven't taken anything out of it, you can save it to let it make money. It might even happen that for a week he doesn't get a single car to drive. After a week, if you take out three thousand every day, even in one week, how much have you spent? It might happen that when I go on the road, I may not earn enough even to cover what we are spending. It is just the money that is with you that is available. So this always makes your capital unable to grow. That's really how it goes up and it comes down again. I mean, I use it up.

MA: If you possibly did get some money in your work, what might you be able to do?

OK, right now, this thing has really been on my mind the past few days. If I had money now, then I would like to buy a **plot** of land. And the second thing is, I would like for one of the children to travel abroad. Today, in this place where we live, if you say you live here and you will really stay here, you will truly wear yourself out. Right now, this is the thing that is really in my heart. If I were to get a little money now, then I would let one of the children travel abroad, to go and come back. After he has come back, when I am an old woman, I will have a place to put my head. These days, this is my heartfelt desire. I pray that God will be good, and I might get a little money to save, and I might give it to the child to leave, and maybe . . . I have been in this work a long time. I have seen what it has come to, and it can't take me anywhere. If I earn a little, and if some of the children can travel, maybe grace will come.

That young man that I recently showed to you, every day he keeps talking more about it. "Auntie, send me away," he says, but I don't have any money. He says it because as my child he knows that I work every day. He thinks I have some, but I am just being stubborn. Every day, when we talk, he says the same thing. "Auntie, send me away." I tell him that I haven't got the money, but he says I am lying. I tell him that I haven't got the money. If I had the money, then I would also want for my child to go. If he has gone, then, when you get old, he can build you a building and say, "Mother, live here." So I would like that, but there isn't that kind of money.

GC: So now, what kind of work is your child doing?

My child, the young man? He is a shoemaker; he is learning to make shoes.

*GC: And the girls, you said they were not clever so you didn't send them to **secondary** school?*

They themselves didn't want to. I mean, when each of them finished, she said, "I won't go on. I will come to the market." They themselves did not work hard in school. Girls!

*MA: Why didn't you take some to go learn, for example, sewing or **hairdressing**?*

Well, at that time, my sister, I never thought of it. What I am saying is, by now it is too **late**. At that time, the idea never came to me. I mean, when each finished, she said, "I will come to the market," and I brought her to the market. Because later, when we got the idea, by then they had all gone and had babies. What could they do then to go and learn some kind of work? This young one had three children, the elder had two. At **first**, we never thought of it, because they all just wanted to trade, and all of them joined the market. *Wahu?* As for people, we get wiser every year. Someone can get smart and by then her chance is completely spoiled.

That's why now, even myself, if I sit and think about it, it pains me that I didn't make some of the children learn some kind of work. We all joined in for only one kind of work. As for now, with their children who are coming along, if only I don't die, not one of the children will keep doing our kind of work. That is what I have decided, if I live long enough. And I have told them that even if I die, everyone should let their child look for a different kind of work, **either** sewing or hairdressing, or any work. They should let the children learn a craft. Craft work is good.

GC: You don't want them to follow you?

Aha, not all of us should do one kind of work like that. This work, when you do it you will never get ahead. Every day, you stay where you are.

GC: Do your sisters all do that kind of work? Do they all sell tomatoes?

My sister? She is my mother's sister. She sells tomatoes, she is still alive. But of my own sisters, none of them sell any. As for my siblings, we are two women. One is with her husband in Mampong, and she sews things. The men also are in Tema. The men are four. None of them are here.

GC: So only you sell tomatoes, like your mother? Since you began to sell tomatoes, what changes have you seen in the work?

In the work? As for changes, this work doesn't change. I haven't seen any change in it. I mean, I haven't seen anything out of it. I mean, the money in this, if you get some, you spend it. You see, my sister, as for work, when you do it and you get something to build up property, then you can see that this is the profit from the work you have done. This work, if you do it, it gives you just clothes to wear and **chop money**. I mean, I don't have any real thing from it that I can name, to say that I did this work, like maybe my house or my car, maybe that would be my property. There is nothing like that, only this **fridge**. It is furniture, we don't count that.

MA: Aha, but she means what changes have come, between how the work of the past was done and today's work. What changes have come about?

Way in the past, as I was saying before, the world was not expensive. So if you got even five hundred cedis, then it was enough for everything. But today, the world is going up.

GC: In the past, would you earn five hundred quickly?

As for this our work, its profit is not stable. If God is good to you, among those of us who retail in this market, you might go and buy and bring it to the market in the morning, and if none has come in, you are lucky and you have made a profit. It can also happen that you buy goods to bring to the market in the morning, and by noon plenty of them have come, and you will lose money. *Wahu?* Someone might even buy some to go away with in the morning, and no more have come in. I mean, you who took some away are lucky, and you will retail it and make money. But our profits are not big, so you can't take them to do something big. If you look over the tomato traders, tomato traders are not people who build houses.

We who sell tomatoes, we are not people who build houses. Someone who sells tomatoes and has been able to build a house, chances are she has another business somewhere that supported her. With tomatoes alone, I mean, the profit is not much. It is not something we can take to build up any property. If someone has sold tomatoes and built a house, maybe her husband helped her and some child went to Europe and so she built it. Now, one friend of mine who sells with us said that her brother went to Europe and took her daughter along. Now the daughter has finished building her house; she is going to move into it. She has come to take her next younger sister there. It was her child that helped her. With this work alone, she wouldn't be able to do it. That's how it is.

GC: Is that why you also want your child to travel abroad?

Yes, **sister**, these days in Ghana, if your child has not traveled, and you stay here . . . Myself, I look at the work that I am doing, and if God is not good to me to let one of these children travel abroad . . . Right now I am living in one room, me and these children; we are full, we can't even fit in. *Wahu?* Only one room, my children are not here, but I am living with all of their children, so we are having problems. So if God is good and someone gives you one bedroom, then you might be comfortable. As for that, it is my heartfelt desire that God may put something in my hand and I may let one of the children travel. But all the children also know the conditions we are living in. Before the child even makes the trip, they all know. If God helps, I know that when the child goes, he will also think about home a little, because all these conditions concern them.

MA: So now, have you got some money, so if it happens that someone is going, could you send him?

OK, I haven't got it, but I am working on it. Right now, the money I have is not enough. I have got a little saved up, so I pray that God will be good to me and I get some more. I have got a little, a little is set aside, so I am praying about it, that God helps me, so I may get more little by little. If someone helps me, and if he can take him along for me . . .

MA: So your husband, now, where is he? If he is working, maybe he might be able to help you a little?

It's the car. With a car, it is like this. If you take one, your **chop money** is one thousand each day. The one thousand, **sister**, you yourself look at it. If he gets only one thousand to buy food, how much will he take to buy food and how much will he bring home? Then, each month his whole wages are fifteen thousand. Ghana drivers' wages are bad. Fifteen thousand, and the fifteen thousand he collects, what will he buy with it? So as for him, there is no hope that he will earn something to bring home.

MA: He also, can his brothers help?

Today, in these days, will your brother take your child to go to Europe? On the man's side? It is not even a woman's child, so she can say that she is going to bring it back to the house. His own two brothers went, but they did not write even a **letter**.

GC: Some of his brothers are in Europe?

Yes, but they have not even written him a letter to ask what do they want. They might have said, "We will even buy an old car to bring him for him to drive." Since they went, they have not even written a **letter** home, so what can he do to say he will help send my child over for me?

So the help that will come is only from myself, and maybe God will help and I will get a little. Recently, I saved up some money and I had nine hundred thousand cedis. Then, there was a man who said if I got "one point five" [million] he would take my son along. At that time, I wanted to go to Bolga. I lost the hundred thousand, and when I came back, I lost even more money. Now the money is gone again. *Wahu?* Now I have got five hundred thousand, so I have put it away. I pray that God does not let Satan have his own way, to destroy it again. I am putting aside a little at a time, so that maybe God will help me. If I get a little, maybe someone will see my helplessness, and then, *wahu?* But I say that now, that is what my heart dwells on, so I pray that God will help me and one of the children will go, whether it is a daughter or a son.

GC: So right now, you pray that you will find a way to send one of your children to Europe. At the time you were a young woman, and you were having them, what did you think about like that? What did you want to do?

What I said was I want a house. I am still wanting somewhere to lay my head; I want a house. I want to get a house and live in it. When you came, you saw that my room has many children in it. It is full, only one room, and we are many.

GC: Yes, so when you were a young woman, did you want to build a house?

I want a house because I can't build one. If the child goes there, maybe he will earn a little to come back with, and we can build and we will have a place to sleep. You see that in one room, the people are about ten. We are much too many. We see to it that we pack the chairs together before we lie down to sleep.

MA: And the work could not help.

The work also couldn't help.

GC: When you were a child, then what helped you in your work, so that the work could improve and you could make it a little bigger?

Aha, I was explaining that my mother did it. I followed in my mother's footsteps just little by little. It got to where I also had grown up and I also separated off from her.

GC: You went off on your own?

Yes, she herself said that it had got to where I had grown up, so it was better that I didn't work for her any more. I should do my own thing, and I should go and live my life. I started off, and I went on with it little by little. I mean, today, I am still going on with that.

GC: So at that time, when your mother let you go on your own, did she still feed you?

I had given birth, yes, I had a baby.

MA: Then the young man was still marrying you?

Yes.

MA: At that time, you might have been able to do a little something. Then, things were not expensive.

Sister, at that time, you see, then money was hard to get. When you got even two hundred to hold onto, it was a big thing. Today I have seen that, these days, it is also hard to get money, but today, people work to get money faster than at first, when the world was not so hard. At **first**, life was not difficult, but money was difficult to get. Today, money is hard to get, but people work and earn money faster than before. Also, at that time, people were not modern [*y'ani mmuɛ*]. You can see that people, as they get older, their minds open and they see good things. At that time, I was not as aware as today. I was not fully modern.

GC: Why does it seem to you that things have changed like this?

What has changed? As for the changes, they are like I said: now people are too many, and everyone is working. People are many, and everyone is working. At **first**, we knew our number, the first tomato people. Because we knew each other, if the queen said that the tomato people should come, all of us were just a few and we easily gathered together. Then, the queen knew all the tomato people. Today, even if someone sells tomatoes full time, she doesn't know her.

GC: So that the tomato people in the past were maybe twenty of you?

Yes, we knew our number. You know that if the queen is calling you, you are twenty that are coming. But today, there might be someone there who even sells tomatoes and the queen doesn't know her face. She also doesn't know the queen at all. I mean, today, there are too many people. So when anyone takes some goods, she is already selling. You can't tell someone that she shouldn't trade, with her situation in the world that we live in! So right now, we are increasing, we are becoming too many. *Wahu?*

At **first**, in the tomato market, there was somewhere we called "in the roofing sheets." Our shed had been roofed with metal sheets. Only in that place were there tomato sellers, there were so few of us. I am telling you, now that you are here in Kumasi, if you go from the smoked game people's place to the plantain market, do you see that small section for tomato people? Today, just look how far tomato people have reached. That small place was the only tomato market there was in Kumasi market. *Wahu?* Today, look how people are reselling tomatoes everywhere, by the garbage dump, at the **train station**, here and there. So, you understand what I am saying? That's why, these days, we are too many. At **first**, if you went from the smoked game meat sellers to the plantain market, in a little place beside the onion people, that was the only place for tomato people. As for you, a child of a Kumasi person, you know it. Only there did you find tomato people.

So then the queen knew me. When we were children, we used to sleep behind the **gate** to buy goods.[12] When a car was coming, we said, "You go jump on it and buy from it." This one comes, you say, "I want the first one!" This one says, "I want the following one!" That one says,

"I want the next one." When our mothers come in the morning, then they unload it and divide it up. Today, it's not like that.

MA: And today, too, there are too many markets. Kwadaso has a market.

There are many markets. Kuro foforɔ mu has a market. Tafo has a market.[13] Here has a market, there has a market. So wherever you go, at our place here, for instance, there may be some people who never go to market at all. She shops right here. At our little place here, where you came, there is beef and all kinds of fish. Whatever you want is here, so there might be someone who lives here, who never goes to market. Here is where she does her shopping. Yes, I mean, today, everyone is a trader. Oh, but at **first**, someone might be from Tafo, and she knows that she buys her tomatoes from me. When she gets down from the Tafo car, she doesn't go anywhere but to me, and she will buy them there. If someone comes from Asuyeboa and she knows that she buys her tomatoes from me, she doesn't go anywhere else. Today, when she gets down from the car there will be some right beside the car, so she doesn't pass through the rubbish to come in here to buy some.

GC: So is there any story left that you want to tell me, so that I understand well?

No, my situation is what I said, that my child should go to Europe. **Sister**, it is hard. I always know that however God has planned it, it is the truth. So if God says that the children should find somewhere to put me before I die, as for me, every day this is my goal and I will get it. If it is not meant to be, one child might even go there and will not be able to come and do anything. So every day, I pray that God should show me the way to the goal that he is keeping me for.

A few days ago, in the house that is next to ours, the child of the landlord was in Japan. He went and he was going to take his older brother over. He arrived at the **time** that the younger brother should meet him, and he hadn't come, so they arrested him and made him come back. The older brother came back, and he was angry. And the younger brother, who was still there, he really struggled again to bring the older one over. They took him there, and in only three months he died. When he arrived in Japan, after just three months that young man died. *Wahu?*

Every day, I tell God that what is good for me is what he has to do for me. If it is right that some of the children may go, he should give himself glory. If they would go, and it would not be a thing that would glorify him, then everything is in his hands. So now, I lay everything before God. Whatever I do, I lay it before him so that his will be done. As for me, I am only human. I have used my mind to say this. If it would not be good, he is the one who knows everything.

Abenaa Adiiya in Her Stall, 1979

The Tomato Association Secretary, Selling Boxes on Commission in the Wholesale Yard

A Tomato Retailer Teaching Her Daughter to Sell

A Company of City Buyers in the Tomato Periodic Market, Navrongo

Gracia Clark with Onion Traders in Kumasi Central Market. *photo:* Carmen Paz

An Enthusiastic Cosmetics Seller

A Prosperous Cosmetics Wholesaler

Selling Sets of Cooking Pans and Enamelware in a Store Just behind the Market

Cloth Traders at a Meeting in the Cloth Line

A Newer Suburb with Half-Built Houses

CHAPTER 2

Maame Kesewaa

Portrait: A Quiet Saver

I had four hundred, so I put it around my waist. I had got real capital I was bringing to a big town.

Maame Kesewaa's shaded, dry cloth stall was one of my comfortable refuges in the market. At a casual glance, her slender, elderly figure looked frail, sitting back among its shadows, and her quiet observation might pass for shyness. Greeting and joining her promptly dispelled this impression. She was a lively and relaxed conversationalist, her delicate wrists flashing expressively. She would joke freely with her market neighbors and friends passing by, and was warm but not effusive when they sat for a visit. When a customer enquired about a cloth, her back would straighten and her rectangular face stiffen into a businesslike frame. She would step neatly forward, always polite and informative.

Her toughness remained mainly unspoken; it emerged from her unheralded actions. Government price control raids figure in her story, but only as a pause in her career. When other cloth sellers fled or shuttered their stalls after violent confiscations cleaned out their stock, hers was one of the few remaining consistently open. She even rented one opposite, for her teenage daughter to sell toiletries at. Maame Kesewaa had shrewdly shifted her stock early on, away from the standard "West African prints," called cloth, which were prime targets for price control. She specialized instead in locally printed and embroidered funeral cloths, which the government usually treated much less harshly. When supplies of these also got scarce, she could wind up her accounts in good order.

By drawing on her substantial capital, she could keep her family going for more than a year without taking the risk of trading under dangerous conditions. She calmly turned her attentions to finishing up the house she was building, drawing on her contacts and experience to locate the needed building supplies. Then she could help her daughter with a new baby. When policies changed, she was back in the market at full strength, even reviving her long-dormant passbook account[1] and restocking her shelves with a full range of cloths.

Describing her rural origins in a prosperous farming family, she sheds light on some of the processes of commercialization and personal advancement as experienced by Asante in the early colonial period. The significant roles played by pawning, shopkeeping, and the first few passbook holders in Kumasi come to life in her vivid descriptions. Her trader mother and storekeeper husband made it relatively easy for her to get established in the lucrative cloth business. Despite these advantages, she worked for pay from a very young age as a farm laborer and a cocoa sorter, to save up capital. Accumulating "little by little" paid off better for her than chasing the quick money she distrusts. Giving and receiving credit on the basis of a reputation for honesty were necessary complements to this hard work, and so was moving to a city like Kumasi where credit was more available. Retiring back to the village would mean failure.

When Maame Kesewaa recorded this story, she was more than eighty years old, but fully active in the market and at home. She had expanded her stall in its original location, when cloth sellers had rebuilt that line of stalls, and climbed the stairs into it almost daily. She still did all the wholesale purchasing, while her now matronly daughter handled retail sales and brought along several young grandchildren for her to indulge. At a party that year, she sat on the sofa with three of them, making sure they had enough food and behaved well. But she also surprised me by being a skillful and enthusiastic dancer, one of the first to get the dancing started and the last to stop.

Her story here shows all these sides of her personality. She enjoys her successes, slips in her understated jokes, and keeps many of her thoughts to herself. Her face wrinkles in disapproval of colleagues who seek public acclaim. Her obvious pride in her passbook credit account and the house she built for herself overshadow her self-image as not caring for worldly prestige. She also presents some of the most coherent strategies for success among these stories, strategies that she has obviously thought hard about over the years. Her attitude toward socioeconomic change is measured, assessing its positive and negative aspects.

Her attitude toward publication was equally considered. When she saw my first book, which includes some of her remarks and experiences, she asked a grandson to read the copy I gave her and to report back on its accuracy. She readily agreed to this taped interview and asked for a copy of the tape, to save for her grandchildren to hear. After some thought, she finally decided not to allow her real name and photograph to be used, just in case the visibility might create unforeseen problems. Cautiously trying new things all through her life, she has been served well by this stance and she was not about to abandon it now.

Story: Someone Has Set Herself a Goal

At first, it was not hard at all for people to eat. If you spent even a little bit of money, you could eat. Nowadays, I and my children, they are five children. With my other child and her husband, every day we spend about three thousand before I can eat. Every day three thousand before I eat. *Wahu?* At the same time, that three thousand is not what you are making with the work you are doing, what you are eating. You will not get profit like that to spend. So all the **time**, this gives you a lot of trouble. It gives you a lot of hardship, I mean, some days maybe you need pepper, maybe you need this. And if you get your money out, and say that you are reducing it too, it will not be all right. Therefore, every **time**, you will give only what you have to give. Whether you have it or you don't have it, you will give it like that. Long ago, also, you could spend maybe four hundred cedis for about six people, and you could eat your fill. *Wahu?* But today, it is not like that. *Wahu?*

GC: Formerly, what did they do to get money to buy food?

In the past, for example, if you worked, then we were not using big money to do business. Me, for instance, I went to get a **passbook** at the UAC **store**;[2] it was two hundred cedis. Two hundred was what I took to get the **passbook**. So you've seen how it was. When you went to the store, they would give you that much in goods. As the end of every month came, it meant that you had to go and pay your whole debt, when they give you credit like that. At that **time**, too, when the white people were here, because of that, if you went, they would give you things on credit. At the end of the month, each one of you went to pay your debt, all of it. When you **closed** the account completely that way, then they gave you new goods again.

Because of that, all the **time**, you were not pinched very much. Every time, if you were able to do a lot of work, when the year ended, even when Christmas was coming, you who were able to do a lot of work, they might cut a half piece of cloth[3] to be given to you free, saying, "Take the cloth, to take for Christmas." But as for today, if you do not have a lot of money, you cannot do business. Right now, as we are talking here, it takes really big capital to do business, but you will not get such big profits.

Then, that [two hundred cedis] was a really big sum of money. I mean, if you tired yourself and wanted that two hundred cedis, you would get it. Now, where I built my house, for instance, they charged me two hundred cedis for the house **plot**, the whole of it. I bought two **plots** for four hundred. There are two, but only one of them I have built on. One is what I have started a bit. *Wahu?* The two hundred, too, today right now, it has gone up to three million cedis. Hmm. The thing that was two hundred has now got to three million. And as for the house, you will build it, and the **cement**! It was four cedis and six shillings. At the **time** I was erecting the **wall**, the **cement** was ten cedis. I had finished the house and I was building the **wall**. Today the **cement**, one sack is 4600 cedis. Now everything has gone up. Today, if you do not have big capital also, your business gets hard. When you buy things, even just a little bit, it takes a lot of money.

GC: When you started to sell things, who gave you money to sell?

When I started trading, at that time, my husband was working at UAC. *Woate asɛ?* When I started to marry him, when I was a **girl** and I married him, then my husband was working at UAC. That's why he opened the **passbook** for me with two hundred. I did the work like that, and I was doing the store business too. I earned money there, and I also set out more goods in the market in addition. So, if I went to do the work, I took some of the things to the **store**, and then I would bring some also to the market. *Wahu?* Then my child would be there looking after it, and I went to the **store**. So any **time** I got things, I would bring some for the child to look after. I was selling only cloth then, and I have sold like that until today. When I was a young woman, all along, it was cloth alone that I had sold like that until this time now.

GC: Before you married, were you selling cloth?

It was when I married that I started to sell cloth. When I was a young woman, at that time, my mother died early. So when my mother died, I was staying with her elder sister. We were going to the farm, in Ashanti Mampong. We were going to the farm. I and my mother went to farm like that then. So when we went to farm, and we brought food, we ate some, then maybe we took some to the market to sell. *Wahu?* We took some to the market to sell. I mean, we ate some too. Little by little, we went on like that.

Someone came to marry me, and then he took me to Konongo. The gentleman was keeping a **store** at Konongo, so he married me and took me to Konongo. So when we went there, we started to work. When we went there too, at that time I was a child, and he too was a young man. Therefore sugar, at that time we weighed sugar by the margarine tin, they weighed it and they weighed it. If they weighed out a **pound**, then if they poured it, it made three margarine tins. So they weighed it at sixpence, yes, sixpence. They weighed it out like that, sixpence a **pound**. So you pour it out and it makes three tins. So, for the three margarine tins you would be able to charge threepence each. A margarine tin for threepence! So it meant that you got your sixpence and you also got threepence on it. You've got ninepence, and if you used the sixpence to pay, then you made a profit. That's what gave me some capital. Eh, so if it was going well, and I finished cooking quickly, then I would go to the **store**. When I went and they were weighing out, then I would go and weigh some. I was also selling. When I finished cooking, then I sold. I sold and collected the money together little by little like that.

So we were there, and when I had spent five months there then they transferred us to Kumasi here. I had got a bit of money saved up; I took it to be about four hundred cedis. I had really got money. Yes, then I had four hundred, and I put it around my waist. I had got real capital I was bringing to a big town, all right. Because of that, when I was coming to start, when we had just arrived here, I started in selling **material**. Then I was selling **material**. I carried them around in a pan. At that time we were arranging them in a pan. We would be putting them there, and then you sold them. *Wahu?* There was some for sixpence a **yard**. **Material, calico**, you know **calico**? At that time, it was maybe sixpence a **yard**.

MA: I even bought some myself long ago, when I was at **Roman Girls' School***. At that time we were buying calico at two shillings a* **yard***, so I was buying three* **yards** *for six shillings. When I went to school then, they would give me sixpence a day, so I ate for three and a quarter pence and put a penny down. When I collected them together and it grew to six shillings, then I used it to buy a school* **uniform***.*

It was like that. *Wahu?* So little by little like that, that let me get a bit of money to save. So when I came here, too, when I started with the **material**, when I went to the **store**, there were some kinds at one shilling a **yard**. Some were two shillings or one and threepence a **yard**. If I went to buy, I would arrange them in a **pan**, and it sat there and I sold little by little like that.

Then my husband went to take a **passbook** for me for two hundred. That meant that now I took cloth to add to the **material**. If I paid attention, I saw that the cloth was better than the **material**. I mean, if you cut up **material**, sometimes, after you cut, you would have a half or a **quarter** [yard] left. Then what remained was useless. So then I stopped taking **material**, to sell cloth.

At that time, a half piece of cloth was called "one pound, one pound." You know that at first there were pound notes? As for me, I do not even know how to say this money now. Three days ago, recently, I gave some to a madman. This stuff! No, then we were not eating **pounds**, but **coins**. Look at this **coin**, it was not even five shillings. Yes, two shillings and sixpence. There was some paper money too, that was one **pound**. Was it not the one-pound note? I mean, when I went to get it at that time, maybe at the **store** a whole piece of cloth would be one pound five shillings. So if we brought it back, then if someone added one shilling on the price for each piece, you took it. *Wahu?*

And you too, if they bought it from you then, you would get your whole daily food money out of it. Altogether it was two shillings and sixpence. *Wahu?* If you got two shillings and sixpence, you would be able to eat off it until the next day. I was cooking for three meals, for two shillings and sixpence. It went on little by little, little by little like that. When I went to Konongo my daily food money was just one shilling. When the month ended, he gave me thirty shillings. One shilling. He was giving me thirty shillings, so for one day, it was one shilling that I used. Also, when I did the marketing then, I would have about a penny left, and I put it aside. When I put it all together, then maybe I could use it to buy a headscarf. By the time the month ended, too, I might have been able to save about one pound. From the thirty shillings, I might have got enough money to buy a headscarf, at one shilling and threepence.

And so it continued little by little like that. We came to this town here, where I sold the **material** and stopped, and finally I sold cloth. At that time, too, with cloth, even cloth from overseas, each half piece was one pound or two pounds. *Wahu?* One pound or two for a half piece. For the full piece, two pounds. If you went to UAC, quite good imported cloth was four pounds for a piece. So if you went to get it there, and someone added two shillings to that price, then you sold it to her. Your profit was two shillings, and the two shillings you got would be enough to buy food to eat. Little by little like that, we did our work little by little, little by little, like that.

Later, I mean, finally, **civilization** had come. And I made up my mind that I would find a place and, *agya,* I would build a little house. If I were gone, my children could stay in it. So we went to take a plot for two hundred cedis, a hundred pounds. While I was looking for land at Mmaakro, one of my friends was with me. She offered that if I was looking for some land there, she would get some for me, and I said I would like that. So every day I went there, but she told me that the one who divided up land was not there. So I gave her the money in pound notes: twenty twice, forty. Then I gave her forty cedis that she should take for herself. It was forty I gave her.

Then on a Sunday, when I went, they had divided up some of the land. They had cut the land. I went to pay two hundred, and that meant they gave the land to me. A hundred pounds each like this, a plot like this one. I bought the two plots for two hundred pounds. At the **time** that we started to build the house, little by little, the **cement** was, eh, in pounds, four cedis and six shillings. We started the building of the house then and there. By the **time** we finished constructing it, and we were coming to build the **wall**, then cement had gone up to ten cedis. The **cement**, it came to four cedis each, then six cedis, and then ten cedis. They had increased it, but we still used it to complete the wall. *Wahu?*

At first, in fact, everything was cheap, but today everything has gone up. The **income tax**, for example, for the work that we are doing today, at first it was one pound a year. Just today, when they came, well, my stall is a big one that is in good shape. They didn't look at the goods that were in it. Only because it was big, they assessed whatever they liked for you to pay. They set what you would pay. So between today and before, changes have come into it. A lot of changes have come into it. At first, everything was cheap. But today, everything is going up fast [*de mmirika*]. *Wahu?* Everything is running.

GC: When you were building the house, did cloth sellers do business like they do today?

Eh, do you mean that when we sold they bought it? Eh, then people bought it! The price was high, but people were buying it. Especially at the beginning, how they bought it! Since money was scarce then, they bought it, but people could not buy it in a rush like they do today. Then, a lot of things were there, but some people here did not even have any cloth covering them at all. I mean, the goods were abundant, but you couldn't get money. You would have to work hard before you got money to buy some; then you were tired. Today, the price of the goods is expensive, but people are really able to buy. They buy more than before. At first, no, people were not able to buy. Today, in fact, they buy a great deal more than when I was a young woman.

It was like this. They were not buying much, so if someone came around, you could give it to her on credit, like a headscarf, for instance. Someone would offer it on credit, at threepence a day. So *wahu,* every day she would collect threepence, like that. Cloth, too, sometimes even the one that cost one pound threepence or two pounds, sometimes you could pay for it at one shilling a day. Yes, you offered credit to people. If they came, they paid one shilling a day like that until the **time** was up. Then you would see that the cloth had become the person's property.

GC: So at first money was hard to find?

It was very, very hard. Money was hard to get then. In the past, there was not much money in the world. *Wahu?* Money was not there in the world. My mother's elder sister, for example, she brought forth twins. That meant that she was looking for people to look after the children. So, for one pound, one pound, two pounds, two pounds, that way she took four children, *wahu?* Four children were what she took. She paid two pounds to the child's mother. If she paid two pounds to her mother, at that **time**, two pounds, two pounds, times four. Four young women were looking after the babies. Mmireku Koko, she brought forth in our house there. She brought forth first, then later she left. *Wahu?* So then, getting money was very hard. There was not much money around. Look, you were able to use two pounds to buy a whole human being. If someone failed to pay, and your people got into debt, when they came to collect the money, then you would bring the child to stand in front [as a guarantee]. Until they paid you the money, the child would be serving like that, until the mother would bring you the money she had come to borrow. She let her serve like that, until the time she got the money to bring, and then she would come to take her.

GC: And if I was the one looking for a child to stay with me?

Ehee, then if I had some [children], I would come to take money from you. For two pounds, I would give the child to you. So the child would serve like that until I would get your money to bring you. I would come back to pay.

GC: So if it happened that you failed to get the money for me, would I keep the child?

Then she stayed there at your place, like that.

GC: As for that, your mother had some money, like someone who gives loans.

Yes, she gave out loans. Yes, then she had money.

GC: What did she do to get her money?

She made it herself; my mother sold things herself. She was selling things. When I grew up a bit and saw it, she was selling salt and pepper and other small assorted things: tobacco, and sugar and **sardines** and other things. A can of **sardines** was threepence; **canned beef** was sixpence, or eightpence. Canned fish were fourpence. She was selling things little by little like that, so then she had money around. She took four children, for two pounds each.

GC: At Mampong at that time, what work was there that you could do and get a lot of money? Only your mother's work?

Some were there trading, just like my mother, *wahu?* Also, she was going to the farm in addition, *wahu?* Like yams, she grew yams in very large amounts. Yes, so when she harvested them, at that time, a DC[4] was there that they said weighed the goods. So when we weighed, when we used to dig up the yams in the farm there, then we set down the machine they used for the weighing, and we put them onto it. So when they weighed it out, whatever amount that we would buy was five shillings. We carried them to the scale, then poured them onto it like that. Then if they weighed it up, what remained was five shillings' worth. Maybe my mother and I carried headloads of yams, two full baskets, for five shillings. Today, even one yam is a thousand cedis. Then, there was no money in it. At that time, we were working for nothing. At that time also, if you took a **by-day** laborer to the farm, someone who would weed, then it was only sixpence. If you took a **by-day** laborer to the farm, he would charge you sixpence.

GC: At that time, which place had more money, Mampong or Konongo?

Konongo was especially good, but each town had the work that they were doing. From Konongo to Agogo, as you've seen, they have plantain. And cocoa, that was also there then. *Wahu?* And in Mampong in particular, it was yams and beans. And there too, they were doing that business. Onions, they did that work there. Yes, they got money. And in Konongo, too, it was plantain and cocoa. And from Konongo to Agogo and going on to Patrensa and all those **areas** too, their work was plantain and cocoa. That was what made them also get their money there.

GC: So which place did you like better, Mampong or Konongo?

Anyway, my hometown Mampong was good for me, because it was my hometown. Konongo, I just went to stay there. It was business that took us there, and then we also left there to come to Kumasi here.

GC: Were you happy that you came to Kumasi, and you wanted to live here?

Eh, as for Kumasi here, I like it better than Mampong and Konongo put together, because this place is a big city. In this place, too, if you do business and tell the truth [are honest], even if you do not have money, someone else has money, and she will go to get things and bring them to you. You also, when you sell them, you will get money to go and buy something to eat. But if you lived there in the village, nobody went to get anything for you to sell, unless you yourself had your money that you could use to work. Yes, here work is easy, if only you tell the truth. As for that, if you only tell the truth to people, the work is easy.

Just recently, for instance, my friend was at Yendi. When the fighting broke out there, that meant she had to come back. Recently, she went to bring me cloth for a million or two cedis. When she came here, she could not get a good enough place to sit, so she went to get the cloth and brought it to me. Two million cedis' worth, she has brought to me. I have not given her any money, but I am selling it. When I finish selling it, then I will give her money to her. *Woate aseɛ?* In Mampong, you would not get someone to bring that to you, for you to sell. In Konongo, too, you would not get someone to go and bring things to you like that, for you to sell. So in the big towns, especially, you will find someone to go and get things for you to sell, so that you too will earn something to buy food to eat. Yes indeed, to build a house. If you only tell the truth, you will get enough to build a house.

GC: Are there people who don't tell the truth?

If a person gives goods to her, when she sells them she spends the money. Then she makes that person also go into debt.

GC: Among the people with whom you started selling here in Kumasi, have a lot of them built houses or not?

Some have built houses, but some could not build houses.

GC: What did you do that gave you enough profit to build a house?

As for this issue, it is straightforward. Say there is a person who sets herself a goal: "Whatever happens, I want to do this." *Wahu?* Therefore, even when it comes to the food that she is eating, she will be cutting it back. So *wahu?* If she needs to buy maybe something at four, then she might buy only two, two hundred cedis. Then you take the other two hundred to hide. I mean, you want to do something, that's why. You will put it together little by little like that. So when you see that it has become considerable, then, if you want to do something with the money, if it is a house that you want to build, then you use it to build. *Wahu?*

There might be someone else who sells goods, *wahu,* she might get money, but all the **time** she sees this thing that she wants, she sees that, and she wants it. She cannot build a house. *Wahu?* If you pay, you work, you pay, you sit down quietly and humble yourself. Then if you see that there is something special, like those **glasses** standing there, then you say, I want to do this, to buy this. You will do it little by little like that, and God will make you become able to buy it. So *wahu?* But there is someone else who, when she sees a headscarf, says, I like it. She sees a cloth like this, and she likes it; she sees a cloth like that, and she likes it; she sees shoes like this and she likes them. You can see that every **time** you get money, you are wasting it wildly [*basabasa*]. You cannot build a house like that. There is also the person whose mouth is dear to her. You will see that as for food, she will eat any kind of food, only the best. She will eat like that, and she will not use the money to do anything.

For that matter, one **girl** in the market near us, for instance, once had plenty of money. When she came to the market, she would tie the money around her waist in a tying cloth. Then she would be going round with it like that, at the **time** when we all went in for buying land, for instance. In our area there, a lot of people own houses, but she did not look for one. *Wahu?* The money was at her waist like that, and she brought it to the market. She went away, then she brought it back like that. So when the currency exchange happened, the money was ruined for nothing.[5] She also didn't use it to buy land, she didn't use it to do anything. Just recently, *wahu,* she wasn't able to buy a stall. She herself had no stall, and she was sitting in someone else's. *Wahu?* She herself, her mind did not think about the money being there, so that she might even use it to buy a stall to sit in. She didn't buy anything, she didn't build a house. There was plenty of money at her waist. When she came to work, she used it to tie her waist very big like that.[6] Right now, it is all gone. Today she hasn't got a penny. Right now, she can't even sit in the market, she is sitting at home. *Wahu?*

Therefore, everyone has a goal that is before her. There is someone who, if she works, she says, I am working. If I make something out of it, then in future, even if I become an old woman, *wahu?* You can build. Even if I become an old woman, I shall be sleeping in my room. *Wahu?* There is someone else who does not care. Whether it is her old age, or whatever, it is not her problem. She will be using her money carelessly [*basabasa*] like that. So when she gets to be an old woman, if she is still living in town here, she will have to go to her hometown. *Wahu?* She cannot keep staying here, because she will not have the money to rent a room. If you become an old woman, and you cannot do any work, then you go to your hometown. No, as for me, I do not want to go there. If

I go there, and if I get old and die, I want all my children, all of them, to stay here. So *wahu?* That is why I want to sweat like that to build a house to stand there. Even if I die, the children will live here.

GC: Right now, if someone sold cloth like you do, would she be able to build a house?

Yes, she can do it and build. If the person wants to build, and only then, she will be able to do it. Little by little, little by little, like that she will build it. Eh, the traders right now do build houses. These days, they build plenty of houses, more than before. Where the Breman house is now, my mother, I was going there then and weeding a farm. In those days I was weeding a farm. When I went there, I took a farm plot. In the morning, before I came to the market, by seven o'clock I was at the farm there. I worked like that, until it struck seven thirty. Then I came home to bathe, and then came to the market. Now, that whole place has become part of the town. It goes for a mile and a half. *Wahu?* So now too, in that whole area they have built houses. They have built houses all over, all over. A plot is two or three million cedis, but people still buy. It goes farther and farther. *Wahu?* They go to buy, and they have built. *Wahu,* if you are in a big town, you want to stay in the big town. If you have no building there, you've seen how it is. The **time** will come when, for instance, the landlord will tell you, "My child who is overseas is coming back, so I am taking back my house." You understand me, he will take it. Whoever doesn't take it back, he will tell you to pay more money. And that money you need to pay, you will not have it. So you will have to move to your hometown. Yes, you say there is no money, therefore you will move to your hometown. Maybe too, you have not decided for yourself that you want to stay in your hometown.

If you live in a big town like this, and you move to your hometown, when you go, then you go to become wretched. *Wahu?* I mean, you yourself have no farm there. *Wahu?* You have no work to do there. If you go just to sit down, who is going to cook food for you to eat? *Wahu?* You also do not have any work. *Wahu?* You will be hard pressed like that, and in only three days you are dead. In only three days you will die. *Wahu?*

Therefore, if you want to stay in a big town, then if you really do your best and you push yourself to work, you know that you will eat. So if you earn maybe four, then you will spend two and save two. Little by little, little by little, little by little, little by little. Doing like that, you will be able to build a house. Even if only one bedroom, you will be able to build something. *Wahu?* So, if you are staying in somebody's house, when the time might come that he says, "I am taking my house," then you too have your own house and you go there.

You've seen where I was at Mbrom, when I was at the Bantama chief's place. It was there I was staying. All the time we were living there, I paid attention quietly, so that I, too, one day, I could find a house to build. I went on and on, I did it little by little like that, and then I completed building the house, but my landlord did not know anything about it. [*Laughs.*] I did not let him see, never. When I built it, I did not let him see it. So when I had finished building my house, one day, there we were like that. **African Bungalow** [Mbrom], you've seen the place in **African Bungalow**.

Then he called me: "Akua, come!" When I went, he told me, "Today we are going to weed the house all over."[7] But the part of the house that went with my room I had already weeded, the whole back and the whole front, and swept my portion myself. He said, "We will weed the house here and all over." I said that as for me, I had already weeded in back and front of my room and finished it, so those that were left should weed their part, too. He told me that it was his house, so we had to do what he wanted. He was the one who owned the house. And I said that, having already finished weeding what was mine, I could not go to weed someone else's part for them. They also were sitting there, and they were not weeding their part. He said the house belonged to him, so if you tried anything, he would be able to evict you if he liked. I did not say anything. By then I had completed my house and brought water and electricity service to the place. Yes, but he did not know anything about it. So when I observed **that day** that he wanted to trouble me, I told him this. The day was a Thursday. I went there and told him, "Papa, I want to leave here this Saturday. I will move out." And he said, "Why?" And I said that I had built a house. The man was about to die.

That man, if you stayed in his house there, he checked on your progress in the market. If you were there, you would see that he was coming. He was coming to look at your work. So if I saw him coming, I used a cloth to cover my head and cover my face. I didn't let him see my stall, never. I had always covered my face. When that happened, only after he had looked and passed by would I look at him. If he did this, if he looked for me, he wouldn't see me. So he never once saw my market location. He was a person who was very envious, so I did not let him see anything.

I told him that I wanted to move out, and if it pleased God, we were bidding him farewell. Saturday I would leave the house there. Now then, do you know what? He was sitting there and he said, "Hmm." First he asked his children this: "That woman, since she came to stay in this house here, when did she build a house? When did she build a house?" They said, "Ah." Then he called my children, too, and asked them, "Your mother's house, is it big?" And they said, "Yes." "Ei, when did she build it?" "She has finished building it and connected the electricity. All of us children, every one of us has his or her own room there." He said, "Is that so? She had stayed here to build a house, and she did not tell me?"

Finally he said, actually at daybreak, he told me, "I am going to Kwaman." He was from Kwaman-Nsuta. "When you go, the water bill has come, the light bill too, they have brought it." So his son, a young man they called Kofi, he was going to pay it, so [I should] give the money to him. And I said, "hoo." That man couldn't stay to watch my head go [to see me off].

Besides, the place I was in, it was only as big as inside the yard like this. So I could hardly get in; I and my children could not all fit into the room. And I myself had built on an addition. When I built it, that man had not asked me about it—what you were paying for it, when you built it, you ran up a debt of sixpence or threepence. So I built it, and then he made me pay rent for it in addition. When I finished building it, then and there he took it to rent back to me. It cost me money. The money I used to do it all became my loss. He took the house that I built to rent back to me. And I said, staying in someone else's house like that, to be building something for him to rent back to me! That gave me the idea to find a piece of land myself to build upon. *Wahu?*

So when I moved, he had taken over the building **free**, and he was renting it out. He was taking it to rent out, but he couldn't even stay to see me off. When I left, he couldn't ever come there [to my house], never. He died recently, and they said they were going to observe his one-year anniversary. He never set foot there, and his wife also never set foot there. *Wahu?* But I moved out.

Therefore, if you are in a big town and you want to stay, you must find the wisdom to want to do something. *Wahu?* Little by little, if God helps you and you get a bit of money and you make it. If you finish building it, then the landlord says, "Give me my house" and you turn his over to him. Then you also go move into yours. *Wahu?* And if you don't do that, then you might be staying there and he would evict you and make you leave. When he **first started** to trouble my mind, if I had not had a house, then he would have troubled me very much. He said that as for him, he had paid money at the **court**. If he took you there today, the next morning they would evict you. He evicted people from the house every day.

My sister came first to sit here [in the market], and got a stall and neglected it [*yɛ nɔ* **rough**]. These days, goods are two million at a time. At first, too, my money was nothing, but she had gone to bring things to give me on credit, because "you have a stall you are sitting in." You've seen that she brings me things on credit. She knows that I will pay her, too.

Then, a stall was not hard to get at all. If you wanted one, you could get it immediately. There would be someone who had moved away. If she could not sit in it, she would say, "Come and take it and sit in it." *Wahu?* And also, if you look at the market where we are sitting, this central area, for instance, they themselves [the city] brought us to sit there. And here, I mean, it was a roadway, and they brought us in to sit there. The place is one big stall now. *Wahu?* And this big stall, if we entered the market then we paid two shillings and sixpence for it. Stall rent was two shillings and sixpence, that's what we paid then. And the stalls were not scarce.

Myself, for example, at the plantain section I had two stalls. I kept staying in them, but then I got up and left there. Then I was selling oil, and I got up and left that stall there. I mean, no one needed stalls then. *Wahu?* So if you sat in it, as I did, then later I just got up and left it there. Today, if I go to do my marketing and I see that stall, I say, "You just look, oh." As for the past, then we were really foolish. Eh, if I had stayed on there then, and kept paying the rent, then by this time it would still have been mine. I got up and left it there. Today, someone has arranged **material** and other things there. She has made it beautiful like a **store**, selling shoes. When I get there, I tell myself, "Just look at that." *Wahu?*

At first, in fact, people didn't know better [*n'ani mmuɛ*], and also, the stalls were not scarce. But as for today, you can't even get one. Today, even if you are sitting in someone else's, she will evict you immediately.

When they raised the stall walls up and up, it made all eyes turn to them, very much. So if you are sitting in someone's stall, she will come to take it back. If you yourself do not have your own, they will take it back right away. Even if you don't want the stall, someone else will want it. Then, you would say, "The people there were bothering me, and I just got up to leave it there." Is this a good thing? But then the thing was that nobody knew that it was going to get like this today.

Today, for instance, I went to get some black funeral cloth at the market, where they are selling **material** and retailing it. Sometimes I go there to buy black funeral cloth from a stall there. At that stall, the person bought the stall for four hundred cedis. Four hundred cedis! What I used to buy two plots of land! She has made the stall beautiful, like this one, so when I went there I said, "This stall is mine, oh. This stall and more I don't see." Then she says, "Why are you looking at it? You've sold it, don't you understand? It is mine." Then she said, "You yourself look out." Just today, I could have gotten one or two million for it. But I sold it for four hundred cedis. At that time, four hundred cedis was a lot of money. Now it is not.

GC: You were talking about when you went to stay home. What happened in the market to make you go and stay at home?

Well, at that time, when Rawlings came and the work [of trading], well, when you sold they arrested you. They were also saying that they wouldn't let us bring things to the market, so we stopped, we stopped doing the work. Everyone went to stay in her own house. You couldn't bring goods to sell in the market; cloth and poplin and other things, we were not to take them to the market. That was why we had to stop. We left and stayed home. For that reason, I did not want to just sit at home, so I went to buy a **fridge** something like this size, for instance, to put in the market, and I put in a water **pipe** to the stall. When you used to come there, the **pipe** [faucet] was in the room there, because then I was selling **ice water**. But at that time we couldn't even get someone to buy water. It was for pennies, but they were not buying. People were not passing by to buy, so sometimes, when the children came, they would carry some around like that [to sell].

As for that, it was **control** time. They sold the things off at **control price**. We all had to go and stay at home. All the money got burnt [finished] and we went to stay at home. When I went to buy my **fridge** and put it there, I said that I would be selling water little by little like that, so I would not stay in the house and brood. Eh, during that time, my child and I both were staying at home. At that time, she was selling [face] **powder**. She also, when she went to stay at home, her whole stock had also been sold off. So then we had nothing. We went to stay at home. I feel like we stayed home for about two years. We came back when everything collapsed completely. Finally then they said everyone could do her work. All of us came back. Eh, we didn't have any money left, so it was a new loan we went to go and find. For the loan, my next younger sister, she was in the Fanti area at Cape Coast then, and she gave me a little money. And I again used it to start little by little.

GC: You say you still go to take cloth from UAC?

Yes, I still owe money on some. I went to take my monthly goods, and then I traveled. Recently, when you came to the stall, we went to a meeting somewhere. I just got back, so I went and paid my debt. That is why I hurried, so I could return soon. Maybe you would come by and miss me. That is why, when I came back from there, when I arrived she was sitting in back, waiting for me.

GC: I remember that lots of people have stopped the UAC business.

Yes, they canceled a lot of the **passbooks**. Ever since I did business with the old **passbook**, I never did draw out any of my **commission**. I did business, but I did not take it out. So if you went to show it, you could **start** to work. With Ghanaian goods. ATL, TTL, and GTP.[8] Right now, I even have some from overseas. There is overseas cloth in the **store** there. Some cloths are at UAC there, and I take some. If I go, and what I like is there, then I take some. The **commission**, actually, is small today. Today, if you do not order one million, they will not give you any **commission**. But if you sign for one million, your **commission** is four thousand, or five thousand. It is very, very small.

I have even got so far that, right now, I can do business up to four million in a month. I am able to do it. Each month, for example, I have signed for things worth about four million. If you are holding cash and you go to the **store**, you will not be able to buy any. They will not let you buy any. People don't buy it with cash there. So you will get your profit, and you get **commission** as well in addition. So when you go, you will buy some. If someone comes from the street outside to the place, they do not sell to her. They cannot buy it at the **store** there, only if you can use your **passbook** to take it. If you use the book to go and take things away, when you go, you will also little by little earn something on them.

Right now the PZ[9] **manager** is my son. The one who is there now is my eldest son. My eldest son is the one. He is at PZ right now, but now they do not get cloth any more. Now, medicine and talcum **powder** and other goods are what they sell.

GC: As for this, you've done well.

MA: You've been trading since long ago and everyone knows you.

Yes, everyone knows me. Everyone knows me very well. Right now, in the market where we are selling things, all of those who are there came to find me already there. Yes, all the stalls, big and small, they all came to meet me at that section there.

GC: As for that, they should make you the queen mother.

As for that, that is what everyone is saying, but I do not want it. Mother! Everyone has what she likes, *wahu?* I do not like things that are any big fuss. All those who are there, all of them, came to meet me already there at that section. At the time I came to the section there, I was a young woman. I have stayed there for a very long time indeed, so those who are there now, all of them came to meet me at that section there. From the big stalls, the back there and in front, and the small ones, all together. They all came to meet me already at the section there. But I do not like it. It's like this. They said I should take the office of queen mother, but I said, as for me, I do not want it. As for me, I like things of the Lord more than worldly matters.

GC: I see that the lady who is the queen mother is not very old. She is not as old as you.

Yes, since she came to take the office, she hasn't even been there long at all. She came not very long ago at all. At first, she was carrying things on her head. She carried things like that to go around hawking.[10] When she got tired, then she would come to sit beside someone there. And then someone turned the stall over to her to buy. When she came there, as soon as she came they made her the queen mother. It was just like Kumasi people; as soon as she came they pushed the thing on to her. We don't like it [being queen mother]. Everyone who has stayed in the market for a long time, they don't like anything about it. I mean, it will worry you. One day, you will be doing something, and they say, "The queen mother must come here." Then you will be walking around. [*Laughter.*] Me, I don't even have spare time for myself.

MA: There are some that like it. It feels good to her. She enjoys being the queen mother. They call her queen mother, and it makes her happy.

As for that, this one especially, she will be waving her arm and doing this and that. Then it feels good to her. It feels good to her. As for me, I do not like it.

GC: So, had she ever been the cloth queen mother for Kumasi before?

No, at the very **first**, **first** she was not the queen mother. There was someone who was there before. After her came another person; they selected her and she too became queen mother. They called her Yaa Mansa. As for me, I do not want it. I do not like any queen mother office whatsoever. I only want my somewhere to sit, like this.

CHAPTER 3

Madame Ataa

Portrait: A Good Citizen

In the past, if you hadn't been to school,
you didn't wear a dress. Now we say,
"Whiteness is in the store."

While Madame Ataa talked, we sat on the heavy velveteen furniture of her living room, kept slightly dark to minimize the heat. Her deliberate, stately delivery gave a dignified weight to her bulky, inert physical presence. She was a good friend and neighbor of my research assistant, Mrs. Appiah, who had suggested we call. They had been neighbors in the market when Mrs. Appiah sewed there as a young woman, and more recently they had built houses in the same distant suburb. They also shared a similar religious outlook. Now that poor health made it difficult for Madame Ataa to go out much, she mostly stayed at home and kept an eye on her grandchildren. Our extended visit was a welcome change, and a gratifying reminder of her success in her more active years.

Her story gives a valuable glimpse of the respectable family and community values of an earlier era, which drew on both English and Asante models. She takes school attendance, living with her husband, and ample chop money for granted. Growing up in a leading Kumasi family, she enjoyed a secure position that her neighbors respected and envied. Hard work and discipline were expected, in her mother's stall and the cocoa shed, but they paid off. Working as a seamstress, she soon had twelve apprentices. With a passbook to sell cloth like her sisters, she easily built a house and raised her daughters for better careers. Ending up in a rural village was unthinkable.

Seeing others caught in the crosscurrents of social change triggered her sympathy as well as her dismay. Her remarks on early pregnancy sound condescending, except that she often uses "we" in speaking of those with moral failings. Reflecting on her own life experiences and what she sees today, she thought hard about what had changed in the conditions of life and relationships between people in Kumasi. She looked for a way out of the current economic crises that would restore dignity as well as prosperity. Despite her sometimes ponderous tone, she showed a strong, sincere concern for her community. The question of whether her account should be published anonymously did not trouble her much. She had little left to fear and nothing to be ashamed of in her long and productive life, which had been lived to some extent in the public eye already.

Story: A Man Would Marry You Properly

Really, in the past, when you married a man, well, if you married, the man would marry you properly. And you would go live in your husband's house, so nicely. Maybe he had hired a room, and you would live in it, with everything as it should be. You and he would have children. He would look after them properly. This means that all the time, you are happy with the man. All the time, you and the man are living together **fine**. *Woate asɛ?* Then, in the past, your husband would take out four shillings each day, and it would be enough to cook food. On Sundays, it would be six shillings that you took to cook food, and that, too, he would give you. On some days, you would even get some to save, and you would put it aside. That means that life was not hard like this.

Little by little, with God's help, I began to do UAC work. There were **passbooks**, and I had a **passbook** with UAC. I took one hundred pounds to open the passbook. At Ollivant, I had twenty pounds. At Compagnie, I took twenty pounds to open the book.[1] Then I had many passbooks to work with. Little by little, little by little, gradually I got some money. I went to work and built a house. At the time that UAC came, with God's help I was able to build a house, the **boys' quarters**[2] style. I mean, I was buying bags of cement for the house at four shillings and sixpence each. So every time, I got it easily. It wasn't hard. I built a house like this, and the whole cost was two thousand pounds, that means four thousand cedis, for a **boys' quarters**. It was cheap.

The world was good. If you went to school, you didn't pay school fees. If you went to **college** [secondary school], they would charge a little bit, not much. It was like that. It was in Nkrumah's time.[3] The whites had left, and just then we had reached independence. And just in these days now, prices of things have become expensive. Just these days, things have gone up. But in the past, it wasn't like that. In the past, you and your child stayed at home, and your husband said, "I am going here, I will come back soon." You lived with your husband, and you didn't do anything. You just stay there. The man goes to work and returns and he will see his wife and children.

Also, today's children that have come to us, they are in a hurry to marry. He goes to a funeral. He has taken a lover. He has taken a woman and got pregnant with her. He says, "It isn't mine." Every day, we quarrel. This is what has made the whole world very hard. Our daughters today have no husbands. Our young men also have children with us and don't marry us. He has children like this, and when it comes time to name the child,[4] he says, "It isn't mine." In the past, it wasn't like that. In the past, you lived with your mother and a man would come to ask for you in marriage. From your mother and father, you go to your husband's house like that. But today, the daughters that have come say, "We don't want that."

Because of this, the burden always falls on the elderly women. It makes us anxious all the time. Your own child has had a baby, with no father; you will worry! So every day, it's like it weighs on you. Today's girls and young men, too, they live all over the place [*basabasa*]. They go to Europe, they go to France. Some of us wanted to go to Nigeria. We went to Nigeria and they beat us. They beat us and threw us on the ground, and we came back. So today, that's what has made living so hard. It is very, very hard.

Today, you take out four thousand cedis and you can't do anything worthwhile with it. If you have many children, you can't even eat with them and feel full with that. As for today, things are hard. Everything has gone up [*kɔ so*]. The past was not like this. In the past, when the white people were here, we bought things very cheap. *Woate aseɛ?* In the past, a sewing machine like this was very cheap. You could buy a machine for fourteen pounds. I even have one put away. Everything, we bought a **fridge** just like that. How much did I actually pay for it? Five hundred cedis, for a **fridge**. Today, if you go pick one up, you cannot afford the price they give you. That's what has made things very expensive.

Today also, the people now, we don't like to work. In the past, many young women and girls were in the forest farming. Now, we are not good. All of us have run away to live in Kumasi. This is the thing that has made the price of food expensive. Who should stay there and do the work? We don't like to farm, so it has made food expensive. We all run away to live in the big city; we don't like the village. And if you don't like the village, am I myself, an old woman, able to do it? I can't make a farm. So it has made things hard. *Woate aseε?* My own hometown is near here, ten miles away. In my hometown, we have all moved to live in Kumasi. That is what has made food expensive, it is all from that. It is not that it came from somewhere else. *Wahu?* We are not good. Our young men of today are not good. All of them have run away into the big cities. That is what has brought problems. *Wahu?* So many problems coming has made many troubles land on us. *Wahu?*

Children today, as soon as they marry a man, just like this they get divorced. As for young men, they don't even marry the woman. Only one here and there has married. Just recently, by God's grace, if Christianity has come, Pentecostals and Methodists and the rest do marry. Maybe they have a wedding. In the past, only adults like us would have a wedding. Today, very young people go have a wedding. The next day, they get divorced. A young child a year old, they go to ring the bell; they only do this and they say they have had a wedding. In three days they divorce, and they come back to sit down.

In the old days, it wasn't like that, *wahu?* You were with your mama and papa. And when you marry and the woman understands the man, so that they are living in peace, it means that you will always be comfortable. Children today, they don't want that. Even if a man wants to marry her, she doesn't want it. Every day, she brings quarrels home. Some are here right now, who have husbands who have traveled. He doesn't answer her. If you live there, a woman without a husband, will it be good like that? Your husband doesn't come. Today the world is very hard. Conditions have made life very hard. *Wahu?* Today also, people are having many children. So you are having children like that and you don't have money to buy something, how will it be? Isn't the world hard? The world will be hard. So this makes plenty of problems come, you see?

In the past, there was nothing like Ghana. Ghana then was so very sweet. Then we got everything cheap. If you went to the farm, food was there. Everything was there. But we are not good. If you leave there to come and stay here, then whose fault is it? If you go to the village, only old women are left. We are not able to work. And if we can't do this work, and the young men go off like that, they live right here in Kumasi, won't hunger kill you? You will be hungry. That is why they travel. They have traveled and traveled. Some go to Europe, some go here, some go there. France. Who? Who? If you live in your hometown and farm, will you travel? If you get something to eat, will you go? You won't go anywhere. That's why the young men and women that have come today don't like to work. Isn't that it? They like to show off. They like **life**. They go sit at **City Hotel**[5] and they drink. Yes, they go sit and drink there. A long time ago, we worked hard. Our grandmothers and grandfathers and our mothers made farms.

GC: And did you farm? When you were a young woman, did you farm?

As for me, my mother and father lived here, so I never went to my home village. I was born here, so I never went to the village. But my sisters and brothers who were in the village have all come here.

MA: Her mother had a very big house in Ashanti New Town.

GC: Is that why you say you don't like farming work?

No, I don't know how to do it, since I have never done any. My mother is here, my father is here. *Wahu?* When my father and mother are right here, how could I go to the forest? It isn't that I haven't married. I also married here, my husband is here. *Wahu?* We and all our children lived here. That is why things were like that. So at any time, trouble will come indeed.

GC: When you married, did your husband come to your mother and father to ask for you?

Yes, at the **time** I matured, when I was a child or a young woman, he came to tell my mother that he wanted me. He told me that he wanted me, and I said I did not agree, since he had not asked my mother. He told me that he wanted me, but I said I didn't want him, unless he told my mother. In the past, you stayed put. If you were standing with a man, they would beat you. They would insult you. If you stand with someone, and a young man stands with you two or three times, your mother will insult you. She will beat you. *Wahu?* "If a young man wants you, he should come and tell me, before I decide to give you in marriage." That means that she is under your control. But today's daughters, if you speak they don't answer.

GC: But that man, had you seen him before? Did you know him, or not?

No, you don't know him. Maybe you would be going about your business and he would come up to you and say, "I like you." Then you would say, "Go tell my mother. If my mother agrees, I will marry you." And maybe my mother will say, "That **boy**, I don't like him. He is not a good person, so leave him." She says, "Oh, as for this person, he is good. He is a good person. He is from a good home." Perhaps he comes from a good home, so she knows his mother. That's why he is a good person. Because if I have a child and he wants to take her in marriage, that means she is going to a home where everything is as it should be. *Wahu?* Some also go to homes that are not good. Some have thieves,[6] some are not respectable. That's how it is.

So when I grew up enough for marriage, I just had done this. I started my periods to become a young woman, and I married him. I was about eighteen. That is, I didn't go to school. If someone didn't go to school, she married early. If you go to school, they will beat you, so they didn't send me to school. In the past, if you go to school, we say, "They will beat you," so you didn't go to school. Your mother would never send you.

GC: Really? Did some of your brothers and sisters go to school?

Some of my brothers and sisters did go to school. Not all of us lived with my mother, so my elder **sister** went to school. I mean, she didn't live with my mother. She didn't live with my father. She lived with my grandparent. And my grandparent said, no, no, no. I will take her to school. My father also, if he had daughters, he did not send them to school. Only the boys. If you were his son, you would go to school. You would finish. But they said, "Even if he sends you to Europe, you are a woman. And if you are a girl and you go to learn things, he won't send you to school."

GC: So if you did not go school, when you were a child did you work?

Yes, you do it for your mother. You do your mother's work. My mother was selling cloth, so she would go and I would follow and go with her. She sold cloth, so when I grew up I also sold cloth. That was the work my mother was doing. I sold for my mother. I was young, and didn't know money. So whenever she went to bring goods back, I went with her. She would carry some, and I would also carry some, and we took them to the market. The stall I am in is the very one she bought. I mean, I have kept on staying there, *wahu?* By now she is old, and at home. I am the one in it there.

GC: When you married, did you leave your mother?

Yes, you leave your mother. When you marry, you don't live in your mother's house any more. You will move out, you will live with your husband. You will live with your husband, and with them all. Some days, if you want, you will go and visit her. So when I lived there, some days if I wanted, I went to my mother's house. My mother is there. I go to greet her. She is still alive. She is an old lady, my mother.

GC: Do all your brothers and sisters live in that house?

We live in our husbands' houses. Each one lives in her husband's house. Some have also traveled. They are all alive. Some sell cloth. We all sell cloth. Some also have traveled. Some are not there. Some went to Europe. My mother had lots of children. Only girls. She had ten. My mother only had girls. *Wahu?* The things we said today, *woate?* Only girls.

*MA: We called her mother Adwokumase. She was a **popular woman**, we called her Kumasi, Adwoa Kumasi.*

Adwoa Serwaa, but since she was **popular**, that made people call her Kumasi. Her name was Adwoa Serwaa. Yes, that was [how it was]: "Adwoa Kumasi. As for your place here, it is very hot [popular]."

GC: So when you sold cloth, was it with the money from that cloth that you were able to build a house?

[With a] UAC **passbook**. I sold on **commission**. Yes, I took it out to build a house.[7]

GC: So, those who sold cloth, about your age, did some of them also build houses?

Yes, some built houses. Some could build multistory houses. Some built many things. In the past when the British were here, things were very cheap. That **time** was when Nkrumah hadn't come.

GC: At that time, what helped you a lot in your business, so that you got money to build a house?

Was it not the goods that I sold? I keep selling things. That means if I make **commission**, if it sits there and you earn the money, you go to get it out to build with.

GC: What made it so that people bought lots of goods like that?

If you go and get some to bring back, in the past, they came from Accra and from Takoradi. Some people also from France[8] would buy things to take back. Formerly, they all would buy things here and take them away. They brought them to Kumasi. So if you came to Kumasi just like that, those who had **passbooks** would go into the room. Whatever you wanted you could sell. You would earn a **commission** on it. You would make a profit. The things they gave you, they gave you at the **control** price. They will give them to you at the **store** price like that. If it is four thousand, this thing is four hundred cedis. Maybe one hundred pounds. Maybe, if it comes just like that, the local cloth, when it is there I go get some. On every full piece, I get one hundred cedis. It is a hundred cedis for me. Yes, in the past, a hundred cedis.

MA: One shilling, two shillings?

One shilling each. One or two shillings. So the **commission** piles up for you, and at the end of the year you go **check** it and you leave it there. Now if you might keep going just like this for two years or four years, then you will get enough money. You won't earn like that in only one day. It will take a long time. In the past, the money didn't come fast like it does today. Little children have got lots of money. You didn't earn it like that then.

GC: You said that before, your food money was four shillings, and now you take two or three thousand. Which is more tiring, that before you had to work hard before you got your four shillings, or do you work harder today before you get your two thousand or three thousand?

Well, in the past goods were lying around cheap. Then, even for *fufu*, how much would we pay? We bought it for sixpence, ninepence, or the highest price would be one shilling. But still, not everyone could get money to buy it. It was difficult, it was just like today. It was hard. I mean, in the past, you worked hard and got tired. I mean, if I was at Kuro foforɔ mu [across town], I might walk all the way to UAC here, to stand in **line**. You see? I come to UAC here, to stand in **line**, and I earn money. So it is tiring. Today and the past? All are the same. I mean, there is tiredness in all of them.

I mean, in the past, I have worked at this cocoa **shed**. In this cocoa **shed** here, I was sorting cocoa. Ninepence they paid me. That was before I got my period, and I was small. Ninepence they paid me. We were picking over the cocoa, [picking out] the bad ones. I came from Ashanti New Town; I walked from there to come to work. Only ninepence, but it was enough money to eat. And we walked all the way from Ashanti New Town. She knows the place. You walked to come. In the past, there were no cars. You walked, and you would arrive, to sit here. For one day at the cocoa shed, they gave me ninepence. Later, they gave us a shilling. They said we should take it to start work. All of us [were paid] just the same.

GC: *Were you grown up?*

I had grown breasts, so my eyes were open [*anibue*]. I had not started my period, but I understood what was going on. And I wanted to trade very much. But we ran! If we came home, we were walking; there was no car. When you arrived, you cooked your food and you would eat it. You came and you cooked food to eat. And we sorted cocoa here. Compagnie was here; the Compagnie cocoa was here. And then also, in the past, [we worked] when they said, "We are building a house." Some days at that time, there was no cocoa. When a **contractor** was building a house, if you went to help them they gave you one shilling. One shilling a day. You fetched water for the **cement**. So we all got tired the same. I mean, we walked from Ashanti New Town as far as here.

So the money of the past was small, but it was enough for us to eat. It was small, but it was enough to eat. Me and my husband, he took out four shillings. It was small, but it was enough. *Wahu?* I told you. He just had one wife. Some people even took out two shillings. It wasn't everyone who earned four shillings. There were some there that even two shillings was enough. Four shillings. Sundays he got out six shillings because he would eat twice, because he stayed in one place. As for Sundays, he didn't go to work. Sunday, he stayed at home. For four shillings. Your husband and your children. As for Sunday, he was at home, and he ate twice, morning and evening. [Other days] he eats one time. He goes to work! So for that reason, he cannot be at home like Sunday. You too, you come to the market.

I mean, in the past, how much plantain were you buying, a penny, threepence worth? *Wahu?* Garden eggs, when you bought garden eggs, they would throw in some pepper. When you buy beans, you get pepper as a **dash**.[9] When you buy anything, they give you a little something extra. *Wahu?* Sometimes, when you even go to buy plantain, they give you two fingers extra to go and prepare mashed plantain to eat. They say, "Go and prepare mashed plantain to eat," and they pick out some of the plantain for you. And when you come home, you start boiling pepper and you peel the plantain and put it in. Then you mash it with groundnuts, and the children eat it and get full. Then they leave for school. When they return from school, by the time they come, you have prepared the mashed plantain and they eat. In the evening, when you pound a little *fufu* and they eat a little, they get full. Today, we don't beg for things. We don't beg for things like, "Give me two fingers of plantain." Yes, that is what has made the world hard. In the past, too, things were abundant. When all of them brought plantains to unload, they would pile up for a long time and get ripe. Sometimes, you would hear them saying, "Take this and go and mash it for the children to eat."

We didn't buy cassava. In the past, even if they ate cassava, my mother told me that when you eat it, it makes you dizzy, so it's bad.[10] In the old days, when we were children, when we cooked food, we didn't add cassava. If the plantain was heaped up, what we would make with the cassava? Yes, we say it is not good. When you eat it, you will be dizzy. Maybe you have never eaten any before. I mean, there was a glut of plantain. There was a glut of yam. Many yams were there. If you bought sixpence worth of yam, you couldn't eat it. Ninepence worth, you couldn't eat. One shilling, you certainly couldn't eat. It would be plenty, because there was plenty of food.

In the past, people did not take cars. You walked. No cars were there. No taxis were there. Only those who were very rich could buy what we called a touring car. And you sit in it and you go. At that time, anyone who did not have one walked. No, you walked to the market. Who would take you? Nobody would take you. Only if you are going to your hometown, maybe a car would charge a shilling. My hometown is fifteen miles away, so the car charged one shilling. That's why I mean that it was hard. We didn't ride.

Much later, Anwona Patuo[11] came, for threepence. Even with Anwona Patuo, some still walked. If I am lying . . . Much later, Anwona Patuo came. It was a small car they used to pick up people. At that time, when it let you off, [you paid] threepence. Then it was sixpence. Even when it became a shilling, we said we wouldn't take it. It was too expensive. We called it *trɔ, trɔ* [threepence, threepence]. You take it to the market, and you pay threepence, and you get down. When it got up to sixpence, and then a shilling, we said it was too much, we don't like it, we won't get in. We walked and came back, and went out again.

This **civilization** that we have now, it came just these days. As for this, even today it is expensive. I mean, as for this **civilization** of these days, **civilization** has really come. There are too many people, and also **civilization** has come. When people become too many in the world, it makes **civilization** come.

GC: And what makes so many people come?

Isn't it giving birth so that makes them so many? They are very small children and they have given birth. In the past, if people hadn't grown up, they didn't do it. There are even some girls who are not fifteen, and they have given birth. If you go to G,[12] if you even go visit someone, some are there who are not yet fifteen years old, and they have given birth. Some are there fourteen years old, and they have given birth.

But in the past, also, when a child grew up, she went to school **fine**, until she completed **Standard Seven**, so that she could speak English. Today, her friend that has gone to **college** can't even speak English. It has gone very far. Excuse me for saying this, but with what she had learned then, the one who has finished **university** now couldn't speak English with her. Even her English is not very good. *Wahu?* Also, in the past, if you went to school, well, if you don't speak English you haven't gone to school. Then also, if you went to school and you hadn't finished, you wouldn't wear a dress. *Woate asɛɛ?* If you have not finished school, you don't wear dresses. You will wear your cloth in a **collar**.

*MA: You will wear only one cloth, even if you are a **boy** and you have grown up. On Sunday, if you go to church, they will give you one cloth like that to let you wear as a **collar**.*

If you have not been to school. If you have finished school, you will wear a **fine** dress [*atadeɛ*]. But if you have not gone to school, if you put on a dress, they will laugh at you. "You don't understand, haven't you seen? You don't understand English, and what have you put on a dress for?" She doesn't understand English. You will wear cloth.[13] I cannot wear a dress. Yes, they would laugh at me. "You didn't go to school, so what are you wearing a dress for? So now you will understand English? You will know English."

Also today, the young women that have come, we say, "Whiteness is in the **store**." *Woate asɛɛ?* In the past, if you hadn't been to school, you didn't wear a dress. At that time, if you hadn't finished school, if you **failed** and you hadn't passed, you didn't wear a dress. They would laugh at you, because you haven't passed, and you are going to wear a dress? As for today, everyone does. Those who have never been to school before just go put on a dress, and if you talk about it, she says, "**Store**, they sell it in the market." "Good family, being a lady, is in the **store**." Someone who doesn't know anything, even, she says, "Being a lady is in the **store**." If you have seen someone who knows English well, maybe she knows all of her speech is very correct. She knows Asante and so she knows everything.

But today, a young child can be about fourteen years old and she has given birth. Today, a very young child has a lover. In the past, you wouldn't want that. Your father also wouldn't like it. If it was like that, he would speak out against the man. The man who was with you, your mother would insult him. "Get away from there. My child is little." The man hears it and he goes away. He says, "Because of your mother, I can't play with you." But today, if you call for your daughter, when you speak she will beat you. What has happened, she says it is none of your business. There is no business that does not concern people. Every problem is about people.

In the past, you were afraid of your mother and your father. You yourself were afraid. She would speak against you, and you were ashamed. Also, if the man who was with you didn't come to see your mother, and you went to his place like that, she wouldn't like it. And also if you were there with your daughter, and maybe your child goes to him and returns, you would be able to tell him that they will summon him to **court**, and say, "He has taken my child, to behave badly." And he would be afraid. *Wahu?* Just like that.

There might be someone else who, he doesn't marry the woman, but he doesn't leave her. Then he goes to take another lover, then this one and that one. Is that all right? And he and this one have a child, and he and that one have a child, and with that one too. Where is the money that he will use to look after the children? But in the past, we wouldn't like this, at all, at all, not to treat our children badly. *Wahu?* Because, I mean, all the time, if there is a man who stands there, his wife is this one, so you don't behave badly. I mean, as for him, his one is there.

If God helps and this child maybe grows up and hasn't been to school, even someone who has been to school, then if the child's body is comfortable, someone will tell her that he will receive her, to give to his son to marry. Maybe he says, "My child, you are beautiful to me. When she grows up, if she finishes school, I will take her to give to my child to marry." Some can do that. That shows that the child, she respects herself. She doesn't behave badly. And it means that the man, when she finishes school, he lets his son marry her, very properly. Some people are married with a ring, and they celebrate the wedding **fine**. You see? Someone brings along an **Air-tight** trunk and a **Bible**, so that you are his wife. You cannot treat him badly. So that means that every day, you see that this is her husband. But as for today, the children that come today don't do this. If you go to G, children less than fourteen or fifteen have given birth.

Rather, in these days, if you go to school as a child, you should have matured a long time before you get married, because she should finish school. She will be about twenty before she gets married. So that means, if she married like this, her body is strong. At any time, it means that she is capable; she can look after the child. A child goes to G and you go to see her; some are fourteen, fifteen and have given birth. If she has given birth, will the child have a father? This one says, "I am not the father." That one says, "It is not my child." And the child is there, confused, *wahu?* So the child is always fatherless, and if you are fatherless in this world, what will you do? You will be messed up [*basabasa*]. Just like that. But in the past, if your mother was there she would not like it. Your mother wouldn't permit it at all. She wouldn't listen to you.

GC: You say that cloth was very cheap in the past. What has made cloth so expensive now?

As for that, can someone know what has made the price of cloth expensive? Formerly, we brought it from Europe. We didn't make any here at all. All of it we brought from Europe. The goods went by **ship** and were unloaded. *Wahu?* But when we threw out the British, then bringing them now makes the price very expensive. Now the good cloth is expensive. When they come, and you take it to the **store**, will the duty charged be a small thing? **Duty**. Right now, the prices are big. Now if you get some, I mean, its price has gone up. I mean, the Europeans themselves, they put their goods in the **ship**. They bring them to UAC, Ollivant, Compagnie, and they share them out to give to their people.

*GC: So you still have a **passbook**?*

No, I don't have any. Eh, I can't work. If you are old, you can't come and stand up in **line** and shout. It is not profitable. These children are grown up. Have you seen that when you come, they are not even in the stall? No one is there. When I came just now, the whole place was standing empty. No one was there in the stall. *Wahu?* This one lives there, this one lives there. And you have got up to go stand for long hours. An old lady stands up for long hours like that. Doing it is a problem.

GC: Have any of your children decided to follow you and learn the cloth business?

People who have married and gone to live somewhere? Some live in Accra, some live here. Some live in Europe. Who will come? Will she be able to come? As for me, it's like I don't work. They have their own work to do. And they are living there. They have all traveled. Even if you tell your child [to do it], she won't bring even her little child to you. She took her to live there, and she has spoiled her. We all take our children away. None of my grandchildren is here. No one looks after [my stall]. None of my children looks after it. Right now no one is there. God looks after it for me. That's how it is.

*GC: So now, do some people still have **passbooks** to work with?*

Oh, they really work. Some are at UAC. They are working very well.

*MA: Was there a time they canceled the **passbooks**?*

Hmm, what happened was they moved us. They didn't cancel them. They moved us from the street there, in front of UAC, in the past. In the past, we were trading there very disorderly [*basabasa*]. So they moved all of us from there, for us to go into the market. They took all of us away from the street there, so we should go to the market. They didn't cancel it. No, no. I mean, they moved us from the place that we were. You couldn't get a place to sit, so you couldn't go get goods and sit down. If you went to sign for things and come back, they arrested you. That meant there was no profit in going to sign for things.

*MA: At the **time** that the government came to let us buy things at control [at the official, controlled price], were you still selling things with the **passbook**?*

Control. Yes, if people were there and we got some there, but only if you went to sign. There were some people who didn't get any to buy, and maybe if they go to buy it on the street they will unload it at **control price**. That's how it was. Maybe you wouldn't get some to buy. Someone has gone to buy it at the store and returned. She won't give it to you. It happened some days also, that if you sold it they might seize it at **control price**. And it was not because maybe they had raised the passbook price. They never increased the passbook price. Maybe in the past when we were in the street there, you go sign for some to display in front there, and they sold it off for you. They said, "We won't let you sit in the street here, and you also cannot take them to go display at home." So you have to stop.

We who are in the market, lots of us are still doing that work right now. My **sister** who comes after me, even she has a **passbook** there and is working with it right now. She does that work at UAC now. She goes to write down things. Even yesterday, she signed for things. Right now, if I had money and went to get some, they would give me some. Right now, I say, if I went to sign for some, they would give me some. Also, the way it is now, if you have money to go and buy, they will give it to you at **control** price. These days there are lots heaped in the room. If you have money and come, they will give you some. Now there are lots of goods. It is there. Some is there. If you go there, they will give you some like that.

GC: So between selling cloth in the past or today, which has the better profit?

Profit? In the past like that, when you get some goods, the **commission** comes in very fast. I mean, as soon as you go get some, when you are still in the room. Maybe, if the people come from Samenama, they might ask for twenty pieces, and they have bought and paid for them. You go sign for them, and you get your **commission** and go. But today there is no profit in cloth like at first. There is no profit in it. In the past, because of the **commission** you would get money. If you were lucky, and maybe you sign for cloth to go like this, you might make a hundred cedis on each. *Woate asɛ?* Controlled goods, you go to buy them at a high price, and where is the profit?

When you went to buy at UAC in the past, some goods would come from Accra, some from Lome, some even from Abidjan. Goods from everywhere. As soon as some of these goods arrived, they would buy it for **cash**. With **cash**, you pay the money to the **cashier** and he gives you a paper, and you take it to the **manager**. If nothing is there and your business is exactly right, and he finishes writing your name, that means you can go and come back, and you will sign again. *Wahu?* Maybe you want certain things, but there are none outside. Maybe, too, someone comes and signs for some to display outside. A person comes and sees them, and she buys them. She buys, but she doesn't add anything to it. When she buys them, she packs them up and goes to sell them. Because of the **revolution**,[14] if you collect some things, if you are lucky you will make money. If you get your **commission** and you have signed for your goods, it means everything is working well. And you are still working, like that. But if you don't have any **commission** and you have not paid some money down, they won't give you goods. A while ago, they said that as for **commission**, we didn't get any. We didn't have **passbook**.

Nowadays, we go buy funeral cloth at 13,500 cedis for one piece. When you sell it for fourteen thousand, what is yours is five hundred. Also, when you cut a half piece, your share is 250. *Wahu?* If you haven't tried hard, what will you do? Also, at this **time** [**time** *yi*] at UAC nobody has the idea that they might buy this or might buy that. I mean, at UAC, if you come like that and you go into the store, as soon as you come like that, someone comes, and she says, "That one, that's what I want. I want that one." She herself will pay for it. As for you, you don't get into the money. She pays with her own money. "I want that one." Ten pieces or twenty pieces. You finish that and he has given you a receipt. He finishes this and they **check** her goods, and she takes her things and goes. So you will get **commission**, you see? Anyway, you have made money. Later she has gone and come back again. She has gone and come back. That's what lets us make money. That's all of it. This is just what makes us make money, just like that. You will pile it up like that. Little by little, it lets us make money.

GC: Did your mother also have a passbook?

My mother? No, as for her, she has no **passbook**. I myself went for it. It was my husband that gave me money. At first, I was a seamstress. At first, when I was young, I sewed things. Yes, I learned to sew and I sewed things for a while. Then I got money, and he added some to give me and I took it to get a **passbook**. I sewed. If I hadn't done that, I wouldn't have saved money.

In the past, **passbooks** had not come for them to get. They didn't make **passbooks**, so they hadn't come. When they first came, people didn't even want them. At that time, things weren't scarce. In the past, if you wanted something, you just go there and buy it. And she bought it. It was piled up and they went buying it. Much later, when UAC came, they said that if you will buy, I will give you **commission** like that. In the past, there was plenty in the **store**. If you go and buy, you take your things and go. Goods were piled up. If you go, you have gone to buy. Then you carry it off, and you go around hawking it. When you have finished selling it, you pay for it and take your share away. *Wahu?*

So that means what came in our time, it was good. They explained to us that you should take your money and keep it here. You take goods for a hundred thousand, oh, ten thousand, no, formerly a hundred pounds, and you bring the deposit there. You have taken those goods and you do the work itself, and when they are finished, they can give you more on credit. Your own money, that is, it is there. But also with the **commission**, if you haven't come back to pay, it can pay your debt. Have you understood? So you do something and maybe you take one hundred pounds to work with, and maybe you **check** this account, you will see that something might have been added to it. If you go write down for goods and it goes over, they can give you some more of the goods, because your money is in the book. If you haven't come, they will take some out to pay for it. That's how it made us able to do the work.

But we used to get tired. Very early in the morning, we came from Ashanti New Town, way over there, to come up here, to get goods. And you returned by foot, on this hill! Today fast cars have come, and we always take cars. Long ago, you couldn't. Today, there are plenty of cars, but in the past, cars were not many. In the past, you could walk just like that, and not see a single car. You wouldn't even hear a car, except for a touring car. Unless maybe you went on the main road. But today, **taxis** are not scarce. If you come from Kuro foforɔ mu and you come here, if you are not careful, a car will hit you; a car will really hit you. You can't walk. If you come fast from Kuro foforɔ mu, walking like that—-beep, beep, beep, a car will even hit you. It will knock you down.

But in the past, there were no cars in the world. You would walk so much. Your mother sent you here, she sent you there, she sent you to come to the market, and you didn't have money to ride a car. You walked on the roadside, and you would go to market and come back. *Wahu?* So that was not anything like you might go look for a car and ride in it. Today, if you send a child and you haven't given her money to go, she says, "I'm not going." It's because she can't walk. In the past, it wasn't like that. In that past time, when your mother gives you money to go shop at the market, that is it, you go to market and come back. You don't sit, you don't look for a car. But today, if you send a child and you haven't given her money, she says she won't go, because she can't. You also see that it's really true. She can't walk to Kuro foforɔ mu like that and come back. There are too many cars. *Wahu?* In the real past, look, from Ashanti New Town to Compagnie here, eh! We came to market and we went back, and we walked.

GC: So, the sewing you were doing, did your mother make you go and learn it?

Yes, it might have been my mother. I took my older **sister's** sewing machine to go and learn sewing. My older **sister**. I went, and she bought it for me. She had married.

*GC: When you sewed, did you have **apprentices**?*

Oh, yes! The **apprentices** were about twelve. I had many **apprentices** there. In the past, you sewed a cover cloth for ninepence. You sewed a dress for ninepence or one shilling. And cloth by the **yard** was one shilling. So if you were my child,[15] and you were going home, I gave you two shillings to take with you. In the morning, you came and you ate something. That's how I did it. And I had lots of children there.

MA: So you couldn't combine the cloth selling with the sewing? Is that why you stopped?

That wasn't it. I mean, the place we were was in someone's stall. In the past, it was not the place there where we are now. In the past, the place where we were was not the cloth **line**. I mean, the thing was, it was not really the right **line** there. Only the enamelware **line** is there. They only sell enamelware where we were. Even in the far past, when we were there, they sold bread there. Bread was what they sold over there. Later, the enamelware sellers came to join us, from where the bread sellers ended. Later, when they moved, meat sellers came to stay there. Finally, it became a cloth sellers' section. So where we were was far away at the top. I mean, in one stall there would be many people. This person passes here, the other person passes there. You cannot sell cloth. You cannot, so what we were selling was calico. A piece of calico was eighteen shillings. Ninepence, maybe one shilling per **yard**. Things were cheap. *Wahu?* At that **time**, there was no modernization [*anibue*] as today. Today, modernity has gone high.

GC: *But why did you stop sewing? Why didn't you want to make it a big business?*

Sewing? At the **time** I went to start the UAC work, but the UAC work could not go with this. You get up early in the morning to stand at UAC to collect goods. Formerly, goods were scarce. You have brought the cloth, then you sell it. Why would you stop to sew? Yes, just look at it again. As for this, it can't be done. When you look at here and there, you can't do the work. In the past, when I went to bring things, I came to sit down and put them there. They would not buy. The other thing was that you should be there in front of UAC, so that if somebody comes and she wants goods, then what should you do? You give her some. *Woate aseɛ?* But if you go to stay somewhere to sew things, when your friends come, they will take her business. A friend of yours has come from a village. "Ei, where is Madame Ataa?" "Madame Ataa is at the market," that person will tell her. "Buy some of mine." She goes away. For that reason, you cannot do two jobs like that, so I stopped.

The sewing wasn't like today, when people charge five thousand and twenty thousand. A blouse was ninepence. There even might be someone who would not come for it after you sewed it. It was one shilling, but she does not come for it. It hangs there and gets dusty. Only people who fast would come.[16] Fasting people would have the work done. *Wahu?* Ninepence or one shilling was what we charged when we sewed. A beautiful dress, what you will call a lady's dress, one shilling or one shilling and sixpence was the charge. There are some that, like if the person is having a thanksgiving service,[17] two shillings was the charge. The two-shillings one, too, you were not going to get it ordered every day. Sometimes, it might be even two months and you had not earned four shillings. Then, that person might be going to **chapel**, so that she came to have you make something. The other woman could not come for her dress.

But over there [at UAC], as soon as you went, the goods were sold out. As soon as you went, perhaps people from Sunyani or from Berekum would come, *wahu?* They were coming to buy these goods and go back. Over there, when you went inside the room, calico and everything could be found in the room. Calico, grey baft [cloth], school uniform cloth, anything you like, you could write for that person to take it away. All you wanted was the **commission**, and that doesn't mean that there would be no profit on it. As soon as the French people come, they have money. They buy these goods well and take them away. They come from Ewe land.[18] All the Ewes come to buy goods in Kumasi. Everyone came, and it meant the goods were being taken away.

They take them from Kumasi here. The goods came from Takoradi, at the **harbor**. They had not built Tema then.[19] They finished building Tema, and then people went there. In the past, the steamers arrived at Takoradi and unloaded, and we took it back here. Tema wasn't there, so everything was unloaded here. All the goods came to Kumasi. So if you wanted something to buy, and you didn't get it in Kumasi, then you wouldn't get it. So when goods arrived here, the people from Accra came here to buy a lot and take it away. Goods went to Ho, to Abidjan, everywhere. People from Sunyani came to take some. Berekum people came to take some. Everyone came to take some. *Wahu?*

So when it happened like that, it was very fine for those of us living here. You walk a little bit and come back; you finish and go out again. If you want, you go shopping at the market and you go home to cook your food. I mean, that was just how it happened. Today, there is not really good profit in it any more. It's just as if you stayed home. But if you haven't come to work, that means things are really bad.

Even if they are expensive, they are still the goods that we sell. They are expensive. It is not because of the women, it is not from [passing through] their hands. I mean, [it is from] the **duty** they charge, the dye they use to make it and many other things that they make in this country which they put into them. And the time it takes before they reach you; it is a long distance. How can the price not be high? It is not the fault of the government, it is nobody's fault. I mean, the things they use to make them, like the dyes, make the price high. And it is not the government that raises the price, they know nothing about it.

GC: At the time you began to sell cloth, would you say everything was fine, or were there worries?

I mean, about the selling of the goods. If you are not serious, you won't get anything. Only if you get tired first can you then get anything.

Wahu? You are at home and you don't come to the market. You don't go to the **store**. If you sit there, will you get anything? You have to exert yourself and become serious. As for anything, we search for it, and God too will help you and you get it. There may be someone in Kumasi, excuse me to say, who is at home and has never worked before. Someone my age, even, who has never worked. *Woate aseɛ?* She has a husband, so she sleeps. She eats and goes to bed. That too is not good. When I get serious, I say, "I will work." God too has honored me. I have built a house. And when you say, your husband will give you, your husband will give you, your husband will give you; if your husband doesn't give you, what then? Aah, yes! Today also, the Asante people, when you have a child and the lineage members are there, he will not give you all the property. He will give it to his family. He will give you some, too, but if you make it yourself, it is yours. And you live in it, *wahu?* When you try hard, then God helps you.

Some are also lazy; they won't do it. A lazy person, will you get any-thing? When you left your country to come to this place, wasn't it that you wanted to work? Somebody else would not have come. *Woate aseɛ?* There may be someone who, when she is asked to come to Ghana, will not come. I live in my country and she will come here? Aah! Do you hear what I am saying? You make an effort. God also helps you. You will get what you want. You were living in your country. Somebody there might say, "I won't come, I won't come." If you won't come, what you want, you also won't get it.

There might be someone who was my age, but she was at home, she didn't work. Yes, there were many. She would not work. Ah, she stays at home like that. When someone cooks, she eats some. When you eat and you are full, then you go to bed. When the sun shines, she lays a mat down and goes to sleep. But while you sleep, will you get anything? You won't get it. That is it. But if you make an effort, whatever you do, God will bless you. What you want, you get it.

When I was a young woman, nothing worried me. My mother cooked and I ate. I did nothing. If you marry your husband, your hus-band will give you money. You shop. Your husband brings money, and when you prepare food, you eat some. You see? So every day, you are happy about the man. If your money is finished, [he says,] "Oh, take this and go." [My husband] was a **fitter** [mechanic]. He also used to farm at Sankore, far away. I went there only once. When I came back, I couldn't go again. The way is far, and I can't walk. When I went, I couldn't go back again. He is gone now, but I haven't married again. We had one child. My own child is working in Accra, with all her children. She has children. I will not marry. I am going to marry again for what? He will make you a glutton. "When you cook, leave some for me." [*Repeats this twice.*] I, myself, will cook my thing to eat. [*Repeats this.*]

I have talked a lot now. I will go. Have I finished the whole story?

A Seller of Funeral Cloths

A Seamstress Displays Her Blouse Designs for "Up-and-Down" Cloth Outfits

A Plantain Wholesaler with Her Children and Assistants

"Essential" Commodities Displayed near an Entry Point

Trucks Unloading in the Wholesale Yard in Stacks of One Hundred

The Yam
Association's
Sheds at Its
Wholesale Yard

A Retail Stall in the Yam Line

A Head Carrier Delivers Twenty Yams to the Retail Line

Amma Pokuaa
Shows All the
People She Feeds

Amma Buo, Amma Pokuaa's Mother, in the House She Built with Her Yam Profits

CHAPTER 4

Amma Pokuaa

Portrait: A Market Daughter

*For those of us who have seen how it was
in the past, the world is hard for us today.
But for those who have not seen the past,
today's world is not so hard for them.*

Amma Pokuaa worked at the center of a bustling family dynasty of yam traders built up by her mother over many decades. Her mother and aunt, her sisters and cousins, and her daughters and nieces all had stalls near each other and took various roles in buying and selling, mostly on their own accounts. Pokuaa was one of the most active among them in 1978, when she was one of my first and closest associates. Her round face usually bore an expression of determination, quick with a laugh or a sharp retort. Her warm affection for friends and her confidence in her own skill and judgment were key assets in all her undertakings, including mentoring a novice ethnographer.

In vigorous middle age, she traveled regularly to buy in farming areas, coordinated several of her daughters' trips, sold in the wholesale yard, and supervised the retailing from her stall in the middle of the yam section. We traveled together to the neighboring Brong Ahafo Region, dealing with farmers she had first met as a baby on her mother's back. Her aged mother sat in the stall most days, but I usually found Amma Pokuaa around the wholesale yard, either selling a truckload that had been brought to her or unloading a truck of her own.

Filling that truck became more and more of a struggle as the demands for capital escalated as a result of spiraling prices and the credit restraints of neoliberal reforms. Her family situation offered no alternative source of funds. None of her three husbands had turned out to be a lasting provider. She lived with her father as a child, but he had left his wealth to his lineage heirs (his own children by a slave wife). Most of her adult children still lived at home, expecting her to feed and house them and their children. The drain on her income prevented her from building a house or reinvesting in her business.

By the time she told me this story, her successful career was coming apart. A life-threatening bout of malaria struck the first blow, forcing her to take her doctor's advice and stop traveling. Her aged mother had finally stopped coming to the market altogether, so she might have stepped into that senior role. But before her mother died, she had withdrawn most of the trading capital, which Pokuaa had been working with and expecting to inherit, and had distributed it to various other relatives. After the funeral, Amma Pokuaa had barely managed to hold onto the two rooms her children and grandchildren shared, in the Kumasi house her mother had built.

She still had rights in a retail stall in the market, shared with some relatives, but she now spent most days at home, frying doughnuts for sale by neighbor children on commission. This was not "real work," and was quite a comedown for a once-prominent wholesaler of yams, one of the most prestigious commodities in Kumasi. She lacked sufficient capital to employ her own daughters, so they dispersed to other work, other towns, and even other countries. The one who had assisted her most closely in the yam trade went to Nigeria with her husband. When I came looking for Amma Pokuaa in the market, her stall neighbors there were reluctant to tell me how she was doing.

Although I remembered her as full of pride before, she looked worn out and deflated to me in 1994. She was hardly defeated, but seemed bewildered somehow by the twists and turns her life had taken. Not surprisingly, her story spends plenty of time tracing the family and marital relationships that shaped her fortunes so much. Only the sections that describe yam trading and the increasing commercialization of farming communities retain something of her original vigor. For her, the life history interview was only a rather pleasant escape into reminiscence of better times; it showed few prospects of improving her life situation. She has little hope of sending a child abroad. Her major worry is how to pass on the family responsibilities that her limited resources make overwhelming.

Story: All of Them Depend upon Me

As for the story of my life, right now before God, it is hard. From my very beginning, I did no other work but yams, because that was what my mother sold, and I also came to sell them. They call me Amma Pokuaa. I am from Ejisu-Onwe. I live in Oforikrom. So those yams, I have really sold them hard, so I could raise my eight children. When the children were little, then life was really good. I had a little money, just **fine**. Once the children grew up, I lost all that money.

The man I **first** married, I had five children with him. He didn't look after the children; I myself looked after us. Later, I married another man. I had two children with him. He did look after the children. His children were two and he looked after us. Then he and I left each other, and later I married another man. But that one, as soon as I married him, about seven months after I gave birth, he died. As for him, no one looked after his child. The father had a lot of money; he had a house in Kumasi, a car, and other things, but no one looked after that child. Because the child was just left with me, it made my life situation hard. Myself, the money that I worked with is all gone. So for about the past ten years, I have stayed at home. Because of the way I have come to hear God's word, for more than fourteen years now I have not had even a lover. I have no husband and I am living for the Lord.

So when life got difficult for me, I started frying doughnuts. At that time, I didn't have the money to go on the road [to buy yams]. I go to buy flour on credit, and I come fry them, and I earn a little money. I and the children take it to buy something to eat. That is how we are living. This is really, up until this very day, the situation I am in. The problem is, I don't have the money to do my work. I am not a very old woman, such that I couldn't do the work, but I don't have money to work with. As for the children, it so happened that I never got a good man, for us to look after the children together. That is why the situation of the children is also not so good. I mean, maybe later help will come from God's hand. Right now, I am suffering a lot. Today, I finished frying doughnuts in the morning, and then I went back to the market to see if we could get some food to eat.

As for the traveling, these days, there is not the kind of money that would allow me to go again. In the market, they give us credit and we sell. When you finish selling, you have your self-respect and you pay for it. That is how we manage to stay on in the market. I wish that I could go on the road, because I am strong, but because of this money problem, I stay home. So I can worry so much, but I can't figure it out, and truly, when I worry, I lay it on the Lord. Only God himself has the strength to help me.

At first, when I went on the road, I even went with Akua Konadu, the white woman.[1] I took her on the road, and when I took her along, the money that I had with me was a thousand. Yes, five bags,[2] a thousand cedis. At that time I could use it to buy yams to fill a whole truck. Today, if you don't have one million and more, you won't be able to load a truck full of yams. I mean, if you really want to do it, you carry about two million before you can fill up a yam truck. That is why living right now is hard. Besides, the price of yams is high today, even out in the countryside. Then there is the money for the truck. When you go, the collector who takes you to the farm, he has what he charges. The tractor you hire, he has his charges, before what the truck charges, and before the ticket fee [at the market]. I mean, if you are not carrying a whole lot of money, you won't be able to do that work. That is why these days, I am sitting at home.

The children also, they don't listen to me. None of them has even been able to finish school. Only one, of the two that I said their father looked after us, one of them went to school and is in a college now. In the end, all the rest are having children every which way [basabasa], and many of them depend on me. Now, I suppose I have reached fifty years old. Now my children and grandchildren, we may number twenty-five, and all of them depend on me. I don't have any work, but the truth is, it is not the work that makes me eat, but the grace of God that lets me eat. Now, as we are here, this is the prayer that I pray: I pray that God gives me grace to earn something, or else that the children themselves will find husbands to marry. The first child got pregnant when she was in school. The young man didn't marry her. The next one she took up with, he had four children with her. Of the four children that he had with her, he has not named even one. Yes, and if I say anything to my daughter, she doesn't listen. Just now, she has had another one, who is depending on me. Because the children don't even have any work to do, they are all messed up [*basabasa*]. A few days ago, one said she would fry some doughnuts; I mean, she is frying a little at a time.

Look at all these people! There are about ten or eight of them like that, and I sleep in one room with them because of our problems. Then I found another small room somewhere, and I rented it to give some of us a place to crowd into. The very eldest, besides all these, well, since my mother has a house in town here, she gave the very eldest one a room. My mother's children, we are four, so she can't give all the rooms to my own children alone. If she gave the rooms to all of our children it wouldn't be a good thing. So the best thing would have been that when the children grew up, they all got married. But when the children got old enough to marry, they went and got pregnant. That is why these days, I am so worn out. I am tired, but what can we do? We don't have anywhere to go. It's a thing that, when I even think about it, I conclude that it is not too hard for God. For a human being, it is too hard for her.

I ask God to let even one of my children travel abroad, that he may do well. Today in this town, if you see someone who has got well settled, it means that one of her children has gone abroad. If her child has not traveled, with conditions as they are here, it's not likely. If you have a whole lot of money that you can work with, it is fine here, but if the money is not with you, then you get tired for nothing. That is how I know it. If you have money here in Ghana that you can work with, it will go well, but if you have no money, you will wear yourself out so much, and all the **time** you will be in trouble. Should I keep adding more?

GC: Well, at the time you were starting to sell yams, was it like today? What changed?

It has changed. I mean, when it was good, when I was going on the road, I took forty pounds to go on the road. I loaded up with *pona* [the best variety] then, about two thousand of them, and brought them back. But today, if you don't take two million, or one million, you can't go. Today, when the yams are just starting to come in, when they are plentiful, you can go if you get even about six hundred thousand cedis. But this time of year, if you don't carry the two million, you can't go. Even two million is not enough. In the old days, even if you were someone who had money and you took good money, it was one hundred thousand. Even that, you couldn't take it along, it was too much. So what has really happened is that today, the world is going up [kɔ so]. Today, it won't come down [kɔ fuom] again.

Today, if you look into it, I mean, modernization [anibue] has come. Modernization has come, so it has made it happen like that. In the past, if you went to a farmer, especially the Konkombas, they didn't hire laborers. They exchanged labor, this one goes to help another, and the other has helped him. But today, it isn't like that. I mean, today he hires a Dakarti man or a hired man to clear for him, and they might also charge him even a hundred thousand cedis before they have cleared the farm. *Wahu?* Before he is finished with the season, the laborers will finish clearing, they will make the mounds, they will weed it again, and his costs will come up to about one million. So before he will run up such a debt, what will he have to do? He also has to earn another one million on top, to make it two million. So when you go to his farm, it goes like, he has paid so much in wages and other things, and he also pays that debt first, before he also earns something on it. That's what has made the price of goods go so high.

And the meat that at first he would buy for ten pounds, today he buys for one hundred cedis. What do you expect him to do? At first, too, the Konkombas, I mean, they were not modern [n'ani mmuɛ], they didn't know anything. They were not even sleeping on mats. But today, you go into anyone's room in the countryside, there is a **mattress**, there are even some metal beds. When you enter their rooms, it's impressive! Even you who live in the big city may not have such things. So I mean, today, modernity [anibue] has come, so it has made things like that.

*GC: You say you started selling yams when you were little. Comparing that **time** to today, were there a lot of people selling yams?*

When I was little, we were not very many. That was my mother's work, that she did in order to have me. At that time, there were not many people, and we knew our number. So it was like this: if we went out and there was one person already there, as soon as I went, I went to her house to greet her, and she would also come to see me. So if I go bargain for these yams, and I offer ten pounds, what should she do? If the farmer does not accept my offer, and if he calls to her, she goes, and if it happens that I offered ten pounds, she will offer six pounds, so that he will call me back.

But today, it is not like that. Today, you will go into a town, and there will be more than twenty people there. So you go this way to buy, and someone else has gone around behind you, and she has offered a higher price. I mean, what you went to buy, if they do that with about three people, your own price will go up before they will give it to you. At first, when you went, the farmer would want everyone to know that he was a real farmer, so a whole car full of yams, he would want to load it all at his farm. But today, it's not like that. Today, even if he could harvest a car full, when you go, he will take out a third of them, and he will let you buy them.

At first, he might harvest all two thousand of them, and he would sort out three sizes. When you finished bargaining, you set the price for the big ones, and then you bargained for the next size. If you bought the big ones for one thousand pounds, the next ones you bought for one thousand cedis. If you bought the big ones for two thousand, the ones that follow you would buy for one thousand cedis, and the ones that follow those, you would buy for five hundred cedis. Some you could even buy for less. Today it would be, in today's money, you could buy it for around 150 [thousand]. But today, it's not like that. If you tried to do it like that, he wouldn't agree.

He will sort them into three piles, one big one, the one after that, and the one after that. So, if it is three hundreds, he takes these big ones for one hundred, then he takes the next ones, then he takes the little ones. So if you buy the big ones, and he gives them to you, and you buy them, you have got tired already. At first, even if there was a full carload on the farm, even if he harvested three thousand yams, he gave them all to you. On credit! Well, he would still sort them, but he would let you buy them all. I mean, when you finish, you will divide them into groups, so you see how much you have paid for these. You have bought these big ones for one pound, the following size for ten shillings, and the next ones for five shillings. *Wahu?* But these days, he won't give them to you like that. Oh, he doesn't do it like that. He will take out three hundreds, and he will give them to you. When someone else comes, then he will take out two of these big ones, or one of the big ones, and one of the small ones, and one of the medium ones, and he will give them to her. All of this put together has made yams very expensive today.

As for me, from my own experience, I would say that it's really today that we work hard. Because in the past, if you worked, as soon as you got ten pounds, you were tired. But these days, even every young child who works today can earn about two thousand cedis a day. But the things he is going to buy, their price is high. At first, if you earned a little, also the thing you went to buy was cheap. But what you did to get that small amount would also make you tired. *Woate aseɛ?* For this reason, for those of us who have seen how it was in the past, the world is hard for us today. But for those who have not seen the past, today's world is not so hard for them.

GC: When you were young and you went on the road, what did you do with the money you got?

I was a nursing mother, and I used it to look after these children. I had no one else to look after these children. So I was looking after the children little by little, so that the children could be finishing school. But the children were disobedient, so no one has finished school.

GC: Before you married, were you working?

I was not very old. As soon as I matured, I married. I was following behind my mother, little by little. I mean, in our own time, they didn't send us to school. Me, actually my father raised me. At that time, as an Asante, you grew up in your father's house, but you didn't stay on there. Your father raised you, and when you had grown up, you came to your home. Also, my father planted cocoa at Kenyase. Aha, so I went with my father to the farm. When I got there, my father had already planted all his farms. I am the youngest child. So I followed my father, little by little, little by little. I mean, he was an old man and I lit his pipe and gave it to him, until I matured and I came to live with my mother. Then I got married, and I also did my mother's work. *Wahu?*

I was working with one of my sisters, selling yams. She also had the same money problems. When the work got like that, none of us had money. In 1983, people really suffered. The big famine came. So she was also like that, she also didn't have money to work. But as for her, by the grace of God, one of her children traveled abroad, So, *agya,* they brought her something to buy something to eat. She even stays at home today, she doesn't work. But for myself, my children haven't turned out well. So, in truth, I am really suffering.

A few days ago, two of them said, "We will fry doughnuts." One of them started, and one other has joined her. In truth, my very oldest child, the oldest, a young man, he has got a car today. He takes it to Accra and back. So his **problems** don't fall on me. And the following one, she also is in the market. She also sells yams. She has also moved away from me. At this time, she is at Adwaase, and she has a room there. But the ones that are left, I live with them. And one of them, too, her father came to take her.

MA: Those staying with you, can't they also come and sell yams? You say that you buy the yams on credit, so they can come and buy some on credit and then fry them.

They say, "We don't want to. We will fry doughnuts." These days, when I fry, then they also take some to hawk around. If they haven't fried any, and I fry some, then they take it to go hawking. These days, I have many children. They are not just my own children, but my neighbors' children. When I fry doughnuts, then they take them to go hawking. If I give them doughnuts worth three thousand, or 3100, then they bring me 2200. If he takes 1300, he brings me one thousand.

*MA: His **commission** is three hundred, eh! And you will give him the ticket and the paper. Certainly, it is cheap.*

They even sell it for fifty. If I give her 1300, she brings me a thousand. But she sells them for fifty each. Many of the ones left for fifty are hers. Some get to the point that she has to reduce them. She reduces to make them sell. She has bought them from me at forty, and she might sell them for twenty-five. She sells two for fifty, but she has bought them from me for forty. And she goes to some places where she can charge fifty for one.

GC: What made you start making doughnuts?

I didn't have money to do my real work. I got the flour on credit, and because I was honest, they gave it to me. When that person gave it to me, I got the palm kernel oil on credit, I got the sugar on credit. I mean, I got everything for it on credit. Also, as soon as I finished frying it, then as soon as the children bring the money back, I put it all together, and I take it to give to the owners. I give this person hers, and that person his. So I just stay at home, and they bring me something. With the doughnuts, if she takes 4200, she will also bring me three thousand.

MA: So she will get 1200 cedis.

Yes, but it is because she gets fifty for some, and thirty for some. Both of them are cheap, and she can even charge two for fifty for some. When she has finished selling, and some left are about to get spoiled, she will reduce them more. When I started out, I was buying the flour at six thousand cedis. Today it is twenty-five thousand cedis.

GC: So between doughnuts and yams, which has more profit?

As for yams, if I had money, that would be my job. And as for these doughnuts, I mean, it is frustration that makes me go do it. But really, it is all right for me. Look at all these many people here. If I get enough for my food money, it is all right by me. As for saving money, I have none; working like this, I have none. Now, I don't have anyone to give me a lot of money, to let me use to do a big business, like going on the road for yams. So with so many children, this is not the kind of work that could earn me money to save.

GC: Before, when you were a child, what kind of work did you wish that you could do?

At that time, when I was a child, they didn't send you to school. What you did was follow your father around. *Wahu?* So when my father raised cocoa, I followed my father to the village. When Christmas came, we returned to our hometown. When Christmas was over, we went back. So I didn't do anything. I only went to the farm to cut some plantain and came back. Then I cooked some to eat, and I sat there. My father called me to send me somewhere, and I went.

*MA: At that **time**, what really good work did you think about, that if maybe you got it, it would be good?*

At that time, when I was a child, what I really might have liked was sewing, but my father did not send me to learn it. Actually, I didn't say a word, but I was very interested in it inside. I liked it, but I didn't speak up. Later on, even after I had got married, I studied it a little. I learned sewing a little, but it was not like today. I saw that my mother's work was with yams, and I had no interest in sewing any more. I had to continue with my mother's work.

MA: Have any of your children learned some kind of trade, like sewing?

Not my own children. Now one of the others, she has learned hair-dressing, and she studied again to do "mesh" plaiting. So her father has bought all the things for her. Just a few days ago, her father also built a **kiosk** for her. That was the one I said he and I had two children and he looked after us. The child after her, she was small when her father took her from me. The father sent her to school, even until she finished.

Today he has sent her to college. As for that child, she doesn't come here to my house at all. So my home folks themselves don't even know her well. Now, she is at college.

GC: When you were a child, what really good work might have been there, more profitable than the yams you sold?

I mean, I was with my father in the village, so I didn't know. I mean, I didn't know about anyone's work. I did know Kumasi, since my mother lived here. But I followed my father, so I was interested in my father's place. You know that when you are in the country, you can't do any business. Maybe once a week, you come to market, that's it. And at that market, as a child maybe what I could carry there was worth a shilling. That shilling, I would stand in the market and eat it, and I would go home. Aha.

GC: Didn't you think that you might plant cocoa, like your father?

My father had finished making all his farms. When I went to him, he had done all the work to make that turn out very well. I mean, I was his last-born, so I didn't go to join my father doing his work. Truly, what I saw was when he would go to the country, then I followed him, and I cut some of the plantain to bring back. I got up in the morning, and I went for water.

MA: Did your father give your mother any of the cocoa farm?

He didn't give her any. It seems to me that it wasn't she who made the farm with my father. You know that long ago, people didn't love their children like their own [matrilineal] relatives. So what he gave us was that he raised us. He had three children with my mother. He gave us a little bit of cocoa planted in our hometown, but it died a long time ago on that land. Today you can't do anything decent with the land; I mean, maybe you might think of planting some garden eggs and tomatoes. That also is not something that we could go live there and be doing today, with all these children.

Actually, he gave all his things to some of his other children. The reason is, they say, when he got married, my father's uncle went to get a house-person and he brought her. Do you understand what a house-person is?[3] My father, also, was an only child, so my great-uncle forced him to marry her. It was my father's duty, that's why my father married her. Aha, so he married her, and he and she had about six children. Because of their situation, they had nowhere else to go. Since it was like that, my father made it so that they should live in the house there, and everything of his was for them.

So among those of us that he had on the other side, who were not house-people, he gave one a small farm, and another also he gave a little something. I mean, when I knew my father, he had farms at Duampompo and Kenyase, and in our town, too. It was all in cocoa. So he gave us a little bit in our town there, but even that little had died by the time I had grown up properly, when Papa died. You see, in the old days if they give you something they say, "When I die, it will be yours." But by the time Papa had died, the farm had already died.

Most of his property went to those other people. His house that he lived in, a story building that he built himself, went to those people, and it still belongs to them today. We ourselves, when we moved away, we came to our mother's house. We couldn't return and join them there again. If it had been today, we would have received some property. These days, if he had had all of us children, we would have received something, but that was long ago. Is there anything left?

GC: When you started to go on the road, what work was going well in Kumasi here? What work did you see that all the people who did that made a profit?

At the time when we started going on the road steadily, well, money was hard to get. So if someone had a husband, if she had a good husband, her husband did not let her work. He said, "Stay home, I will buy food for you to eat." Am I lying? Truly, it seems to me that in Ghana here, it might be that everyone respects you if you are selling cloth, you are an established person. If you are selling cloth, it means you are in society, you have money. And finally, if you also sell yams, then you might be an important person. It is good if you sell plantain; if you sell meat, it used to be good. That is how all of us were living then. Really, these days, now that cocaine and importing are the going businesses, I mean, what we are doing is no business at all. It is not real work. I mean, today it is only if someone gets a little money to travel with that she can make enough money to build a house.

MA: So you said that your mother had a house? Did she share it between you?

Her house is there, where we live. She gave it to her children. Well, when she died, mother herself, she had made a will. But when she died, the will was not good. We couldn't make it work, so we shared the property out. When we divided it, we were giving all the brothers and sisters some. We said, if we do it like that, it won't work. Today everyone has children. So for everyone, what God has given the mother belongs to her children. So we and our brothers and sisters divided it. Even what we and our brothers and sisters divided, it didn't divide up well.

Also, it turned out that, if you looked at the will carefully, [you could tell] it was not Mother herself who made it. It was her sisters. The eldest sister's children are well educated. If you look at it really carefully, the **will** is **strange**. So the family sat down again to divide it, but the way we divided it, most of it went to their **side**. My mother's child, yes, she made all of it go to her side.[4] The rooms in the house are nineteen. She alone got nine for herself. We are also four, and the eldest has two [rooms], the second eldest has four, the next one has four, and I have two.

When the family met, and we said we would do it like this, they said that it wasn't right. So they should give me two, and later my little girl, the one that I said her father had died, we gave her to the chief of our hometown [as a promised wife]. So if the child will go and marry him, I mean, we should give her property. So if that's how it is, we should give her the one room. My sister said she agreed, meaning, when the child grows up and if she goes, then she would give it to her. That's cheating!

Then my brother who I come after, he said the cocoa farm was his. Our uncle who died, it belonged to him. The family said, if we do it like that, it would not be right. He also said the market stall belonged to him. And they said, if we do it like that, it would not be right. All of the ones that Mother gave birth to, we are all alive, so let's share. In the house in our hometown that Mother built, when she was alive we each had one room. That is why, now that she has died, that brother could not do that; but the rooms that are left over are his. The family has said it isn't a problem, we should give them to him. So we gave them to him.

GC: And where is your mother's money that she used to go on the road?

That money, well, my mother got old. And when she got old, also, one time, my older sister, she really forced my mother to take the money to buy a ticket for her child to go abroad. Eh, she is strong. Yes! When her child got to Europe, people said they arrested him on the way. They locked him up for six months, before he returned. So after that happened, Mother had no money with her at all.

Yes, as for today, it is only the money that counts. When I started to go, the work was good for me. At that time, when you came back you would earn for each thousand, how much? If you even got ten pounds, you wouldn't be losing money. Your food money wasn't much, just a little of it, so for me, when I started, it was fine for me. Was it tiring? As for tiredness, going on the road, you are bound to get tired. But when you tire yourself and you come and you earn a little profit, you forget.

Then I did make up my mind, I decided that I would build a house. I went to buy a house, a plot at Tafo. But later, when my mother went to buy this one, I went to look at the house there. I was then living in Fanti New Town. I went to look at the house, and I didn't like it. I even said, "I'm not going there." But my mother insisted and made me go there. That's why I planned that I would pull the house down and rebuild.

At that time, there was one brother with us, so we were five. If we had built, I had planned it as a five-story building. When I had built the bottom floor, we would live there. As for the rest, I wasn't strong enough for it. After a while, you might be my sister, and if God is good to you and your children are good, if God puts it in your hand and your child has added on to it, then we might keep adding on to it like that and build the five floors. Then each of us would get one floor. So that was the idea I had in my head. When I went to give the landlord his due, I had collected the money, but he wouldn't sell it to me. When I came back, I was so interested in that plan. Then troubles really hit me, right up till today. So I might have had the idea of building a house, but not the strength. You see, there where it is, it's only a **plot**, it's not a house. If we got the money, then we would build it well, and it would be a good place.

Today, the only [yam trader who is prosperous] is the one whose brother has traveled and brought her money. Only if her child has traveled, then she can build property and maybe her living conditions will be good. Or else, maybe, the one whose uncle has died and left her cocoa farms, or her brother or her mother, then she is doing well. But of those of us who stayed on like this without any help, some are even staying home now. Someone else can load up four trucks and bring them there to the wholesale yard, and she started out just like us. Today, some of us have even gone to live in the village. If someone moved away, even her food money was hard to get. She could even be paying rent, so she moved back to the village.

Everything was cheap then [when I started out]. At that same time, it wasn't that people had some really big money. You see, it seems I have sort of forgotten that time. It was from then that the awareness or the idea came that everyone had to see that they built a house. But not everyone then would think about a house. But truly, I realized early that I should have torn it down and built one, but I thought about the old lady's house, that I might tear that down and rebuild it. I mean, if your mother has it, it is really yours. But these days, even if I had the money, I wouldn't rebuild it. I would rather build mine for myself. If I had built my own, or bought at Asawasi at that time, it would have been one or two thousand cedis. If at that time I had been at all prosperous, and I had even bought one house, it would have been profitable, but it didn't happen like that. Then, I thought that I and all of my brothers and sisters were really united, and since it belonged to our mother, we would do it. But these days, even with you and your mother's child, she thinks of her own, so you have to think of your own.

There is work here, but there is no money. If you go look for a job for a child, or else you want the child to work, there should be money, and I don't have any. Today, the thing you bought last year for ten pounds, you will buy for two thousand. So right now, as I was saying, even just a while ago, when I started buying flour, the flour for doughnuts cost six or seven thousand cedis. This very day, it has reached 20,500. These very money problems are this life. These money problems are this life. Right now, I am crying that I am in trouble, but somebody else is happy. She has money to work, so she is very happy. So this same money is the life problem that has changed.

When I came to meet my grandmother, my father's cocoa farms were huge. In those three towns, today all of it has become cassava farms. The cocoa gets to a point that it dies. People have become so many in the world today that if you say you will even replant it when it dies, you won't get food to eat. In our hometown then, for example, if you went off to farm, for about four or five miles it was solid cocoa. A little while ago, when my mother died, I took that road and it was all cassava. If you say you will plant cocoa, we will not have food to eat. So if you take the villages around Kwaabere, for example, we have to plant cassava, so we will get food to eat. These days, even out there in the countryside, there is no new forest anywhere for anyone to cut. Only where they planted cocoa and it died in the forest, then they can replant cocoa. But as for Kwaabere here, if you plant cocoa today, you won't have cassava to eat. If you have planted cocoa, and you have made money, what food do you eat then? Do you understand that? That is why you have to plant cassava that you can eat. Maybe not in Ahafo, but in Kwaabere there, where I **first** saw cocoa, if you plant cocoa today, you won't find food to eat. But at **first**, cocoa was the number one thing in people's lives.

In the old days, if you saw a person who had ten children, everyone respected her. *Wahu?* Then, there were not many people in the world. But today, plenty of people have come into the world. People are so plentiful that the world is getting wider. At **first**, for example, you might go to someone's farm and see there was some plantain there. You could cut some, and when you got back, you went to tell him. "Oh, I went and cut some." He would say, "Oh, it's nothing." Today, if you even go to touch someone's greens, without God's help you will go to prison. The reason is that she and her children do not have enough to eat, and you have also gone to eat some. So today, people themselves have become too many in the world. Today, in our town, for example, where I used to see backyard cocoa everywhere, today we have built houses all over that area. Me, I want some, you also want some, but this field is only one. It isn't the real town, but we will move ahead into the farms, into the cassava farms, to clear land to put up houses. Only in the country-side, where the land has died, the cocoa has died, can you plant cocoa. Actually, all these days, we are still going on planting, but it seems like it is all between these houses. If someone plants it all in cocoa, what will he do to eat?

Right now, in Ghana here, if you have money to do business, money is here. There is money here. But if you don't have money to do business, that is it. You will have so much trouble. If God hasn't helped you, you can only die. Nobody will help you. If I could say that when I fell down, I had someone to give me money to go on the road, then today I would still be just **fine**. But because it happened like it did, today even my body has changed. It's like this: even when you go into your room, if you are worried, you can't sleep.

For now, I have finished speaking. I have said what I had to say. You also came to see a bit of Ghana. When you came you saw how the world was, at the time when you came. These days, too, you have seen how it is. So all of it, it is God's problem.

CHAPTER 5

Auntie Afriyie

Portrait: A Shrewd Dealer

My mother had not gone to school. Her wisdom, that she used to live in Ghana, that is what I studied.

Auntie Afriyie is first and foremost a hardworking trader; her short, dark form seems always in motion when I see her in the market. Her fierce concentration can be intimidating, and her flinty gaze often suggests impatience or reserve. The occasional sparkle of dry humor or mumbled wisecrack reveals a skeptical streak, turned most often on others. The ups and downs she experienced through frequenting village markets doubtless fed this skepticism, while the resulting detachment helped her weather their daily volatility.

When I first knew her in 1979, she kept a grueling schedule, rising early most days to ride out to a weekly rota of periodic markets. With a busload of colleagues, she bought farm produce at markets that were each held one day a week, in villages or small towns near enough to Kumasi that they could return to the city the same day, early enough to sell their goods at a decent price. She almost always bought palm nuts and red palm oil, from farmers or village processors, which she resold from her own stall. Besides these, she kept an eye out for a good deal by monitoring prices in Kumasi for a wide range of standard vegetables, including plantain, cocoyam leaves, and garden eggs. Thus she could quickly spy a local bargain, and usually brought extra goods for resale to her specialist friends in Kumasi, turning a quick profit.

When I brought up the idea of coming with her, she first warned me off, saying they left at 6 AM and I couldn't stand to get up so early. One morning she had agreed to take me along, so I traversed the misty dawn of the waking city. Dutifully arriving at 6 AM, I found the area of her stall completely deserted. As her market neighbors began filtering in toward 7 AM, one eventually explained to me that the buses were loading up in a gas station down the street. I got over there in time to catch an astonished wave from her before the bus pulled out, and joined her on a later bus and on several more occasions.

Auntie Afriyie managed to build up a substantial business in one of the more ramshackle fringe areas of the market, on a steepish, eroded slope near one of the truck loading areas. Her neighbors still sell their raw palm nuts from low tables of rough wood, or even from burlap bags on the ground. This area was cleared completely in the 1979 AFRC demolitions, including a shack the local watchman had built so that he could charge for secure overnight storage. Auntie Afriyie rebuilt a much larger shed in which she stores her own palm nuts, oil, and equipment.

By local standards she is an entrepreneur, one of the few traders to move into food processing from retailing. Her palm oil press was made locally, as an outgrowth of an intermediate technology initiative at the local university. In the space just in front of the shed, her hired laborers boil and pound the palm nuts to prepare them for pressing. By expanding the oil side of her business, she has been able to cut back on her personal travel to weekly markets as she gets older. One daughter still runs her retail stall, although she has greater hopes for a granddaughter.

Auntie Afriyie shows her self-confidence and drive, but talks about her wisdom. Her story gives a unique perspective on indigenous concepts of intelligence and training, as formulated and experienced outside school altogether. She explains how she learned by attentive watching and listening, both at home with her mother and in the market with her group leaders. Her story also models that process by telling me many legends intended to teach, both Asante and Biblical in origin.

By calling herself a "house wisdom" (fiɛ-nyansa), she marks herself as a custodian of indigenous knowledge. Her story of her puberty ceremony reflects the value she places on respecting traditional norms and the elders who upheld them, rather than going her own way. Those who rebel are condemned as *basabasa*, or disorderly, a condition that makes them useless to themselves and others. The seasons of maturity for people, as for foodstuffs, are ordained by God, and profit comes from fitting in to their rhythms. In comparison, the fruits of progress or modernization seem dubious and unreliable. There is no hint of a contradiction between Asante and Biblical principles.

When I returned for the life history project in 1994, she was equally serious about her Jehovah's Witness affiliation. She explained that she was no longer "of the world." Before agreeing to record her story, she consulted her local preacher, who fortunately allowed it. Her life story confirms that this commitment keeps her from taking up a leadership position in the market, but apparently does not keep her from taking full advantage of her commercial position. When I returned to go over the text with her, she declined further involvement. Although I could still publish what she had already said, she asked me not to use her real name or picture. The images illustrating the story here show some of her colleagues in the palm nut trade.

Story: If You Have Wisdom, You Can Do Many Jobs

In Ghana, now, it has turned around and gone so far . . . During our time, they were buying pepper and garden eggs by the halfpenny. Even when you bought the pepper, if it was from someone kind, she might throw in the garden eggs for nothing. We were not buying beef, except with an egg. When you bring the butcher an egg, he will cut some meat for you. Cassava was selling for a penny or threepence. Plantain was also sold by the penny or threepence. Beef innards were twopence. They cut up the internal parts of the cow, the intestines, and called it twopence, twopence, *wahu?* The word *nnamma nnamma,* in Frafra language, means twopence, twopence. When you were going to find some to buy, they would say, I am buying some of the *nnamma nnamma,* and the money used to buy it has become its name. We used to buy it twopence, twopence, *wahu,* and today it is said *damma damma.* So the past is actually alive today.

Formerly, every year, prices went up. Even the Bible says, every year we shall miss the old year. What did Kwame Nkrumah say? He said, we are fighting to go forward and we shall not retreat. So you know that time is passing. For our grandparents, living was cheap. Now, our living conditions are not cheap. Ah, if a case lasts too long, what do we call it? Ancient, ancient, ancient. As for the ancient culture, it is still there; we don't throw it away. For instance, the *trotro,* why do we call it *trotro?*

MA: *In those days the car used to take threepence.*

Today how much does a *trotro* cost? One hundred, or two hundred; 150, *wahu?* As Kwame Nkrumah said, we fight to go forward [*kɔ y'anim*].

Our hometown is named Asonommaso. Do you know why they call it that? In ancient times, they came from Denkyira to settle at a place called Ampon. At Ampon, they came to meet an elderly man called Donsoahene. That name means he came to carry all things there, so that place became a town. When they came to stay with him, they also came to hunt at Asonommaso there.

Those who have picked up guns to go to the bush to kill animals are called *atweɛ, wahu?* All hunters are called *abofoɔ.* A hunter gets up very early in the morning and goes to hide in the bush, in search of an animal. All of them are called by the same word, *abofoɔ.* But the [ones who are] *atweafoɔ* [plural of *atweɛ*] also, if the animal is hiding in the bush, people slash the bush, shouting and making lots of noise. The animal comes out and they shoot it. They call this beating the bush to look for an animal. But the other *ɔbofoɔ,* he goes walking very quietly and stands still under a tree. Here is the path of the animal, and the hunter comes to stand beside it and waits. He will see when the animal is coming and bam! He has killed it. That is why the elders came, and they saw that a baby elephant was standing there, bam! We had killed it. Then we went to tell the elders that we have just killed a baby elephant.

We would stay right there and cut it up. They stayed with us and we cut it up, and they made us put up a house right away, and we lived there, and it became a town. They said then that they would not go away again. They would stay with the baby elephant. *Woate aseɛ?* That is why the town is called "At the baby elephant." They came there and killed the baby elephant. In Twi, every town name has its meaning, so this was "At the baby elephant." Because we had made it beside the baby elephant. *Woate aseɛ?*

Because between the old days and now, everything has changed. Listen, the Bible says that when the end of time comes, hard times will come. It happens that many people say that this government has made life become hard. If you study the Bible, you understand that it is not them. It is the Almighty. The words of his mouth that he has spoken have come true. The Almighty has said that it will happen like this, and it has happened through him. So if anyone says, it is because of one chief, it is untrue. It is in all the countries of the world, not only here. It will come to the whole world; it is not only in Ghana here that there is trouble. You have seen that in Europe, you look at many towns, they take out guns and just shoot! In this town, also, they shoot guns and kill their brothers too. We keep on fighting and fighting, *wahu?* It is the Almighty that has foretold this fighting, not a person. It pains me that, when I was coming here, I didn't bring a Bible or the Book of Revelations. If I had, I would explain these things, that are not from the government, but from the Almighty.

GC: *One day we will do that with you, but if you tell us some of this for now, one day we will do that also with you, so you can get ready.*

So right now, mudfish, seafood, **fish, fish**, how much did we pay for it? Threepence, penny. Today, you pick up one fish and how much is it? One thousand, two or three thousand. The other day, one fish was five thousand, about this big, and I cut it into pieces. Five thousand! So if you look at how Ghana is going, it is going too far and not coming back. It will never come back. All the **time**, it gets farther ahead. How much do we pay for Fanta? **350!** In the old days, how much did we pay? I first found it at fourpence. So when you work and you get tired and you get somewhere, "Ah, drink some of this Fanta, fourpence," she says. And you take one and drink it. Today it is 350. Isn't the world going forward [kɔ n'anim]? These onions, tomatoes, peppers, and garden eggs, they were all put together as one bunch and sold to you for a penny. Today they are sold separately. Now tomatoes alone are grouped for five hundred cedis. Four little ones are two hundred, *wahu?*

If you look at Ghana, well, this papaya has its season to bear fruit. Now, when the rains come, it has started flowering. The hungry season has come, *wahu,* and there is no fruit on it. This means that it is not for her to take care of human children; it is not her duty to look after human children. As soon as the plantain goes away, the papaya also goes away. As for you, look out and watch when the rains are over, there is no papaya on the tree. You can see that now the flowers are very little. When those little ones grow up, and the plantains have sprouted anew in the eighth month, then it grows and you cut the plantain and divide it up. These days today, what we heap up for a thousand cedis, we will come to heap it for two hundred pounds, four hundred cedis or five hundred cedis; then plantain has really come in.

Oranges, too, have their season. Today they have planted the **agric** type that yields a lot.[1] So there is a **time** that oranges come and a **time** that they go. Because in the seventh month and the sixth, oranges have started to flower. So by the ninth month, we start harvesting. We keep on picking until Christmas time, the twelfth month. By the twelfth month, we have finished harvesting, and the flowers have come out again. It does that twice. They say the harvest is divided. It matures little by little and we pick it and then they gather them up and bring them in. Oranges, they come twice.

It was like that when we met our grandparents, because for everything, God arranges its time. All these deeds, they make the world keep changing and changing. So you see that this papaya standing there, if the time that it has to fruit is past, its time is finished, and it will yield very little. It always comes along with food. If there is hunger, you won't see papaya fruits ripening at all.

When we came and met our elderly grandparents, in our grandparents' time, when you sit down as a woman and they are going to make your *bragorɔ, wahu?* You don't go to a man, until the time that they perform the ceremony. When they initiate you, they beat the *donno* drum and perform the ceremony, they beat the other drum *gongongon* [*imitates the sound*]. Your cloths, your headscarf, your loincloth, your beads, all of them will be displayed beside you, and what does that say about you? You follow the words of your mother's mouth. You have plenty of things. In the old days, if you are someone that they beat the drum for, you are a person that respects things. You listen to your mother's words, so every **time**, you are not the person to behave badly. So she says of you, "Ah, as for this child, she has a good character. I have a relative there; I will go and bring him, to let him marry you." You listen to your mother's words, that's how we do it. You take your good friend, and she goes to bring her relative and he comes to marry you, and he and you make very good children.

Today, this no longer happens. When you explain something to your child, she says, "Oh, don't bother me." She won't listen to what you say. She goes and stays away for a while, and when she comes back she is pregnant. This is what has made the world full of pickpockets. I mean, you don't know his character, but still he and your child are having a baby. When the baby comes, he doesn't look after it; he goes away. From you yourself, she will take a small calico cloth. If you go to market, you can see that it is like that. If a little girl is carrying water and carrying a bag, wearing a secondhand dress, and she has tied a child to her back with a calico, as for them, they did not listen to their mothers. All of them like that, they walk around Kumasi hawking in the streets. They weren't people who listened.

But as for us, they beat the drum, and they put our cloths, our beads, our loincloths by our sides. Then the young man comes: "Mama, I beg you, this child of yours, I want to marry her." Then you also observe the man's character closely, and ask what house he is from. He says, "I am from Maame Asomasi's house." She says, "Oh, I will give her to you," as soon as you say that I am from Maame Asomasi's house. Or she says, "Ah, Maame Asomasi, as for that house, my child is not going there. They don't have good character." She will not let her child go to that house to marry and have children, and bring that kind of children back to her house. *Wahu?* That is why people then lived a good life. If you use a hook, you will get a good mudfish.

You know that I did not go to school. Why didn't I go to school? My mother, I had pity on her. She goes to make a farm, and when she goes she doesn't have anyone to help her lift up her load. She gathers a lot of plantains, and she won't have anyone to help her, so I followed after her. In those days we took thought; as for us, we were thoughtful. So every time Mama was going, I used to follow her. So when she gathered up the things, then I would hold it and she also held the other side, and I would load it on her head.

GC: Did any of your sisters go to school?

Yes.

GC: Yes, you alone followed your mother around?

Yes, I followed her like that. I am the last-born. The older ones, some of them helped out, they served. Some also went to school. My mother gave birth to nine children. I am the seventh, and the two after me died, so I have become the youngest. When my mother was going somewhere, I would follow her. The **first-born**, she didn't go to school. She was grown up already. She followed my mother just like that, she didn't go to school, but she was a woman by then.

Besides, we have house wisdom. When we grew up, we became the house wisdom. The eldest was a house wisdom, and what did I do? I also did house wisdom. Only now I am going to school. I learned little by little, *wahu?* When I went with her, my mother would gather things; she gathers a few things and I can load them up. If something is lying on the ground, I take it and give it to her, and she adds it on top. Like that we get plenty, and she gets up and we come home. It continued like that until I grew up. So when I grew up, I knew my mother's wisdom, that she used to live in the world, and I have taken it. My mother hadn't gone to school. Her wisdom that she used to live in Ghana, that is what I studied. So right away, I grew up and had not gone to school, so the trading that my mother did, I observed and learned it.

I sold oranges, but it did not do well for me; then I went to sell bananas, and then I went to sell palm nuts, which did well for me. The oranges, it is not my work, that I came into the world to do. *Wahu?* If you are doing some work and you don't get money from it, you sell and you lose money, then it is not your work. *Woate aseɛ?* My mother traded little by little. So when I grew up, I started trading to see. What did well for me then, I am still in it today. When I buy palm nuts, when I sell it, I mean, I get customers. You saw that, when you first came, and we went to Anyinamso and Nkawie with you to buy palm nuts. I bought it in big quantities. *Wahu?*

Now I have sent two of my children overseas. Two are in Holland, but one of them was sent back. As soon as she arrived, I made her **papers** and she went to America. So she is in Accra. She arranged so that she is leaving this Sunday. The one who went to see her off has not come back yet.

It is wisdom that we use to live in the world. So by selling these palm nuts little by little, now I have bought a palm oil machine. You see that I did not go to school at all. I bought a machine and built the building that I was inside. It belongs to me. It is my own thing. It is wisdom that I used to make palm oil. The day that you come there, I will let you take photos. I will let them stand beside it and they will do it for you to see and take pictures. So that palm oil I kept making little by little, little by little, little by little, little by little.

When you come, you will see that I take a drum, and I pour the nuts into it, and I put a board on top. I lift another drum and I put it on top, and I stand up. I take another thing to put there, and I put another thing on top, and I stand up and press it little by little. I pour [the oil into a drum] until it is full and then I put a board on to cover it. It will keep like that for two years without spoiling, inside there. I have pressed it and boiled it and poured it back in the drum. When palm oil is too plentiful, so they don't buy it, I store it.

I take the palm nuts that I have pounded, and I put it in the machine and press it. Then I go and boil the palm oil. I strain it, and draw off the soup at the bottom to go throw it away. The fibers left from the fruits, we roll them up; some are over there. I have finished taking out the oil. I have extracted a lot of oil. The **first one** and the second one, *wahu?* So what is left, what is it? The fiber. It is fuel. It lies in the sun and becomes dry, and becomes very hard. Then I fold it and fold it again, and put it into this fireplace. I take any small stick and put it on top. It will be flaming just like that, and the palm nuts will be boiled. I boil them with that. I don't go and buy a lot of firewood. I put very little, very small firewood here and there, and I light it with the fibers beneath it and put more on it. It will be flaming like that and let the palm fruits get cooked.

Would I have been able to do this in Kumasi? It is wisdom; anything is wisdom. That was my mother's work, it began when my mother had wisdom. I also listened to my mother's words. She sat down and talked about things, and I listened and took it in. That is why I have written it all down in my head, and I also am using it to do my work. That is why my mother herself built a house in our hometown for us, and we lived in it and grew up. So right now, I have built one in my hometown. I have worked to build one. I worked and built a second one. One of them I am just now starting. The one that I have poured a cement floor in, that one I have given to my child. I have not finished yet, and whenever I say I will go finish it, then I have sent one of my children overseas. When I finish with all of them, only then I will work on the house. It is in town here, behind Prempeh College. I have gone to receive the **plot**, and laid the whole **foundation**.

This is because only now have I started to sell palm oil and use the money to build. This palm oil, I poured it into drums two years ago and just sold it this year. It is the good kind for eating, that does not spoil. If you look and it has solidified, even the solid one hasn't spoiled. When it doesn't look quite pure, then I buy it up. Right away I take fresh palm nuts and boil them and press them, and I pour the oil into a metal pot. I take the old one to mix with it and boil it, and it has become fresh again. That's how I do it, *wahu?* So I have palm oil at all times. It is wisdom.

When I had sold it, that child of mine also came back. I cannot save the money to build a house and let my child remain in Ghana. So I have made her [visa] papers for her. Now she is in Accra, and she said maybe this Sunday. They say that the Ghana Airways plane is spoiled, so she will take a plane to another town for about thirty minutes before they fly out. The one who went to see her off has not returned yet, and until she comes we will not know whether she has gone or not.

So everything is done with wisdom. If you have worldly wisdom, you get everything. You have seen that I never went to school. The one who went to school also has wisdom, but I might have more than her. This wisdom, it is not only when you have been to school that you will have wisdom. It is the mind and eyes you use to keep track of small things and they add up. I think, if I do this and that, it will become something big, so I will do it like that to see what happens. *Wahu?* Someone used their mind to make this bottle. Someone used their mind to do this, someone used their mind to do that. *Wahu?* That's how it has become wisdom. The shoes we are all wearing, someone put their mind to making them. So it is something that the Almighty gives to people, and if you have the intelligence, you can do something.

That's what, right there, gave me the idea about the palm nuts: if you buy some and they are not buying it, buy a machine. I didn't have the money to buy the government one, that is **electric**, so then I went and bought the **manpower**. The one I have, we call it **manpower**. Our strength, you see? In addition, I hire people. At first, I was doing it myself, little by little, but my own strength was not able to make a lot of it. Then I hired some Northerners. They pound and press for me, and I pay them three thousand cedis every day. Those who pick out the kernels, too, I give them five hundred cedis every day. *Wahu?* So when I finish, like just now when you came, I was taking out the oil inside the room. When I draw it out in front of the house, then I go pour it into a drum and fill it full. When it gets to this time of year, I sell very little and I use some of the money for food and I take some to hire workers. *Wahu?* I cover the drums up, and when oil becomes scarce what do I do? Then I sell it. That's how I do it little by little, little by little, little by little, little by little.

If you have that wisdom, living in Ghana here, everything of yours will make you get ahead. But if you don't know this wisdom, if you live here today, you say that Ghana is hard. It is wisdom that you use to live here. A person like that, if there is someone like me, she will be proud. The government doesn't help me; the government doesn't do that. You yourself take your aid to go help the government. You will help it. When you get some money, what will you do with it? You will send it to the bank. When you take it to the bank, the government will use it to work to help the nation. Yes, don't say that the government should go and find money to bring to you, for you to use it to work. It is all wisdom. If you are wise, you too, you will help the government. *Wahu?*

Plus, the people who are in the government, they don't pay attention to things. They don't do their work well. *Wahu?* People like us, they should build a relationship with us, and ask us for the wisdom we use to live in the world. For example, who gave you the idea, that if you go and buy palm nuts and people don't buy it, and they are getting rotten, then you go and throw them away?

They said that they would tax us, and we said that we would not pay, because this is food, it is a tree fruit. Recently, a bag of garden eggs was forty-four thousand. *Wahu?* There was none at all. After it rained twice, garden eggs came in. A bag was three thousand, five thousand, or four thousand. Even some we bought for five hundred cedis. That came in fast for one month, then it disappeared. We don't have a machine to put them in, like a cold store. We have none. When we do the work and they get too ripe, then they get rotten. Recently, palm nuts are abundant. We buy them for three thousand; today it is one thousand five hundred, for a plastic bucket.[2] Then we also sell it for three thousand. But if I were not wise . . . Did you see some shells over there when you went into the passage? I have boiled the palm nuts like that and I have thrown the kernels over there. When palm nuts become scarce, they will buy the kernels at a thousand for a plastic bucket full. Just the other day, somebody came to offer me eight hundred cedis. So if I have extracted the palm oil, and the kernels have been bought for eight hundred cedis, do I lose?

The fibers, too, are there. Do you know that our pastors do not eat meat? When they come to buy them, they go and put them here and there, maybe under this papaya, and they put on special fertilizer and mushrooms called *domo* come out from them. They grow mushrooms with the fibers that I have put over there, so they buy them. So, there might be someone that, when he comes to buy them, I say no. I don't have firewood; I am using it as firewood. They say there is a fertilizer to use to grow mushrooms. They even use it to grow snails. They put the fibers there, and they put the chemical for snails on them, and they hatch snails. They fence it, and the small snails crawl around and grow big. Do you see that is what they do?

Yes, if you have wisdom, you can do many jobs. Intelligence lets you go do many kinds of work. It is wisdom, that the Almighty has given us for free. But as for some people, who are stupid, it doesn't work. They don't use it to do good things, out of laziness. You see, at my age, I am old, but I can work.

Now, pepper is plentiful. It has been plentiful for the past five months. When you come to market, I will show you. I have broken off the heads and I will put them on the fire. I will not put in water, but I will take a sheet of **polythene** to cover the pot. The fire heats the bottom of the pot gradually, and makes steam. Then I will remove the **polythene**. I mean, when we entered the car, did you notice that the inside was hot? When we rolled down the windows, air came into it. So when I go to remove the **polythene** sheet, even the top ones are all cooked. They are cooked and I pick them out and take them behind the roofing sheets and put them down there. In about three days' time, they will become dry. If it doesn't rain, to wet them, after three days the sun has made them dry, and I will collect them and put them in a sack. I keep doing that, and maybe I will gather about twelve bags. Recently, when pepper became scarce, I was selling them. *Wahu?* It is wisdom. Someone else doesn't know; hers can ripen like that and she goes to throw it away on the garbage dump. She has no wisdom like me.

Recently a man came, and said he will take me to the FM radio station. What have I done? He said that when I dry pepper it smells bad. I said, "Sir, you have made a mistake. If you get one wise person in Ghana in addition to me, it would be a blessing. Why? In Ghana, I am gathering together what is spoiling, and when it becomes scarce, I can bring it out for my sisters and brothers to get some to eat. If everyone could store some, and it later becomes scarce, as soon as everyone brings out theirs, it will become abundant. Its price will not be expensive. But since it is getting rotten for them to throw it away, when it becomes scarce there won't be any left. So when we get a little to buy, the price goes very high."

Look at garden eggs today; recently the plastic bucket full was three hundred or a hundred pounds. Two hundred or three hundred cedis. Today, how much do they sell it for? A thousand two hundred each. It is now coming, but it is going away. It came in abundance in the fourth month. In this fifth month, it is gone; it is going. The plants are very old, and it rained on them and fruit came up in large amounts. This harvest is called *atufuɔ-huru* ["teasing wholesalers"]. It comes fast in large quantities and bears fruits. After a while, it dies and they plant another. Do you know that they are planting new tomatoes, *wahu?* Now is when they are planting the new ones. It is like this. Immediately the old ones go away, then the new one takes its place. That is how it is, *wahu?*

So when the crops come all at once, I do this very very fast. Every day I put some of the palm nuts on the fire. If I don't work like that, they will rot. The other day, for example, they brought me bags and bags of palm nuts—-ten, seventeen, or eighteen bags. There are six plastic buckets full in each bag, and eighteen in all. So I paid **thousand five, thousand five** for each; I checked the whole amount and it was **one-fifty-two** [thousand]. When I was coming here, I gave the money to my mother, so that if the farmer comes, she could give it to him. I was going to boil them all. Yesterday none came in, and I sold it for **two five, two five**. For each one, how much did I make? **Thousand**. For each plastic bucket full I made a thousand cedis.

MA: You get even more than the farmer.

Just so, Just so. When I boil it, too, and extract the palm oil, I also take the kernels to store. When it becomes scarce, I sell that, each plastic bucket for a thousand. I mean, they say they will come for some on Sunday, so I have given them each bucket for eight hundred cedis. You have bought something for **thousand five** and you have taken the palm oil out of it. The fibers, too, I have tied it in balls for five hundred cedis each. *Wahu?* Like that for five hundred. That means I have wisdom. If you don't have wisdom, you can't work like that. If you have wisdom, a very small thing, you can make it very big. If you aren't wise, every day it will stay very little. If you know wisdom, every day it will get very big. Just like that, little by little.

So these days right now, in our time, good advice is there. Then you don't go get pregnant carelessly and have children every which way [*basabasa*]. You look over the house and you take your child to go there. This is the house that I want my child to marry into. If someone's child is in Europe or America, and he writes to me to find a woman for him, I have seen that you are a good person, so I will come and receive your child for my child to marry. When she goes, she does not behave badly, *wahu?* He does not treat her badly. They will agree with each other. They will have children. The child and its mother and father will all have one mind. The child will not misbehave. His father does not smoke weed, so that he might smoke some. His mother does not smoke either, to let him smoke some. *Wahu?*

But if you haven't made your child go to a good house to marry, then she walks in the street, and a **boy** who makes **high time** sees her and cuts his eyes, saying, "Come here." "Oh, I would like that," she says. "There is a way to do it. Let's go." She has gone with him, and he goes to steal money and gives a lot of it to her. Then he takes her, and they get pregnant, and they have a child. The child, well, the work his father does he will also do. That's why in Ghana today, there is chaos [*basabasa*] everywhere. Today, in the whole nation there is chaos.

You see, my son acted like he wanted to marry a Dutch woman. You see? A white wife. He wanted a white woman to marry. The white woman has taken his money and run off. On top of that, she made my son go to prison. You see? By saying she and he would get married for papers. My son went, but hasn't come back. The woman has run away. She took the money and ran. She didn't marry him. Then they said, it was not a proper marriage anyway, so go back to Ghana. So they deported my son to make him come back. Do you think that if he had a good white person like Akua, that had wisdom, she would say, "Hey, I don't want you, go away" so flatly? That one didn't like him, but she had taken his money. When they were making the marriage, you didn't show up, and they took my son off to prison again before they deported him back. That woman's mother, she didn't take a good man who was wise to conceive her, *wahu?*

That's why now my son says he doesn't want a white woman ever again. He will look for a Ghanaian, whose mind will agree with his. Some Ghanaians also are like that. It isn't only white people who do that. Ghanaians also are just like that. She says that she will marry you, she will make you spend your money to do everything; when she goes out, you won't see her again. You have lost money. That's why it makes wisdom. If that one did this to him, that they put him into the cells, to deport him and make him return to his hometown, tomorrow, when he sees a white woman who says she will marry him, will he marry her? He will not marry her. Everything makes you wise.

That's why in the past we, when you matured, you would be given to your husband. Before going, you would be given these things, that your mother would buy for you. A headscarf, take it with you. She would give you beads. She would give you a loincloth. Then she would get all of them out to pile up in the evening, when the young man would come and sit down. In Ghana, we make your *bragərə*, so you know whether he is somebody's husband. We will do it, we will play the *donno* drum, and you have seen your blood. How do you call it? When you are a child, they do it for you. Yes, they did that for me.

I mean, if you are one that we do this for, you respect your mother. Any word that your mother says, you say aye. No! If you are one that acts like that, we won't do it for you. Your mother says something and [you reply] "Oh, not for me." You who are acting like that, we won't make you any ceremony. Your mother says something, you say, "Yes, ma'am, I have heard. Mama, what are you saying?" If you haven't heard well what she is saying you say, "Mama, excuse me, what did you say?" She says, "I said, tomorrow we will go to the farm." You say, "Yes, Mama, I'm sorry, I have heard you." But there are some children, some young girls, that when they are little their mother calls them, "Akua, come." When she comes, "Tomorrow we will go to the farm." "Oh, I'm not going. You can't make me go to the farm. I've gone and gone, why?" If your child is like this, her mother will not go buy cloth to pile up, she won't go to buy these things to pile up, so that when you mature she can give them to you. She won't do that for you. When she wanders around like that, her mother won't help her.

The girl herself will walk around that way. But when she comes home, if her mother has put *fufu* aside, she looks, and if her mother is not there, then she opens it and she eats it and she runs away. That one, we call her a bad child. It means, she doesn't listen to her mother. A girl like me, if I come in from outside, maybe I went to sell things. If my mother has finished cooking, and she has eaten and has left some for me, then I go to ask her, "Mother, please, where is my food?" She says, "It is what I put in a dish over there. One is for Akwasi, and Adua, yours is also there." Then I pick it up and I go and show it to her saying, "My mother, please, is this it?" She says, "Yes," and I go to sit down and eat it. I am a good child. But the bad child, when she has come and the food has been shared out over there, she was not given some, because she was a bad child. So when she sees that her mother has gone into a room, she goes to take Akwasi's portion, and takes some and eats it very, very quickly and goes away. She will be doing that until she has grown up.

She won't bring forth a good child. She will not have a good child. The only thing you will see is that she has brought a belly home. "Why?" She says, "I am pregnant." "With whom are you pregnant?" She says, "I don't have a husband." You can ask her and ask her forever. Maybe she will show you someone that you can't stand. Like a black monkey, what white people call us when we are Northerners. *Wahu?* And we also call them, those they have scratched.[3] The world! Maybe you say, "Where is he?" and she says, "He has run away." Then the child is going to be born, and when the child is born, it has no father. All the burden comes back to fall on the grandmother. Then what happens is that when the baby is born and is a few days old, the grandmother says, "I say get up and go to work to earn your food. I am not the one who is going to look after you. Me, I can't even care for myself and I am going to take on this in addition?" So it becomes like she bought this bowl. *Wahu?* She has filled it with water and it is big enough for her, and she will pour it out. When she pours it out for you, you give her something. That way she takes it to look after herself. Those that act like this, they are not obedient. You tell them something and they don't listen. That's why you see people who walk around like that.

I mean, if she had been obedient to her mother, she would say, "Oh, Akua, you are my friend. Since you came, you have come to look for me and I also have come to stay by you. So when you go, take this child of mine; I give her to you as a gift." You too, because of me, you will treat her very, very fine, and you will give her to a wise man. Then she will have many children. So whenever I see you, I have to laugh and be happy. You have helped me. I mean, my child also has helped you. When she went, she did not, she did not insult you, she didn't behave **rough, rough**. Whatever you said, she says, "All right, I heard it. Please, I heard. Excuse me, I heard it." Then you push yourself to go find a good young man for her.

GC: So your mother found a good man for you, from your hometown?

Just like that. He was from my town. So with that man I had four children, and then he died. I became a widow, and I remarried the second one. The one who died lived in the village. The next one lived in Kumasi here. When my husband died, I came to Kumasi. When I came, I met him here and we got married. But he is also from my hometown.

When I came to Kumasi, I came to join my sister. Yes, she was staying here and I came to join her. But even when I came to join her, she could not stay on here and she left. She went back to our hometown, and she married and went to live in Ejura. She went to stay there, so when she and the man got divorced, she could not come back to Kumasi here. So right now, I am the one that, when I get cloth, I send it to her. It was because of her that I came, but now I have overtaken her. Work stays with me. She doesn't have the wisdom to do work. Me, I have had the wisdom to work well.

Our mother's sister also came to stay with us. But our mother's sister also, she didn't have wisdom; but me, I had some. Then, she started talking about me, that if she didn't send me away from her, I would turn into a witch. You see, in Ghana here, what happens when you have wisdom. My own mother's sister. If she doesn't move us away, me and my sister, I will bewitch her. I wouldn't let her do well ever. So, when I heard her, I left her [stall] and I moved there behind the gate. I was at the market before, *wahu,* inside the main market. You see that when we go to the markets and back, I arrange my things and I take them into the main market. When I left the main market, I left my mother's side to come here, and I built a stall. By now, I have got a little place. She also, her stall is still very small; it is as big as two of these chairs. Only she herself sits there, *wahu?* I have about fifteen tables. I have put my children and grandchildren's names on them. *Wahu?* It is wisdom. *Wahu?*

GC: In the days when you left the village and came to join your sister, were you selling palm nuts?

The house that I left the village to settle in, well, when I came, it was not because of my sister. But there was a young man, who was from Abira, and he was working in that town, and he got to know me. I am from Asonommaso and the man from Abira came there to build a house, as a contractor. He saw me and he married me. I had four children, and I came with him. I had one child with him, too. He came and rented a house for one cedi. It was small, a kind of kitchen room, and I lived in it. Little by little, little by little, and the man and I had had one child, and he said he would not marry me [any more]. Then the child died, and he divorced me, and I went to marry a person from my town. Our children have been added to the older ones. As for him, I have had children with him **fine**. Some of our children are even in Europe. So from the one-cedi house that I lived in, little by little, little by little, now I have built three houses. One is in my hometown, and two are here. I have not finished building, but since I have got the land, I will build it. It is up to Jehovah, *wahu?*

So everything is wisdom. If you don't have wisdom, you will not get that kind of awareness. It is because, like, the friends I came with, when we came we met some people. I even met one who asked, "Where are you going?" I said, "I am going to see this friend's house." So she said, "All right." Then I went to buy some things there, and I went to the market. I stood with her in the street looking for a car to come to Kumasi. We stopped a car, and all of us got in one car and we came. Then all of us slept in the room that my husband had found to give me, we slept in it. So you see, we came to live in it. And I took my children, all four of them, to my mother. I went to have more, to make them be ten in all.

At that time, when I first came, I said I would go to buy bananas to sell. And then I went to buy avocados to sell, but there was not much profit in it. I bought them here in Kumasi. Then I went to buy cloth at Asafo Market, and the whole piece was two pounds and ten shillings. A half piece was one pound and five shillings. Then I arranged them and was carrying them around to sell. If you go to bring European cloth, the border guards will catch you, so I was always breathing hard. I was afraid. When they get hold of it, then they take it. So I said to myself, as for this work, I won't do it any more. I want some quiet work at home, for which the police won't arrest me. That's how I started selling palm nuts.

So when I was selling palm nuts, I went to the village markets: Nkawie, Anyinamso, Kunsu, Adugyama. I was buying cocoyam greens and palm nuts and avocados. When I came back, I unloaded them and went home. I kept doing this little by little, little by little, little by little. So my mother that that I settled with, when I came to join my sister and we stayed with my mother's sister, by now her stall was too small, and I moved out of it. Then I made a big stall for myself, and I press my palm oil little by little.

So when she comes by, she says, "I beg you, today I am hungry." As for me, when I first came she didn't treat me well. I thought it over. I said, this woman, *wahu?* If I had stayed there, she would have said that I with my witchcraft did not allow her to do well. What about after I moved? Have you prospered? You did not prosper, because you did not have good ideas. Maybe I have taken money and given it to her. Recently, her child had a debt, and for that I have given her ten thousand cedis, and she went to pay it. As for me, I have brains in my head; there is no evil there. *Wahu?*

GC: What did you do to learn how to sell palm nuts?

It is wisdom.

GC: Is there any relative that came to sell palm nuts, and you followed her?

That sister of my mother's, she came first to sell and I came to join her. It was my sister who came to join her, and when my sister came to join her, she herself sold avocados and oranges. So I too, when I arrived, sold avocados and oranges. But when I examined it carefully, it was not good. But I sold some of the palm nuts, and they did better than the avocados. What came into my mind was that I should go and sell palm nuts. When my mother was selling it, I watched her. My mother's sister that I came to join in Kumasi here. Before, when I was a small child in my hometown, I watched her. My mother's sister that I came to join in Kumasi here, when I was a small child in my hometown, we also sold it there. The men went to cut the palm fruits from high up, and the women went to buy them. Then they cut the nuts from the bunch and picked them out.

Also, when I went to the farm with my mother and went where they had cut them, and there were some left behind, my mother would go on and I would sit down to pick them up. Maybe I would get about a basketful. I had not yet come to Kumasi. So when I picked them up like that, and took them to show to my mother, she would pick out some and we made soup with them. I would go out with the rest and retail them for a penny. That made me know that there is profit in palm nuts. When they are in a basket and you mention the price, it is very small. But when you divide them up, there is profit in it. That is what made me know how to sell palm nuts. When I was a child, I put my mind to selling them, and it made me know that there was profit in it. *Woate asɛ?*

GC: Your machine, that you bought to press the oil, are you the only one that uses it, or can someone come to hire it to press hers?

If someone comes, I will not give it to her. For people can come to tell me that they want to hire it and use it, and I say you won't get a chance. When the palm nuts are plentiful every day, I will boil them. So you want to take my machine to put yours in it? I will not do that, because when it breaks down, it is **manpower**, I have to send it off to **maintenance**. So I use it myself for my own goods, little by little. I am not going to give it to you to process your own goods; it is not yours. If you have palm nuts, what are you going to do? You will give them to me, to buy very, very cheaply. If they are about to rot and you give them to me, if you bought them for **thousand five**, I will give you **thousand**. Maybe if it was very good, you would get **two thousand**. Like you, if you bought it for **thousand five**, then you would look to put something on top.

It is because [the nuts] were rained on. When the rain falls on palm nuts, they get very hot inside the sack or the basket. If today it gets rained on, the next day you put your hand inside and ah, it burns you and it clumps together. It is not spoiled. The water has cooked it, *wahu?* It hasn't spoiled, it isn't rotten. But the person who is buying it will tell you that it is rotten. So then, I gather my goods and put them in a pot, and when I put it on the fire, it cooks very fast. Then I pound it and pick the kernels out and I press it. *Wahu?* So I am always wiser than them. That's why recently, when palm nuts became abundant, they said, "Eh, Nana, come! How much will you give me?" There may even be someone who will pour it out and give it to me free. When I finish making it, I measure a little of the palm oil and give it to her. It is wisdom, *wahu?* If you are not wise, you cannot live in Ghana. *Woate asɛ?*

MA: And now, how did you become the queen for palm nuts?

The palm nut queen? All right, when I started selling palm nuts, I was a person whose eyes were open [*anibue*]. I am wise. So the market queens, when any problem came up and the elders were going somewhere, I would follow them. If she lifted this up and said, "Hold it," I would hold it. So if we were going out, everyone else was selling their things and they would not have spare time to go. I was the only one that would follow them. Hold it, and I hold it. She would say, "The government says that all the palm nut sellers, everyone and every queen mother should come and pay money." Or tomorrow, "We shall go and meet with the government. We need to collect a little money to buy something, to go and greet them." This one, she says, "Am I the one to go collect dues for this old woman? As for me, I'm not going." She is also too old. But I follow them and I collect all the dues. So they observed quietly, and they said, "Whether we die or live, hold the office that we have until you die." Just like that. So they themselves took it in hand to give it to me. Then one of them died soon, and one has died just recently. The whole time that she was bedridden, when she was so old that she could not get up, then I did the work for her. I did the work for her, and I took the money to give her, so that she could take it to buy food to eat. It was like that until she finished dying. I did it for about one and a half years; it was not for long.

During that time, too, I said that I have known the Almighty, his knowledge and his wisdom. So that work, I was not going to do; market queen work, I would not do. Now, I have removed myself from it. *Wahu,* when we were coming, they were starting to hold a meeting. They called me; I said I would not be coming. Also, if I am not there, they can't say anything.

Right then, at the time that the Almighty said that Solomon should go and rule Israel, and he was king, then Jesus Christ had not come. The Almighty himself made Solomon king, so we had a king on this earth. And between the king and Satan, Jehovah Almighty said that he would not let this earth be taken by the Devil. Then the Devil was up above, doing foolish things, and he was making the angels do them and he was complaining to them. Oh, eh, Mark and the angels threw him out and he fell down. So when he was removed and brought down, he came to the earth. So that meant that the Almighty said Jesus should take his holy blood to rescue mankind alone. Then he let Jesus come. So Jesus

Christ came, and the Devil took him to the top of a high mountain and tempted him, that he should bow down. They would give him the kingdom of the whole world. From that time on, the kingdom of Solomon did not function again. *Wahu?* As for this, the Almighty himself established it.

So for now, he has installed a new king, who is the Devil. When the Devil came into the world, the kingdom of Israel was not in force. It was the Devil who was coming to be the king over it. So this earth, it is not the Almighty who is ruling it. He is the ruler, but he has given it to the Devil to do whatever he wants. *Wahu?* Let's say that this is my town, and Akua has come to stay in it. I say that Akua should take this town; I myself have given it to her, and Akua should do whatever she likes in this town here. But some time is coming, that I will drive you away, Akua, and make a big hole and put her into it and cover it, and she will not be Akua again. That is how the Almighty has fixed it for the Devil. So when you say that Solomon was a king and I, I will be a king, is it possible? No, no, no. Do you understand that this king that we have here, he belongs to the Devil?

GC: So, when you stopped doing it, who is the queen mother now?
She is there.
GC: Didn't you get a new one to take her place?
They even say they don't like her.
GC: They don't like to be queen? Is it because no one has time to do the work?
It isn't that. Me, the Devil has admired me. My wisdom measures up to being the palm nut queen. I do things very well for the family, that is, the palm nut people. Right now, they can't get anyone who can do that. So, if they look around, I am the one they want. But I have also seen Jehovah; I am not going to do that kind of work. It is against the laws of Jehovah.
GC: Do any of your children sell palm nuts?
Yes, the one who came here to do my hair and put a watch on my wrist; she sits with the palm nuts and sells them. She is my third-born. And the tall, dark one with her is my great-granddaughter, my grandson's child. She is also from Jamasi, and her mother married and gave birth to her. That's why I have taken her on. My grandson had her, then I took her to be with me, along with my children. Yes, and I am train-

ing her little by little. So she is the person that, if I pass on, she will do the work. None of my own children can do it. As for her, she can do it, because she watches everything that I do.

GC: And why is it that none of your children follow you as this one follows you?

Of my children, only three are women. The women are three. One is a sick person; she can't use her legs. And I have sent one to Holland; she has four children. And one also is the one who was sitting by the palm nuts selling them. She also has one child. But maybe when I die, she will get serious, so maybe she will do it. But now while I am here, she knows that any difficult task, I can do it, so she will not do it. She won't do it. Maybe when I am not there, she will do it. Now I feel tired. Everything is lying there. If you won't do it, and you will let neighbors do it, I don't care. Because I have done my all and put it there.

GC: You have done so many kinds of work; what has helped you especially in your work?

Among the many kinds of work I have done, it is palm nuts that have helped me most. With the palm nuts, I sell some; I also make palm oil from it and I sell the kernels. So the palm nuts have helped me very much. I also sell the fibers. As for palm nuts, they have helped me a lot. I have studied the wisdom about palm nuts, so they have helped me a lot. As for the work, it is because I am honest. I am honest with the farmers who bring me things, so that doesn't allow anything to bother me in the work. So when I get up, because you have a farm, you come. You say, I am looking for money to weed the farm. So I give the farmer some, and with it you go and clear it of weeds. When you cut it, you bring it to me. So nothing troubles me in the work.

GC: Is there anyone who takes your money like that, and does not bring the palm nuts to you, and goes to sell it to someone else? Don't some do that?

Yes, they do. They do it, and it is like, in this world, the elders have a proverb that "If you are afraid of a long speech, you don't understand the elders' dealings." As we sat here, we have talked like that. We are listening, and you have heard some. Like about the town Asonommaso: it was a baby elephant that they killed there, because the name means "At the baby elephant." When a hunter goes to the bush, he goes to stalk an animal. And people who hunt in a group, too, are those who use dogs and guns. When they also go out, they surround the bush and two of them are clearing and cutting up the bush. So if the animal is hiding in it, it comes out and they shoot it and kill it, or the dogs go and catch it. Those ones are called beaters. And the hunter also takes a gun and puts it around his neck. He has also noticed that an animal seems to be eating at this place, so I get up in the morning and go hide there. He goes and it may be standing there in the farm eating, and then he shoots it. That one we call a hunter. *Wahu?* So, all of this is a story that I am telling, and if you don't take the time for it, you will say, "This is enough for me" and you get up. And what will you do to understand? That is why elders say the proverb "If you fear long speeches, you will never learn the elders' dealings." Every story has its meaning. *Wahu?*

In Kumasi, everywhere you go they have made something to stand there.[4] This is Komfo Anokye, and the mysterious things that he did. *Wahu?* They made it at G, very tall. And at **prison yard**, they have made a leopard with a person sitting on it. Have you seen it? That was the place where the royals, the Asante kings, lived. And that animal, it always went to catch them to eat. So a hunter went to hide there and caught it. Have you seen a person sitting on the animal, they call it a leopard? And the person on it, what do they call him? Kyeretwie. The leopard, its other name is *twiɛ*. He catches the leopard. So, the elder sitting on it was the one who caught it. The very same day, Nana Ntim Gyakari was born. That same day we gave birth to Nana Ntim. So he said, go and tell them that I have captured it [*m'atim no*]. What he named him was Ntim Gyakari. *Wahu?* He said, you go and tell them that I have captured it. So if he sits on it, he is killing it. Ntim Gyakari. So they said that if he has been born, then they should name him Ntim Gyakari. He has caught it. So, in this town everything has its meaning. The one sitting on it is called Kyeretwie, and that same day, too, Nana Ntim Gyakari was born. He has captured it. They said then, if he has captured it, and this child has been born, we should name him Ntim Gyakari.

Anywhere that you go, at Dunkirk,[5] everywhere has a story to tell. That is why the white people have looked in the books and we have made a mysterious thing about it and we have put it there. So that any place that you go, you remember the particular thing that they did there. You see that over there, he was pouring libation; with the water pot and calabash, he was pouring libation. At Ashtown[6] also, you will see a man holding a knife. All of them have a meaning on the Kumasi streets.

Kumawu and Kumasi are one. Why are they one? They planted some seeds, for two *akuma* trees, one in Kumawu and one in Kumasi. When they were planted, the one in Kumasi flourished, and the one in Kumawu died. *Wahu?* What did they call this place? This place is called "Under the *akuma* tree"; it did not die. Under the *akuma* tree. And the other one, they call it Kumawu; because it died, if you listen to its story.

MA: They say that it was the one at Kumawu that flourished.

And they uprooted it, Komfo Anokye did, and exchanged it with the one at Kumasi, and he took power to the place. All of it is the Devil, do you see? That is just how it is. So this place should have been called Kumawu. They changed the royal place that received the power. It was because Komfo Anokye liked the Asante. He did like the Asante, though he was an Akuapem person, from Awukudwa. So he took the power of the house and he brought it here. As for this town, it is very ancient.

Those drains in all the Kumasi streets, what do we call them? The drains, any big **gutter** that is there, what do we call them?

MA: Don't we call them "gutters"? I don't know another name, except for the Subin [River] itself.

Kofi Dankate.

MA: That's right, I have heard that before. I have heard it before but I don't know what it means.

Kofi Dankate has grabbed me. *Wahu,* Kofi Dankate has grabbed me. And they also used to say it, and I didn't know the meaning. But that Kofi Dankate, he was a contractor who had the contract to make the Kumasi roads. He was a Northerner, a Dagarti. He was an educated man, a Dagarti. So he put his mind to it. He was a **professor**; he was intelligent. He thought it out and he put in all of the big drains in Kumasi. Today we wouldn't be able to do it. The gutter that Kofi Dankate made, the Subin gutter, could we make it these days? No one could make it. Just now, they are redoing Kejetia[7] here. They should have made a huge big gutter and connected it to the Subin. We couldn't do it. Also, since they could not construct the small gutter to go deep enough to let them cover it over well, every day the mud would come to Kejetia. Kofi Dankate built them very big and covered them up well.

So if you fall into a drain, you say I have fallen into Kofi Dankate's trap. Everything has a meaning.

Because of this, when his mother died and he went to the North to bury his mother, then he said he would return to Kumasi to have the funeral. And the Kumasi people made a huge gathering for him. And then he bought drinks and they were drinking, and we played the ceremonial drums, and the women shouted "Yea, Yea." The Creator made the world, and since the Creator made things, have you seen a Northerner coming from the savannah to come to Ashanti to show off? "Kofi Dankate, he has ripened and we are eating, yea, Kofi Dankate, he has become wealthy and we are enjoying it." *Wahu?* He said, "Oh, my mother! Help me, father! I am worn out [*maberɛ*]." But the words they were saying, he didn't understand. He didn't speak Twi. If you understand what they were saying, they said, Kofi Dankate, *waberɛ;* it is like a plantain tree stands there and it has ripened yellow, and people are picking it to eat. *Wahu?* Because he has got money and is boasting, we will spend it. So the drinks and everything he had done, it just made him look stupid. The Asante were singing for him, and he was crying out, "Oh, mother. I am tired, I am tired." He doesn't understand, you see. They say that he is ripe and they are eating him. But he also says he is tired. He is tired, and they are spending his money, *wahu?* They also are talking to him in proverbs, saying he is ripe and we are eating him. It means that he is foolish; we are taking his money and going away. *Wahu?*

Everything has a meaning. It is **history** that comes from Asante. That's how it is. If anyone does anything, there is a meaning in it. That's why if you cross any gutter in Kumasi, they call it Kofi Dankate. He is the one that took his intelligence to do it, before the white people joined him, like that. When the white people came, and they used contractors at all, he was the person who took the lead like that. Because the white people found him already here, and for construction, he had the ideas. He was constructing the roads, before the white people came to take over and build all the roads. As for him, any village road that you see is from Kofi Dankate. In Kumasi here, any gutter here was constructed by Kofi Dankate. I mean, you see that they are small and wander around. He thought of them. So when the white people came, he had finished covering them up.

That is why today, if white people come to take over Kumasi here, we say that the Central Market, that is why they can't rebuild the market. The water runs all over it. They dig gutters all over. And then the women, too, make them. Our cloth market and the stores, we don't want to demolish them. But every time the rain falls, then it spoils their goods. What they should have done was remove the goods and break down one half to rebuild it. Then they would move again to the other half; we would understand. That's why all of the time they have so many problems. They have to let us demolish the market and rebuild the huge **gutter** and seal it. Then if the rain falls, it flows in and goes away. Have you seen that the Subin River, it is only rainwater that goes into it? If it floods, a lot of it overflows like that. So they have to rebuild the **gutter**, the gutter that goes to join the Subin and it takes it away. If they haven't done that, every day their goods will get spoiled. That's how it is. So now, I will leave you right here.

Wholesalers of Oil Palm Fruit

Palm Fruit Retailers at the Market's Edge

A Row of Cooking Oil Stalls Built by Traders

Rebuilding the Main Sewer without Moving Traders

A Hawker Sells Oranges at the Yam Yard

An Onion Retailer Working with Her Niece

An Onion Stall Deep inside the Shed

Onion Sellers outside Their Shed

A Wholesaler
of Wrapping
Leaves, Sold
in Bundles to
Wrap Retail
Purchases

A Mixed
Retail
Area at the
Market's
Edge

An Orange
Wholesaler
and Her
"Boys"

CHAPTER 6

Sister Buronya

Portrait: An International Observer

You have exhausted yourself for nothing.

Sister Buronya's slender arms were her most memorable feature. She moved them continually, like a dancer, in graceful curves that complemented her graceful turns of phrase. Her compact, neatly rounded figure, medium height, and reserved demeanor made little impact in the market. Since her stall was next to another orange trader I visited often, we had known each other for nearly twenty years but rarely spoken at length. When I invited her neighbor to record a tape, Sister Buronya came along to keep her company. We watched this friend fall sound asleep before she finished her soft drink, twice in a row. Meanwhile, Sister Buronya readily started a conversation and began to analyze the country's economic problems. Soon, she suggested that she could tell her own story.

She seemed to have thought about national issues more than most, perhaps because she had plied the international trading circuits for years. Without the usual preliminary remarks, she presented us with lengthy, connected explanations. Her expressive face and slow smile bolstered our impression of thoughtfulness and careful consideration. She turned out to be an exceptionally articulate and skillful speaker, moving myself and my assistant deeply by the time she finished. As she picked her way delicately through life experiences marked with loss and tragedy, including a brother's suicide, she maintained her dignity and self-esteem.

Detachment also appears in her account of the many different kinds of trading she had tried. Her voice takes on a tone of sophisticated cynicism in the stories of her cool and clever handling of the border crossings that terrified other narrators. Although several other narrators echoed a local stereotype that girls automatically follow their mothers' trades, she spoke as if she had never imagined that such an assumption existed. She had ended up in orange trading, but showed no particular attachment to it. Even though her mother had sold oranges, she did not identify the work as a family business. Most of her brothers and sisters actually sold fish, a line of work with a completely different geographical and technical orientation that was common in her home area. Her lack of schooling is due not to poverty but to rebellion, and she strikes an ironic note when she reflects that her mother sent her brothers and sisters to school.

Her world-weary attitude denies that any of the trading niches she has seen hold much potential for sustaining real prosperity, especially without either capital or education. She reports bad credit, unscrupulous characters, and other disasters lurking in every option. Even the everlasting quest for emigration overseas is described as a series of dead ends even worse than remaining in Ghana.

The only way to preserve her self-esteem is to remain aloof, maintaining her own standards of good behavior that put others to shame. Yet she is the one who talks most eloquently about the need for love in the world, and recommends generosity and respect for other people. She argues that living according to solid traditional principles will bring both material and psychological rewards. Such principles bring good customers and steady income on top of happiness and community respect.

Story: If I Had Money, I Would Go

As you are living here, and you are staying in this room, let's say you came and there is a chair inside it. When I came here, I have got a chair to sit on, you have given me water to drink, and you have given me food to eat. I feel comfortable, so I am happy. But if when I came, I did not get anything, would I get up tomorrow to come again? Because of that, I wouldn't come tomorrow. Eh, when I went to her house, she didn't even give me water to drink. I didn't get a chair to sit on, I did not get anything. Then tomorrow, what will I go to her house again for? I cannot go there again. "Oh, come to visit me," you say. I came to visit you before, but I didn't get anything and I wasn't happy. Why should I come again today? So I will not come. All right, she will think that maybe she will not come. She says, "All right, I will come," but thinks, "I will not come." She will say to herself, "Oh, but why is it that your friend is saying to go, and every day she says, come, and you also do not come?" She will say, "Ah, the day I went, she did not even give me water. Also she did not even give me a chair to sit on. If she did not even give me water to drink, and I go again today, what am I going to look for there? Therefore I cannot go." That's how it is. If you came, for instance, if you were not offered a chair in the house here, would you sit down? If you got a chair to sit on in the house, and whatever you liked, she did it for you, you were happy. When you came, for instance, if you didn't get what you wanted, would you be happy? You would not be happy. You would even say that you are leaving. Those who brought you also would let you leave, so you have walked there for nothing. That's how it is.

GC: And you were saying that people do not feel happy in Ghana?

Presently, all of the Ghanaian people are unhappy. He is not happy; I mean, he doesn't get any work to do. Today, when a Ghanaian young man gets up, he roams around in the bush. He will go to buy cassava, he will go off to buy plantain, pepper, or garden eggs, before he brings them to sell. After all that, he might get his food money and maybe one set of clothes to wear. If he has a wife, he will get something for the wife. If that is not so, he will have to get some government work. That's how it is.

Someone else has forest farms, so he will be weeding and preparing the farms little by little to plant tomatoes, pepper, and garden eggs like that. What has he accomplished? Not much. If the crop grows well, he will get some food. If he harvests it for the market, too, what does he do? He comes to sell it, and then he earns a little from it to eat. Maybe you are not lucky, and where you planted the tomatoes or other things, there was too much rain and it flooded. Then the crops are destroyed and you have lost money. What will you do? Maybe when you were doing it, you ran up lots of debt for laborers who did the weeding. You will be paying for the hired hands, for the things you needed to do the work, things you bought when you did it. Maybe you have put fertilizer on the soil, to make the land good so that all the work will go well. But the rain falls heavily, and if the water comes to flood the crops, they are altogether spoiled. Then you have run into debt, and it troubles you. Some people who have been able to work and the work is spoiled, then they can even worry themselves to death. They will drink poison and die.

Look, some of them do like my brother, who said he would go to a foreign country. He sold all of his things, everything: his household goods, even the land he had bought. He said he would build a house there, but he was not getting enough money to build it. He said that since it was so, he would sell it in order to go, to buy a ticket to go. He would go and hope for luck. He had some brothers over there. If they helped him a bit, then he would use what he got to build a house. He went and they sent him back. They turned him back at the **airport**. They would not allow him to go there. When he went, too, he said then that right now in Ghana, he could not see anything that he was going to do. His children and his wife's money, too, he had used it all up. And the things he had that could help him here, he had sold. So now, if he came to Ghana, what would he do again? He was just standing there, and he died. He had completed school. He had completed school. He stood there until he died.

So now for sure, in Ghana for sure, the children are suffering. Some people who want to go away won't even get the chance to go. Then maybe they will arrest him and put him in a **cell**. I mean, maybe his home folks think about their child who was traveling. Maybe the people [already there] had not written that he had not come and they had not seen him, and that maybe he had arrived and he was in the **cell**. You might have a feeling that I have gone in order to return home peacefully, for the home folks to be a little comfortable. But if you haven't heard about him, you also don't feel comfortable.

Right now, here in Ghana, we are only praying to God that God will rain good water onto this earth, making it turn new. For the sin is too much for us. Sin has become much more than at first. Then, in the world and among all the people, we had love. There were some people, like for instance, if I came to visit you and you had pleased me properly, if you came to visit me, I would also come, eh! "That day I went to Akua, Akua prepared for me nicely, she looked after me nicely, so if she said she would be coming to me, I will really prepare for her, to make her feel happy, too." Eh, you had told me yes, you would come. The **time** I set for you, like the day that you set our **time**, for instance, you came exactly on **time**. You have come to take us there. Maybe I too would have fixed a **time** for you like that, like maybe I would come to pick you up for us to go. If the **time** arrived, and I had found some place to go and sit, and I didn't come to pick you up, would I have done right? I mean, what she would do for you, she wouldn't also receive. But she couldn't say, maybe, "Akua, if you come, I won't have anything to give you, so maybe your coming will even trouble me."

In the world, if I say so myself, it is not money that we need to love people. Sometimes, as we are sitting here, even, just conversing like this, it is happiness, it is beautiful. Sometimes you might be sitting there worrying, thinking about something, and sadness will come into your heart so very hard. But when you see someone come to see you, and you are conversing with them, then you feel happy. The sadness you are feeling completely leaves your heart and you become **happy**, that's how it is. It is not money that we use to love people, and it is not food that we use to love people. When the good news was going into people's heart, then people had some happiness, it is with them. That's how it is.

GC: And you told me that nowadays, if a person even finds work, they don't pay you like before. You said that even if a man is working, the money is not enough. Please, say it again for me to understand better.

It's because the man, if he works, doesn't get paid properly. Ah, long ago there were no jobs in Ghana, and today there are no jobs, no jobs. Today it has got so there is only day laborer work in Ghana here. If someone wants to hire you, he might say, "I am building my house, this one here. Come and see and build it for me, or you can carry **concrete** or you can carry **block**. Maybe I will give you, for one day, four shillings, maybe I will give you three shillings, maybe I will give you two shillings." This is the work that now a good half of the women are doing, and some of the men. Today, if you say you are looking for a real job, you won't get it. Right now even the work for the town council, for instance, that they are doing these days, they say that the pay doesn't get you anywhere. We don't get any jobs, and they have sacked half the people, even put them out of business. So the people who are walking around in the world, what will they do? That is why house robbery has become so common in Ghana here.

But when you wake up like that, and especially if you are not too greedy, you will find a way to get food in your mouth, you will see. Someone who gets up, who gets up early in the morning, and he is a young man and nice. He will get up, and you will see that he has got dressed to come over. Some come up when you have bought your things to put there and say, "Madame, where are you taking them?" You say, "I am taking them to board a car, over here." He says, "Let me carry it over for you, and how much will you give me?" I say, "You tell me, if you take them, how much will you charge me?" He says, "Maybe I will charge you a cedi." You say, "Reduce it for me." Eh, he says no. "Maybe I shall give you fifty pesewas." He says, "As for just fifty, it is small. Add a little to it for me." Then you add a little to it and he takes it away. Someone will do that, little by little, until it gets to about four in the afternoon, and then he has got money. Then he has got some money.

Someone else, he would be ashamed to do that work. Some people are so serious about traveling overseas. The same laborers' work that they would refuse to be doing in Ghana here, if they go over there, they will do. It is laborers' work that, when you are living in your hometown, if some was available, you would not do it to pay your rent. Maybe your mother has a house, or one of your fathers also has a house. You will be able to sleep somewhere for free, and you will get up for free, so that for sure, you say you don't want to do it. "My mother has a house; my father has built a house. So should I go to the market? Should I go do laborer's work before I get money on me? Why are they saying that?"

But if you travel and buy a ticket, it takes a lot of money to board a **plane** to go overseas. When you go, right away you will be doing that same laborer's work to get money. If you stayed in your town and did that laborer's work, which of them is more profitable? Since it is your own town, there is more profit in it than if you travel and pay a lot of money to go. Today, right now, if you want to go overseas, your **plane** fare alone is more than one million cedis. Besides that, there will be lots and lots of small costs you will be paying before you get the chance to go; it is not a small sum. Sometimes even, if you are not lucky, you will go and then they will return you, and the money is all gone for nothing. This same money you are talking about, if you used it for a luggage carrier's work and used it to do something, couldn't you afford somewhere to live? You will get somewhere to live, *wahu?* But in Ghana, we do not like it like that. We prefer doing it over there, because we can say that we will not be there for long.

Today, money from overseas is worth more than Ghanaian money, too, so that is what we want so fast. But also, what you have already, for instance, if you sit down and figure and think about it, you will know that right here is better than over there. When you figure it out well about this place, and you sit down, you know that it is better here than there. Nowadays someone, you know, will go there just to wear himself out like that. The things that he will return with, he also has to sell them here to get some of his money back, before he can do anything with it. Someone might come from overseas, and he will come with a **fridge**, a **TV**, or a CD **changer**. Maybe he will get to the **airport**, and even with the many small things that he has brought, and all of those he has sold, it will not be enough to pay for the goods that he has to unload. It won't be as much as the advance fees [for customs]. Even with the things you will sell, too, the money is not enough to pay for the advance fees of the things you want to unload. What profit is in it? You have exhausted yourself for nothing.

*MA: And why do they not make a **factory** here to manufacture **fridges** or **TVs**, or the small things that they bring from overseas when they come?*

I mean, as for goods made here, some people will open such things here when they come back. They will do just that. Half of the people from home today, when they come back, they want to open **factories** here. Right now today, near the Accra **airport**, half of them open **factories** all together there. They open their goods, I mean, when they open, whatever things in the **factory** that you like, you can buy them. You will go there and buy, to do everything. That's how it is.

GC: And what should be done, so Ghana will have progressed more like that?

Ghana's progress [kɔ so]? It will be good, little by little. Little by little, it will be good. If we bring ourselves together, all of us. I should become determined that if I have this cloth business, let me try hard, so that I also have made up my mind that I too shall find pennies to buy things. And for all of us, if we become one, also, it will be good. You wish that I should not be better than you, and you also, you are not better than someone else. If you wish that one should be better than another one, it will not go well. All of us, we become one, and we all think of each other. For that reason, when you come and we share something, it has become beautiful for us. When some more people come, they also get some to eat. It is good.

I mean, if you give it to us all, we all eat it. Some come later and maybe get a little bit, so you gave it to them also. But what will the others do to get something to eat? Some of them will not get anything to eat, and that is not life. Therefore, little by little, little by little, little by little. The mentality comes, it will come, for Ghana to get a change, to get love.

Not long ago, if you were living there, you might come to this house. Someone might say, "I have seen some white man's child there, and I am very happy about her, what she says and what she likes in life. I want to take her to stay in my house to make her happy." You will not pay rent, you will not pay anything. Maybe he will be able to give you food to eat. You see? But today, he will say, "Eh, should I be the one looking after a white person who has money in her own hometown, and I should be looking after her for **free**? What kind of work is she doing for me? And how much?" If we do it like that, it won't be good. They say, we should have love, we should take it to live with. If we take love to live with, everything will become completely **correct** for us. It will be good.

The whites went away. At **first** it was the whites who opened **factories** and big **stores**: the Syrians, Portuguese, and all. When you went to town, you felt happy. But when they said that each foreigner had to go back to his own town,[1] Ghana here got spoiled. Now, little by little, little by little, little by little. This man who has come and is running things, he also will make everything become good. Now, he will make everything a bit better. It is all standing on love. You, if you love me and I too love you, everything will be all right.

GC: At first, then, what were people doing in business that was not like today?

At first, there was love in it. I mean, there was something in the work that we don't see any more. At first, there was love in the work. If there was a **factory** here, for instance, and things were in it in abundance, eh, when I got up I would call, "Oh, Yaa!" and she would say, "I'm here." "Get up and let us lift this up, let us pack and put them here." Then all of us, "Eh, come, eh, come," then we all would pack it nicely, then we would arrange it there nicely. We would arrange it there nicely.

Today, if you even call your friend, she will say, "Eh, if you have some work that you are doing, and you are doing it, do it yourself; me, I am tired." She will not help you. And you too will not do it, if I am calling you to come and carry it, for us to do something. If she doesn't come to hold it, and you also say that you are doing yours, when you call me, will I come to carry it? I will not help you, so that you will also use all your strength to do it, the same as I did, when I called you and you did not come. So that you also, if you have got your business, you too use your own strength and do it. Those ways, if you use them to build a nation, it will not do well.

When we were young women, all of us, it was only this work that our mothers were doing, and we were selling too. At **first**, then, we were selling oranges. We did it little by little, little by little, little by little. They too did not leave us, and we stayed in it with them like that. Until by now, I cannot say that I am going to stop, to go and start a new kind of work.

At **first**, too, there was cloth in town. If you went to **UAC, Ollivant, Compagnie**, there were **passbooks** there. Some were two shillings and sixpence, or else five shillings and sixpence. They would give you goods to the value of that, and you would use them [for work]. When the month ended, then you would go to pay for the things you took, the exact amount. Then you would go to make **accounts**, and you would go to show what was left. Then they would give you more goods like that. Today, they have stopped all these things. Today as well, you who want to do it, the amount of money that they will write down for you to go and pay, you will not get all that money to pay for it. How much will it be? It is better that you stop and sit down where you are.

Today, everyone must get moving. When you get a bit of money, you say, "Ah, let me use it to go on the road. I will get some cassava and plantain somehow to be selling," so you take it. When you go and get some, then you buy it. If you make a penny on it, you use it to go and buy food to eat with your children. Eh, with cassava, you will get a little to take home. Plantain, you get a little to take home. The little that you earn, you use some to go and buy meat to make soup and pound *fufu* to eat with all your children, and then we feel happy. If someone gets on like that, then she says, "Somehow, I hustled and I got a bit. Somehow, when I came home today, I and my children had got something. If I had not gone out, I wouldn't have got anything." Somehow, God helps you. Tomorrow, if you go again, then you get some more. That is how we are going on living. If they say you should sit down, then how are you going to get anything that way? You will not get anything, and you and your children will be having real problems.

Today, this school business is also hard. Today, if your child is going to school, you have to dress her up nicely before she can go to school. When a child goes to school today, we shine her shoes. If they are not nice, the child will come and say to you, "Mother, one of my shoes is not beautiful." At first, it was not like that. Myself, when I grew up enough to be going to school, I would put my mother's cloth on like this to form a **collar**. The girls and boys both would do this, and then we would go to sit in the school building and learn. Even like that, they were teaching us well then. Today is not like long ago. **Today** if your child is going to school, you must make her **neat** before she can go to school.

School **fees** also [are a problem]. If God has not helped you, and you were not able to do your work, for you to get a bit to eat and get a bit to put aside, you will not be able to send a child to school. The school **fees** you need to pay, you cannot pay. You will say, "Well, I haven't got anything to pay with." That means the child has to stay home; but if he stays home, too, then you have made trouble for the child. *Wahu?*

Those of us who did not go to school like this when we were small, we only knew that we were frustrating our mothers. We didn't know that we were frustrating our own selves. At that time, if I refused to go to school, my mother would beat me like that! I said I wouldn't go, and then I would run away and go hide somewhere. I didn't like school then, and I would run away to go and sit somewhere. Eh, my mother! Eh, if I went to my father's house, my father's mother would give me food. When she came, she would give me everything and fix me up nicely and then she would put me to sleep. I enjoyed that a lot, and so I did not go. Eh, my grandmother would not give me trouble because I was not going to school.

Today, since I didn't go to school when I was growing up myself, when I was going to Lagos to buy things, when I got to the border, then I also regretted it personally, thinking that there is a lot of benefit in going to school. When I was going to Abidjan to buy things, when I got to the border, then I became very convinced of it. If my child also refused to go to school, I would beat him very well, even to the point of injuring him. Because of this, each of my children went to school. *Woate?* Each of my children went to school. Now with my grandchildren, all of the tiny ones, if any won't go to school, when I get up I will take a cane and I will whip them with it. If you go and even if it doesn't do anything for you, even if you are able to **sign** your name and that is all you can do, it is profitable. If you go anywhere, you will not be troubled. If you move around everywhere, you will not have problems. For if you can't do anything at all, that especially is a lot of trouble.

One day, I went to arrive somewhere and I had put my **passport** down. "**Sign** your name!" I can't **sign**. Then and there, they put **ink** there and you place your hand on it, before you can stamp on it that you are bringing in money. They said, "Take your money, and write the amount and fold it in a **paper** and sign it." All of this you can't do, except if you tell the customs man, "This is how much money I have." Then the customs man charges you money before he writes it down to give you.

As you get to every border post, they say, "Do you have any money?" You say, "I have money with me." "Bring the money here." Then you pull out the **paper**, to show to him that this is my money, it is with me. He will tell you to take out all the money. I said, "Why? Where I just came from, there at the **border**, they also wrote it down. My money was then folded in a **paper**. Why should I pull out all the money to give you, before you also see how much money was there? Look at the **paper** first. You let me pass." Now when I said that, he said, "Eh, Madam, this one, you are a hard case." I said, "I'm not a hard case. I came from a big **border** post before coming here. And you who are on this small road, you are also coming to tell me that I should get out my money that is with me, all of it, to show you; but you will not take the **paper** that is in my hand and look at it?" Finally he said, "**Old lady**, just go; take your things and go."

Then he made me pick up my bag. The girls with whom I was walking all together said, "Eh, Auntie, are you going?" I said, "Ah, I am going, why?" Then some said, "Auntie, say that this bag is yours." I had got it, and I was going, I took my bag over across the **border**, then I came back to take the girls' bags also. He said, "Madame, why?" I said, "These are my things." Then he said, "Ah, come and take it away." Then maybe someone would help me carry them. The customers, the women and maybe the young men that helped me, I would gather them to **cross** together. When I finished, then maybe I would give out a thousand to them. "Eh, madame, bye bye! What day might you be passing by again?" Then I said, "**Next time**." I would come back, and they said, "Oh, when you are coming, then come to offer us something." I said, "All right."

Therefore if I went back like that, I took a container I had, tall and big like this, and I would pack it full of oranges. When I went, I would take it with me, and distribute some to all of them, those who were in all the rooms. I would get some for them and then go to Bonduku. We passed Sampa. Sampa was nice for me. When we got to another one of the villages, it was also nice for me. One of them would come and say, "**Hello, my dear**." I replied, "**My dear**." "You have come? Eh, where is your **passport**?" Then I would collect all my sisters' things also, and add them to mine. He said, "But where are your sisters?" I said, "Our things are many, the bags are many, so I said they should take them and take the lead. Then let me get the **passports** stamped, for me to take the goods to them." He said, "All right." As I went, I would take out a thousand and put it there. I would say, "**My dear**, take it to buy porridge and drink." Then he would take the **passport** and stamp on it, and he would give it back to me.

In this world, if you are walking and you brighten your face and respect yourself, everyone also respects you and feels shy of you. Someone else, when he got there [to the border], what he would say was "Why won't you stamp my passport for me? I came long, long ago." You came to find someone already there, so have patience and sit down, so the other person who also came can feel happy. He too, his happiness is nothing to you. If you take your heart and chest to walk [arrogantly], the man will also spoil your business for you. That's how it is. Therefore, in this world, school is really important, very, very, very much. When I am traveling somewhere, then I myself regret that I did not go to school.

Yes, I stayed with my grandmother, and then I didn't go to school. My mother tried and tried, but my brothers and sisters went. At **first**, I was over in the Fanti territory, over near Cape Coast. There in my hometown, forget it! They went to school every year. If they were going to school and finished, so that they took those examinations, not even one of them would fail.

One of my mother's children, our last-born, when he was going to school he did not miss even one day. But to look at, he was very, very small. When they were all going to school and they were calling out the results of the **exams**, they took him to stand on a **table** to announce his name. They said, "Eh, a small child standing on a table, the one there? They say he has passed." He went to school and he passed three times. They made him repeat his exam three times, because they said he was too small. Then they said they would stop for him to learn a vocation, and they made him go to a **typing school**, and he completed just like that.

When he completed, then he said he was going over to France.[2] When he went to France, if he wrote down his papers like this, in French too, they said, "Eh, you, is this really your paper?" If he was speaking French, you couldn't tell that he was a Ghanaian. He spoke French so well, you couldn't tell he was a Ghanaian. Then he said he wanted to work in banking. The French people said that he wasn't a French citizen, and his mother and father and his whole **family** were not citizens. Therefore if they gave him a job in a bank, if tomorrow a court case came out of it, who would support him? So that work, he couldn't get. So, anyway, he is now sitting in front of some **store**.

When I stopped school, did I do any work? I was only selling things. We were selling fish then. We were bringing fish up here to Kumasi. My mothers, some of them, were staying here then. If they brought fish like this, then I would come and sell it. When I collected the money here, then I would go home and come back. Sometimes I would be staying here for two weeks, sometimes a month, and then I would go. If the fish came in, then I would come. When the fish came, I would come here, like that. I sold fish for a long time. By now, I stopped selling fish a long time ago. My brothers and sisters, though, all sell that fish. Only I don't sell any.

Why? No special reason. **Sometimes**, for instance, there is no fish at all. The fish can also come in little by little, little by little, little by little. You might even come to the market and not get any. Maybe you wouldn't get any to buy, and when you come back home, you have your children there, and they are going to school. When you come to market and you get no money, you still go home. In the morning, if you want to get out something to give to the children, what will you do? This especially can become difficult, so you will be hanging on little by little, little by little, little by little. If you have not got anything at all, then one day you will get a sackful to buy. When you sell it, you will only get a bit to buy something to eat. That is why I say that I will never sell fish again.

Fish, also, it shows its mouth [is seasonal]. At **first**, there was money in it. Money was really there. But when it goes away, then you get tired. Right now, there is not much fish. I mean, at **first**, when there was fish we could only get it at the coast. There was no frozen fish whatsoever. In those days, the **cold** storage was in the **ship**. If we went and bought it, we took a lot of the fish, to bring up here. But today, the white people have also made **ships** that go very far. The big ones are going all around the sea. They go over to Europe or to the French border to fish, and bring it to Tema. Therefore today, right now, the fish business has become hard.

But long ago, it wasn't like that. Then, so much fish was coming in that in Kumasi here you couldn't do anything with it. Today, it is all finished.

MA: My friend, why did you say that you were going to sell oranges?

Oranges in particular, it was my own decision to sell them. As for that, there can be some work that is for someone. If you are doing some other work and this is what is in your heart that you want to do, you can stop and just look at this work and go do it. That's how it is.

As for **passbooks**, I have sold some cloth, cooking utensils, and plates, but I was not taking out a real **passbook**, only if there were some goods. In the past especially, in Ghana, if you went into any **store**, there were plenty of goods and they would put them on sale. We might take it like this. "Woman, come, look at this, we have reduced it. Come and take it, and go and sell it." Then I would collect some. Maybe, if I came to the market regularly like this, they would give it to me for sixpence or threepence. Once I came, I would also add a penny on to it. Threepence and a penny, threepence and a penny, ringing a bell about it like that. Right away I would sell them all, even about ten **dozens**. After finishing up the goods, your profits might be four shillings. In the old days, if you had a profit of four shillings, it was more than ten thousand cedis in today's money. The four shillings then was more than ten thousand today. Yes, but today there is nothing there like that.

In that time also, Nkrumah's **time**, we started to sell utensils in Kumasi here. By then I had stopped selling fish.

GC: And why did you stop selling utensils?

Right now, they are expensive. The price is high. Also, when you sell something, the buyer herself cannot afford it. Before, the **silver** [aluminum] cooking pans that they buy in a **set** all together (eh, how much money is in there?) were seven shillings and sixpence, seven shillings and sixpence today. The other day, when you asked the woman about it, she said the **dozen** were how much? Twenty-eight thousand, today, for **silver** cooking pans. Then, in our time, we were buying the whole dozen for seven shillings and sixpence. Today, twenty-eight, and if I do not have the twenty-eight, how can I go to buy it?

Look, at that **time** I and my sister were sitting in the market and people were bringing cloth around. They said some half pieces were for fifteen thousand, some were for sixteen thousand cedis. I said, "As for me, I won't buy." My sister said, "Eh, let us buy it, for they will give it to us on credit, we would be paying for it little by little." I said the price was much too high. In the old days, that same cloth, I would buy the half piece at maybe four shillings and sixpence, or seven shillings and sixpence for the whole piece. Also, look today at how the money has become so much, when you reduce the old one, and you look at today's prices. If you have any money, it must be because you have some help that someone is giving you. By yourself, with only your own help, you can't buy anything right now.

Well, let's say that today, right now, I had gone to buy this **glass** for sixpence. With that sixpence too, I had added a penny on it, so it had become sevenpence. Maybe you want it, and I have given it to you on credit. Maybe you will take about a **dozen**, because they look nice to you. I have given it to you. I say, "Oh, every day I can take sixpence, until the **time** comes when you finish paying all of it." What will you do about that? You say, "Eh, today, I came to the market and I did not get a penny. They didn't buy anything from me, and my goods were all just lying there. I didn't sell anything, so I could not earn enough money even for my food shopping." Could I tie you up? I couldn't tie you up. You would be cheating me like that, but meanwhile I had used money to buy it. Maybe my boss, where I went to get it, she is asking me for the money. I might have gone for a loan, to go and buy the things to sell. Since you are not paying for it, what will I do to get the money and make a profit? Is it in there? That's how it is. Somebody will even buy and not pay you at all. Then she will run away to stay somewhere, thinking only of herself. Somebody will buy a cloth today, and having bought it just today she will go and give it to a **tailor** today, to sew it up. She will wear it and she hasn't paid for it yet! If you go to demand your money, she and you will just exchange blows in addition. I can't come to blows. I cannot fight; talking doesn't count.

And then, this is a penny, penny, penny business. When you see someone who even has a penny, if she is holding on to it, will you be able to give her something? Somebody else doesn't even have any money. She comes and says, "Mother, I do not have money. I am buying some, dash me one." Eh, can I take out three to give her, saying take and go eat it? I can do that in the orange business; I can give. But with goods like these other things, I cannot do that. If I do that, where will I get the money to pay for it? But also, this orange is a tree fruit. God has given it to us. Therefore, what the person who gave it to me, what she has given me, I can also sell it and have some to give away. I will still get her money for her, and I will also get a bit to eat. These things, we do not become hardheaded about. If you are holding onto something, and you give your friend some of it also, then God blesses it for you, to make it grow big for you. That's how it is.[3]

GC: You said that long ago, four shillings then was like ten thousand cedis now. At that time, you would feel very tired before you would receive the four shillings, and now you will feel tired before you get your ten thousand cedis. Was there more tiredness in this then or now?

Well, during this time there is more tiredness than in the earlier time. At first, envy was not there. Especially now, there is more envy than at first. Before, for example, I might be gone and my sister here had come to market. She didn't earn anything, but if I had earned something, what food I would buy we would divide in two. "You didn't get anything, but I have got some, so let us share it. Take this to go home, and let me take this also to go home, for us all to give to the children to eat." Especially **today**, that doesn't happen, except once in a long while. In the past, there was love, more than long ago. Today, if someone says that she loves you, then she loves you dearly. She has a lot of love.

This also happened: let's say I have a sister. If she is going somewhere, she will say today, "I am going here, and I do not want to go alone. Tomorrow, get yourself ready, and I will also get ready. We will go and come together. If we don't leave early, how will we get back?" That day you came to see me, you said, "Let's come over here." We would say, "Ah, Akosua said we should come, what will we do?" I said, "We should go, because you gave us a **time**, so that at this **time** you would come to take us away." Today, when we were in the market there, even when I asked whether our **time** had come, my child said that there was a little while left until the **time** had come. Then I saw that, eh, you were coming. We said, "Ah, business has come, so let us go." That is good. But in the early days, somebody would say, "You have your person who wanted to go, so you and she can go on. As for me, I cannot go; I am selling my things." But if love is also there, if it is both of our hearts, then we all have to go, very pleasantly. If love isn't there, then I will tell her that I can't go. "My goods are lying there, I am selling my things. Someone might come by, and if I am not there, what would she do? She would go away, she wouldn't buy, therefore I won't go." But if love is there, we will go. That's how it is.

When I was a young woman I was selling fish. They were all helping me then. Today, also, with this work, if you look at it, each of them, you will pass. I do not get any today, I will get some tomorrow. You have to look at it like that, that's how it is. Maybe today I will not get any, but tomorrow I will go, and why shouldn't I get some? You are in debt, but you keep going. Today, even with car fares, you are going around like this and you don't earn any money. Are you able to go on? You cannot go on. Today you have children. If they are going to school, you hand out money for the child to take to school. When the month ends, you pay the child's school **fees**. If you do not get help with a bit of credit, if you do not have a purpose in mind, what will you do to be able to take care of your children, and to look after your children? You cannot make it like that.

I do not have a helper. My husband is dead. It happened long ago, but I shall not remarry. I alone am looking after the children. I pay the school **fees**, I pay the rent; I do everything. If you have a husband, for instance, the man will give you **chop money**; he will pay the rent, he will do everything. You also, when you get a little something, you will also use it to help. Maybe today, when the children say, "We are going somewhere," you can also say, "Take this and go." If their father gives them something, they will also take it like that. All of us help ourselves, and if it doesn't happen like that, then you yourself alone will be looking after them. That's how it is. If a man is there, he helps you and you also help him.

When my husband died, the children were very young then. One was ten years old. The others were around seven, six, and five, and smaller.

Then later, I married again. When I remarried, then I had one more. With that one, when I looked at how I was living, well, with the man the way he was, it wasn't likely he would look after me. Eh, he wouldn't even look after his own child, let alone look after me. And those children of mine that were there before, he would just stare at them. Then I said to myself, if that was how it was, I would stop. I would just sit there. If I got anything, then I and my children would eat it. It is God that I am praying to. It is sickness that spoils human beings. It is death that cuts everything off. *Agya!* Little by little, little by little, little by little, little by little, that's how I have been looking after my children.

These days, with men in Ghana here, when a man marries, he will make a fool of you. He comes home, he gets dressed, so proudly, proudly. He has come! When he comes, he sits down, and he crosses his legs. "Hey!" You go to see, and you take his bath water to the bathroom. When he has bathed, he sits down. You set the food on the **table**. Eh, what money has he given you for **chop money**? So much that you want to see they have set the **table** for you to eat? Eh? For that reason, the amount of money it will cost you that way, if you used the money to look after your child it would be better. The child has sense. He will see that his mother has worked hard to look after him. "So I also, when I have grown up and find some work to do or get a place to stay, I will use it to look after my mother."

GC: You said before that you have done many kinds of work. You sold fish, and you sold utensils, and you sold oranges. Which work was the best, or did the best for you?

Which work was better for me? Right now, no work is any good. Look, the trading business is no good. These oranges, for example, bring in pennies and threepence. Every day, if someone walks by, even if he only has sixpence he can buy some oranges. You will earn something. If someone sells things for two shillings or four shillings, can the same person buy them? He can't buy. But penny things, they are better than things whose price goes **high**.

If you have some money, or if someone says she will help you, so that you will take the money to go and buy some oranges to give her, will you go and look for another kind of work? As it is today, without help and money, without one of your brothers helping you, what will you do? That's why you will be doing this penny, penny work. Right now, one of my brothers goes to Abidjan to bring water bags, the [plastic bags] we fill with water, and also toffee and **biscuits** and cough drops. If it looks good, he says I should come with him. If I had money, I would go, but I don't have money.

GC: So is the Abidjan work what you really like? Is there more money in it now, or in the past?

Mmm, there was more money in it then. If you go and come back, maybe it didn't manage to go well, but then little by little, you sell this. Maybe, when you come, you pay **duty**, you pay everything and the goods will arrive. If you give them to people, you might sell each box of things with a markup of even one thousand each. If you had bought one hundred of them, and got the one thousand, or even five hundred each . . . **Check** for me, how much would the money be for one hundred? But right now, in Ghana, in order to get that money! You will have gone and come back, and someone will tell you, "I have received them, so in two weeks or a month [I will pay]." In a month she tells you, "Maybe in two weeks I will bring the money to pay you, check with me in a month." By the time you get all the money in your hand, it is more than a month, and the profit that you have earned is reduced. Only a small amount is left, so what will you do with it? You would do as well sitting down doing nothing, and yet you had gone and brought things back.

Also, today the exchange rate is too high. Whatever you buy, when you come back to Ghana here, you won't see the profit that you should get. At **first**, when I was going to Abidjan, you would change one **sack** of money, in Ghana, you would change it for 1100. These days, for one **sack**, if you change it in Ghana here, you change it for two thousand. What things can you go buy, so that when you come back you can make a profit later? Now, there is no profit in it. If you come, you will pay **duty**, and the **duty** you pay, they will not charge you just a little money. If you check, there is no profit. Today, the things that you buy in Abidjan, maybe what you would buy for ten **sacks** here, you would buy for five **sacks** there. Adding paying the **duty** when you come back, it comes to a lot of money. And when you arrive, maybe they aren't buying well. They won't pay for it for at least a week, so that maybe you can get the cedi or the penny that you will make on it. *Agya,* I came, and cedi by cedi, even what I am having now, it is money that I have earned that way.

I was in that business just recently. I went to Abidjan to buy, but it was enough to make me stop doing that business. I bought **biscuits**, and I brought them here to Ghana. The **driver** went to unload them in

Accra and give them to a woman there. When he got there, the Ghana person said that if I brought them to her in the market she would buy the goods. She bought them, too, and she sold them in Accra there. So about three years have passed, and I have never got my money. The money is gone. What can I do to go again? When you go to ask her for the money, she says she has lost money, she will pay; she has lost money, she will pay. Did I make you lose money? It's like, I even brought you the goods in Accra; so I am coming to get what is mine. You say, "I have received it, I have sold it and I will bring you the money." But **still**, if I bring more goods back, I give you some here for you to buy. So will I tell you that I won't give you any? I will give it to you.

Right now it looks like I won't get my money. This sister, that day, she sat here and talked and talked. She begged my pardon, saying she would bring me the money. Now the money is lost. She has got work to do; she will bring me the money; she said so. That's exactly what I am talking about. I haven't received the money. Someone says I should go make a **report** and let them arrest her. If you arrest her, will she pay the money right away? So I give all my cases to God. He will collect that debt for me. As for me, I don't have the strength right now to demand payment. It might even have been stolen money, and I took it and a person had given it to me![3]

God knows how I managed to get a loan to make the money that I took to do that work. One of my friends, when I was going, gave me one hundred, and when I returned I took it to pay my lorry fare for going. As for that friend, **every day** at dawn, she would stand at my door and knock, with me in the room. "Knock, knock." "Why?" She would say she has come for the money she gave me; the owner has come to take what is hers. I worked little by little, little by little [*repeats this seven times*] and I collected people's money little by little, and when it grew to a hundred I gave it to her. Even that hundred, when I gave it to her, she said if the money had been with her, she would have done work with that hundred to get some profit, so it would not be a hundred. She took some extra. But now, the money just stays with people.

That's how in this world, in Ghana, we have made some people this way, so they say, "This one doesn't like to work." It's not that she doesn't like to work. What her neighbor puts her through, that's what makes her fed up with work. Also, the road is so long that you will ride in the car for too long. When we were **first** going, the "she's bought salt" car[4] would take us there. Only after we arrived in Bonduku did we get a **Transport** [government bus] to take us home to Abidjan. And when you were in that car, you got to some roads and the car would tilt over like this! Only God would keep you to get you there and back.

If after all that, you go to bring things back, and your neighbor buys them and hasn't paid you, will God do good things for her? Every day I sit here, it is nothing. Sometimes my children say, "Mama, you went and brought goods for your neighbor, what has your neighbor done? She has sold them and kept the money to look after her children. But you have not told anyone or gone to demand it from her." Then I say, "Myself, who even gave her the money, I am not going to get it. So if you go, who are coming here now, will you be able to get the money to bring me?" That's why Ghana here is hard, Akua, it is hard. Nowadays, I ask God himself that little by little, little by little, he will answer my prayer and everything will make progress and I will improve quietly, quietly, quietly.

The day she came to me, I told her that her debt was no problem. Each month, if she even brings me fifty cedis each, the debt will be reduced a bit for me. You see? We talked together. She went away. Now that she has talked and left (how long ago? It is almost a full year ago!), she has not brought me even a penny. It is not a small problem at all. Look, at first, that money, it was like, Akua, I thought like that, I spoke like that, but then one of my children said that it was really nothing. If you had that money, and they said that you were dying and we should take it and manage to buy things for you, that money could not buy your life. So don't worry about it, and just pray for that person, that she and poverty spare you. If you worry about it and you die, you have died for nothing, there is no benefit. So don't worry about the money, and pray for her. Eh, now it has been almost four years.

Eh, when she came, this sister, she came and really sat down, and we chatted just like we were just talking together. When she got up to leave, one of my children said, "You are too good, mother. When someone comes who owes you money, you leave her alone. You even chat with her, ask for money and she goes." Then I said, "What should I do to her?" A person who comes to you like that, she has something to say. If that thing is bad, eh, then you have a problem to discuss. But for what she is talking about, you cannot tie her up, you cannot restrain her, you cannot do anything to her. What should I do to her? It is true that if I say I will give her to the police for them to arrest her, God will find a way to let me give her to the police. They should arrest her and they should take what is mine to give me. But if she wants to tell me something, I cannot turn her over to the police right now.

Everything has its time, little by little. Everything has its time, so little by little we can do something about it. So patience, everyone has patience. They say that if someone is doing something, you don't say he is making a fool of you. You show good sense, you show your wisdom. She will think she is smart, that she is fooling me, she is fooling me. She is only making a fool of herself.

She might do that, and then she has gone to live in someone's house. She has hired a room to live in, and fixed it up nicely, pleasantly, with **light** and water, with a **stove**, or whatever, I don't know. Eh, she went out on an errand, and when she came back all of the things in her room were burnt. The landlord told her that that very day she should move out of the house. If she lived in his house, she would burn down the house. Don't mind her. That really is just your burden to bear. That is all your trials. That's why she came to tell me that she apologized. But the problem that has fallen on her is not a small one.

I said then, "You take someone's money, it is money they have worked for. Then if you say you will take it for **free**, that thing, you have done it yourself. So you say you will not pay me my money, and you have not brought me the goods either. The goods are still in Accra. Someone has also said that she hasn't found any goods in Kumasi, so she will take Accra goods. She sends me a message that I should unload my goods. You say that you received the things that she brought you, and you sold them and got your money. But you haven't brought me my money. You used it to pay your own debts; you used it to do whatever you liked for yourself. Meanwhile I should be feeling upset? You will see the result. Even with the trouble that I have, what will hurt you will be more than mine."

The other day she brought me fifty, and I just said "ah!" She arranged a time with me, but the time that she fixed with me has already passed. Just yesterday, I said, "Maybe I will go and look for her trail," but I haven't had **time** to go. If you go, and you haven't gone after her early, you won't find her at home. Even if you go early, she says, "Eh, Auntie, at this **time** right now, when I am still asleep, you knock on my door and you wake me up!" And I will say, "Look, why? If I am feeling good, would I get up at dawn to come to your house? What would I be looking for at your house? I'm uncomfortable! If I was comfortable, I wouldn't be getting up at dawn to come to your house and knock on your door. You owe me money. That's what makes me come. Those things, I didn't give them to you as a gift. Those things, people brought them to me. I didn't unload them in Kumasi, but I took them to put in your stall. I went to unload them somewhere. You yourself made an effort to take them. And I am finding a way so that I can take you with me to the police. They will arrest you and put you in prison before you pay me my money. If you are doing something together with someone, and the person gives you a chance, what do you have to do? As you see it, that's how you look at it." Now she also says that it is not important. I really should have patience with her, and she will pay me my debt. The speech she makes to you, you cannot nod your head to say that yes, it must be so.

God is the king. He makes angels for messengers who collect debts, so I have given my troubles to God. It is he who will fight to get the money for me. I do not even have the strength. If I had the strength, some day I could grab her roughly. "Give my money to me, bring me to do this." "I shall not give it to you. I am taking it." Who is the strongest? It is "I will not give it to you!" that is the strongest. If I am taking it and she doesn't have any, can I tie her up and take it by **force**? It will not work. In this world, too, if you just take your trouble to God, then you have finished everything.

Eh, Sister Comfort! Did you come here to sleep or what? Woman, yaa! If we stop to sit down a little, right away you fall asleep. If we are in the middle of doing our work like that, you won't feel sleepy. If you stop for a little, then you feel sleepy, and then you will fall asleep. I mean, we get up early. We get up early. Some days, somebody will take goods from the village to come in. If the person comes and doesn't find you, and you don't look after her, she will complain later that she even brought something for you, and you didn't come to look after her. She will sit there so long, then tomorrow she will not bring the goods to you. That is why we get up early to come in. Sometimes, too, you do come, and then she doesn't come early. If she comes late in the night like that, you don't have a place for the two of you to sleep. She also has no place, unless you take her to your own house to sleep. In the morning, she bathes and you fix her up, before you take her to market.

CHAPTER 7

Maame Nkrumah

Portrait: A Grateful Sister

That house that I earned, it is how I know that I will always be a Kumasi person.

I came to know Maame Nkrumah as a small, plump woman, usually to be found beside her equally short sister, the commodity group leader or onion queen. She seemed a bit overshadowed by her tough older sister then. Her face was a little rounder, brighter and softer, with a readier smile, and she usually had a grandchild on her lap. Her tables and tins were neatly arranged, when the toddler was not crawling over them, and the full sacks piled behind her suggested economic security. Their stall sat across from that of another trader, a friend who had already taken me on a buying trip with her. This friend was now in ill health, so I often dropped by to visit, deep within the cavernous onion shed. It was dark enough to make photography difficult, but I enjoyed its quiet, shady refuge from the boisterous outside passageways of the market. These were the same conditions Maame Nkrumah complains so bitterly about in her narrative, for reducing ventilation, foot traffic, and visibility.

She spent long hours in the market, picking over her goods between customers, so she usually seemed glad of my company. She readily discussed supplies and suppliers, current trading conditions, and the variety of uses and seasonalities for onions of different origins and quality grades. She often pressed on me a handful of onions or peanuts as I was leaving for home, and advised me how to take care of my health and manage my work.

During times of crisis, such as the 1979 currency exchange, she was always at the side of the onion queen, repeating her explanations of the value of the new notes and how to exchange them to the other traders, and collecting their complaints and problems to tell her later. As her sister grew older and began to stay home more often, Maame Nkrumah took a more active role in attending meetings and speaking out, but without formally becoming her deputy. Since they shared the care of their children and grandchildren, she could easily report back to her sister overnight and bring back her advice on disputes, commercial procedures, or new policies.

When invited to narrate her life story, she turned out to be articulate and comfortable as the focus of attention. Her life had been eventful, but her description of those events is calm, with an understated drama that makes it even more impressive. The unconventional choices she made show that she was not timid or apathetic, but willing to take substantial risks and accept the consequences. Her quietly astute comments on various life changes and historical events show a quick intelligence that comprehends without feeling compelled to judge.

Her childhood exemplifies the ideal Asante pattern of village tranquility. The detailed description of her puberty ceremony conveys pride in this endorsement of youthful virtues, with pomp and substantial gifts that top up her savings. Her father looms large, insisting that she marry his nephew; his significance perhaps inspires her favorite interjection, *agya* (father). The role her older sister played in the family demonstrates the alternatives a close-knit lineage can offer to the orphaned, divorced, or childless. Yet she is glad to be able to end her years in Kumasi.

Order has served her well, so disorderliness (*basabasa*) explains much of her world's current problems. Honesty and respect for rules would bring prosperity almost automatically. The major blight on her life is due to corrupt bending of rules about building extra stalls around those originally planned. She feels that the resultant overcrowding significantly threatens her business and her health, by cutting off foot traffic and ventilation.

Clearly Maame Nkrumah is satisfied with her life. She has bought her house and seen her numerous children start to prosper. She was also apparently satisfied with her self-representation. Although she had more patience than most when we read back her transcript, and listened to most of it, she was not concerned to change or suppress anything in it. As long as it was accurate, she was quite willing to be identified with it, under her own name.

Story: She Has Cared for Me and My Children

Yes, it is true that life in the past and life in Ghana today are quite opposite, but what has arrived now is what we say is good. What it was like long ago, when we were young, was this: if you were a young girl, you had grown but you were not mature. Our mothers insisted, if you were not grown up, you didn't even trim your nails. They would say, you haven't grown up yet. If you trimmed your nails, you would be in trouble. You would start your periods before they trimmed your nails. Today, they don't wait to grow up. A girl is just standing there, and you will see that she is pregnant. If she gets pregnant, she even travels away so you won't see it. In the old days, we let the girl mature.

Then your father would give you in marriage. "If this is the one we like, marry him. He is from that house. That house is good, so if you go to marry him, good will come of it," and you went. It was really true, too, that in the old days they didn't have children every which way [*basabasa*] at home. You observed a house closely then, and the people there, you watched how they lived. But today, someone just goes out. She herself walks out and goes to bring, I'm sorry to say it, but she catches an evil disease from that house. And it comes back to your house and you get it.

When today there is a child and you say you will do her *bragorɔ* for her, she will not even stay there to let you perform the ceremony. In the past, though, when they made your *bragorɔ*, they took you to sit on the roadside and they beat the ceremonial drum and they went to bathe you in the river. They said, she has finished her *bragorɔ*. Then, when you are going out to marry, at night they take you there. Today, this doesn't happen, but all this, in the past, was the good way. Besides, today, *agya!*

Because of what else happened, we say it is bad. If you hadn't finished the ceremony and you got pregnant, we held a ceremony to denounce you as "before puberty" [*kyiribra*].[1] They would expel you from the land of the chief. He would come, and they would make you sit there, and then sacrifice a chicken. *Agya!* You and the man that did the crime with you. I mean, like, the man, sometimes he runs away. In our hometown, we did this to someone, and the man had run away. He went all the way to Koforidua, leaving the woman alone. They took her to sit by the road-side and they shaved her head. Then they killed a chicken and took the blood to show you that if, as a child, you say you want that red thing,[2] you will see what happens. Then they took her and threw her outside, and jeered at her three times. On the spot she went off to some village. You don't come back, I mean, until you have given birth, because you have done a polluting thing. Then they purified the gods of the town with water. But today, they say the whole thing is bad, so *agya,* they have stopped it.

Today, whose child can you tell, "You haven't had your *bragoro,* so we will expel you"? There is no one even alive that will mind you about this thing, and it has gone. The way we are living today is not like the past. When a woman came of age, someone came to ask for her in mar-riage. As for today, even my own grandchild, I'm sorry to say, she got pregnant with a Northerner.[3] You have finished school, you have gone to learn hairdressing, you are doing it, and you take a Northerner as a lover! We had quarreled about it, and she said no, she had left him. Today they have got pregnant. It is not what you want, but today you have it. That's why life in Ghana, we say it is hard. But still, we will take it like that.

In the past, when I married my husband, he was a policeman and we lived in the police station here, at Firiidae. At that time, if you were a policeman, your salary was something! That man was not an educated person; they were the ones that wore khaki. The ones who all wear black today came to join them later. In the past, when you were a policeman and not literate, you wore khaki, with a thing hanging at your side like this,[4] and you wrapped strips on your legs. But all of them were with the government, in the big building there. I got tired of living there because my husband was one.

Two shillings [he gave me], and he avoided *fufu.*[5] So from that two shillings, he would eat twice a day, and go back to work. At that time I was a young woman, and I would walk to the CCA's bungalow.[6] When he went there to work and I prepared food, I would carry it. It was not like today, when you can take a car. At that time, where were the cars? So we came with it from Naro, and we took the food to the police station. He gave you two shillings, and that was enough for meals. He liked to eat *ampesie,* maybe *kenkey,* and I would make stew. You go and buy shrimp; they are sold by the penny. Cooking oil is sold for threepence, and I would come back with it to make the stew. And I would also buy fingers of plantain, for a penny, more than I could use. I was the only one, with just one child, and I cooked. It was enough for us. There were even days when I made a penny out of it. If you saved up those pennies, it got to the point where it was real money, that could buy something.

But these days, there is nothing like that. As I am living now, if I don't take out about two hundred cedis, it won't be good. Right now, one of my children that lives there, even, who cooks something for me to eat, *agya!* When she is doing it, I add about a thousand cedis to it so that, *agya,* when you finish, serve me a little, *wahu?* So with living conditions today, it is true that there is lots of money.

Me and this sister, we were talking about it, comparing this time with Gold Coast time, when we were trading. But when we first came, we were selling oranges. There are oranges in our hometown, so we bought the trees with the oranges on them and my sister would pick them. At that time, we lived at the Zongo, near the Catholic church. My sister would bring them. She lived here, and sometimes I would go and pick them. I hired the men, and when they picked them I put them in a car and we would unload them here. The farm didn't belong to us. The oranges in it were ours. Everyone had the oranges that they planted there. It was there that they sold them to you. You bargain, and then when you have finished bargaining, they write a notice to put on it that these oranges have been sold. If a child wants to pick some, we don't like it, and people obeyed. Then we keep picking them like that. I worked with her like that until the end of the year, which means the oranges were finished.

We would get a profit (you couldn't even say what it was in today's money) of two hundred pounds and four shillings. We took it to the store, and we had come to buy ABC cloth for one hundred pounds and two shillings. We bought a whole piece [of cloth], and my sister and I would share it. We bought it outright, and my sister and I would go and divide it. At that time, too, ABC was a good European brand. Yes, and we wore it, and, *agya,* there were a hundred pounds left, and we saved it.

In that time, also, I thought that people then said that we were not sophisticated [*y'ani mmuɛ*]. And really, if you earned even anything small, then you would be happy with it. It wasn't like today; the people that have come today want very good things. The old days were not like that. The way people are now, if your cloths number about four or five, you know you have some. In the old days, there were people who didn't even have any. As for today, you see that everyone has cloths. No matter how poor a person is, she has six or seven cloths. Long ago, there were people who didn't even have one, *wahu?*

Besides, with all that we have, we say it is better for us. But this Ghana has got to the point now that, if you see how it is progressing, we say it is good. With the money like it is now, even a little child selling water will earn some money, about a thousand or two thousand cedis. Right now, this water that people go sell, those of us that go around hawking it, they live with us. If someone is coming home, she will be holding about two thousand that she will save. If at dawn she goes again, she has plenty of money. In the old days, even to get threepence was a hard business. So in this Ghana we say that, if this is bad, well, we will take it just like this.

Look, in our time, a person could just sit down like that. She didn't know the market at all. If you took her to sell things in that market, where would she go with them? In the village where she lived, she could only make a farm. She would farm, and if cocoyam was in season nobody would buy it, because everyone else had also grown some. Nobody was buying plantain. My mother used to farm because she had many children. She might go harvest some cocoyam, but we were living in my father's hometown. Then she took the cocoyam and arranged it on a flat **pan** to put under a shade tree. It might sit right there for three days. If a visitor passed by, we were only taking three- or sixpence for it. Perhaps one day a visitor comes, and maybe she wants food to buy, then she will come and pay threepence. That's why, in the old days, if you did farm work, you didn't get anywhere.

Kumasi here, only today has everyone seen it. I mean, in our hometown, we came to market only in Efiduase. It was like, maybe on Sunday you had harvested your cocoyam, and you look and you don't have any meat. Then you bring it to Efiduase to a Northerner called Ayaaba. The Northerners, they know how to cook that food, and she took it for her chop bar. So you would get to Zongo and put it down there, saying, "Ayaaba, look at mine for me, Ayaaba." You have filled a thing full of cocoyam, and maybe get ninepence, maybe eight. Even myself, when I had grown up, if I went to harvest a little of mine, enough for me [to carry], it was maybe worth threepence. Then you buy one penny of sugar cane on the way back. We would walk. The sugar cane for a penny was a long piece. You would chew it as you walked along, and it would last until you got back.

So if someone lives there, not doing some of this work, she won't have any work to do. So maybe she is staying there, and her husband, at the end of the year, he would give her one cloth. So she will not be able to get four or five to put away like that. Except for one or two people who might have some of the cloth I was talking about. But today, right now there are plenty of them. It is expensive, and no one can afford to buy this cloth. No one can buy any.

So we will act like Ghana is good. It is good, but all the same, our little problem is that we Ghanaians don't obey the laws, up until now. We don't speak the truth, *wahu?* Maybe something is there, and they put that thing here. It is in the rules, or even the government has said so. The person gives it to me, but look, let's put it over there. She doesn't mind going and taking money from someone, to let them put it there. The government, too, stays at its own hometown; they might not know that prices are going up. In Ghana here, conditions are only like this; that is what is ruining us. I mean that if we could follow the laws, then how we are living, I believe it would be all right.

Right now, this old lady that I am, *agya,* if I can get up and come to the market, the little that I would eat, I would earn it. In the past, before you would come to this market, you would be eating. Today this food is plentiful, but then, if there was some there, even if you could buy it for a penny, you wouldn't get the money that you need to buy some. Today, too, the cassava that is here today, we sell for five hundred cedis. When it cost a penny, too, you wouldn't get money to buy it, but today, at five hundred cedis, they buy it. This plantain, at five hundred cedis, they are buying it.

Only honesty itself is scarce in Ghana here. If there was honesty, and we didn't go where we shouldn't go, where there is no way, if we would drop it, then Ghana would be really good. We would have arrived at last at a good place. But as it happens, there is no honesty. If we just speak the truth, even for me it would be good.

I say, if I were in the government, and an influential person, I would write to the government that there was a law in the past, that if I had an uncle who accomplished something, I knew that he was doing it for me. Recently, a Ghanaian law has come; they say we don't do that. If you have a maternal uncle or a brother, he and his wife live together. They are striving hard together, so we should inherit our father's property. You have changed it for us, and we have agreed. On the subject of paternal inheritance, a person goes to his work, he says good morning, I have given this to my wife, for her to take it. The lineage, too, maybe they should take that property. In any case, we don't decide that one person should take it all. You would see the lineage relatives going to protest, and we would meet to decide that this property was not even made by the young man. Maybe he has not inherited any property. The man has started as a young man, and he has got ahead and married his wife. Then he went to his work, and he gave some to his wife and his children, and he also said that his relatives should take this, and they have filed an appeal.

It will drag on like this, and it may be that the appeal will not be settled today or tomorrow. It might be ten years and they have not finished settling the case, about the legacy of one person who has passed on. Maybe this woman, like me, has no money. The lineage members have got up to speak; the woman has got up to speak. They have investigated it thoroughly, and the truth that they decide tells you that, maybe the woman should let the lineage take it, and go live somewhere else. With the corruption there is in Ghana here, I am saying that it is destroying the country. They will draw it out like that, they will not settle the case, and you, the woman, get deeper into debt. If you get tired enough to stop, then you stop. Me, I have even seen someone whose case was decided. They went into the matter and decided it for her, but appealed the case to Accra. So if the government has made it so that there is no family property, so that I alone, myself, am concerned with it, what I would tell the government is this. If anyone gives his own property as a gift, there is no appeal.

MA: Only if he inherited it.

Yes, they should do it for that; we should do it. They should go hire a **lawyer** to argue that what he gave me was too small. Except when someone has been able to come forward to say, "My uncle so and so died, and this is his cocoa farm. And they gave it to this brother of mine to inherit him, so it was the family property that he used to make this property that is there, so we cannot give this to his wife. If we give his wife any at all, because she was working with him, then we will give her a little." That's what I understand.

Just recently, there was a young woman who went to our church, and she and her husband did everything together. **First**, they were living in the North, where they had a store. The young man had not inherited from anyone. It was a store that they built up little by little, and then they brought the business to Kumasi and the man expanded it. This same store, even in the market here they have about two stores. He sells metal roofing sheets and other things. This man got sick, so the wife had to take care of him. The man had made his **will**. The man had got so sick that his wife could not trade. *Agya,* he was at the store, and this woman cooked food and took it to him, and he ate it for lunch. The young man's illness had made him unable to eat a lot of things. Just recently the man died, not long ago, about six years ago.

The man had made his **will**. His house that he built, a three-story building, he took the **quarters** that had six rooms in them, and he gave them to his sister, his mother's eldest child. Then the main building has three floors, the top, the middle, and the ground floors. He was living in the top with his wife. He gave that to his wife and children. The middle floor, too, he gave that to his former wife, with whom he had children; he has given it to them. The ground floor, he has given it to his lineage. He helped one of his brothers to make a cocoa farm, and his own wife didn't go there. So if there is this cocoa farm, the men should take it; his brothers should take it. He raised some cattle, and he said the cows also belonged to his wife. Also, the store which he and his wife and children used to bring goods to stock, the children and their mother should keep on trading in it. But if it happened that the children had to move somewhere else and stop trading, then the store would belong to his wife.

As many years as he had been alive, it has been in court. Now there is nothing in the store, the woman is also destitute, without a penny. The case has dragged on and on. Finally, they have told lies about him, that he inherited someone's property, and no one has come to challenge them. He didn't have anyone's property. He himself had accomplished everything. They talk about his wife. One young man involved says that he wants the top floor, where the man and his wife lived; he won't agree that he gave it to her. The case has gone on for six or seven years, and the whole thing is bad.

Once the dead man has said so, it doesn't call for a lawyer. The way it is now, the lawyers are the ones making money. Each one has taken a lawyer, and they will not speak the truth. The lawyers, too, they meet and they talk things over. They know what the right way is, but they don't do it. If day breaks and he is going to court, it means you pay money. If they meet off and on for a week, their gas money alone is two thousand. All of this is a waste of money that doesn't need to happen in Ghana here like this.

The government has said that we should inherit our fathers' property. If we have understood it, we should inherit our fathers' property at once. Besides, there is nobody, if he does [make a will], who will say that he will give all of it [to the wife and children]. Yes, he gives some to you. And if you have got some and someone else has got some, should this go to court? The government should have stepped in to say that when anything has been done, there should be no litigation about it. If you are a poor person, you will face real problems like that, and if you cannot, and you stop fighting and go home, then you become depressed. For the effort that you made, with your husband and your children, has all been for nothing. That way is not good. They cheat women, and give them problems, *woate asee?* There are many things in Ghana, that maybe the government itself has told us to do. Those that we put in office, too, they are not honest. Money is the thing that Ghanaians want, and they are collecting it. If you are a poor person who has struggled, I mean, if you try and you can't, then you quit.

Look! This stall that we stay in, the government has built it. Long, long ago when they built it, the garden egg sellers were at the end where we came to pass through. Yes, that was the section for garden eggs, and the onion sellers were from them to our place here. Even at that time, when we came to this place, Yorubas[7] were selling the big kind of onions. Men, Yoruba men, were occupying these stalls. When we came, if there was someone leaving, and you gave him even one pound (in those days, money was not like this), even a hundred pounds, then he gave it to you and went away. The government unfortunately allowed some people to build behind us, and some other people to build here, and those of us in the middle here, we had problems. Now, here we are in the middle, and we just sit here [with no business]. In just a little while, we will get up and leave.

But it is because Ghanaians go after money. I mean, there is someone who goes to give them money for the front part. One day, the issue came up and made even Kwasi Agyeman[8] remove them once. Those who first built them, he pulled them down. But Ghanaians are stubborn, because they have money. When you pull them down, it will be at most four or five months before they raise them up again. They go and give them a lot of money, and they come back to build, *wahu?*

In this Ghana market, if they are selling stinkfish, then someone says, "This stall is mine," and she is selling cloth there. With all of them, as you walk through this market, you won't see where the white people's goods are, and you don't find whatever. In a market, we arrange it so that those of us selling pepper, well, our onions are there, and if pepper is there, garden eggs are there; they are all from the farm. Even if any foodstuffs are there, it is all right. Just recently, in our [onion] market here, there was someone who said, this stall is mine. She wants to make a kiosk there, and she will sell her cloth. There is also someone there who is selling cosmetics, the ones we put on our bodies.

So in this Kumasi market, right now, even in the plantain section, they have made it so that they are selling dress materials and other things, but they should not arrange the market like that. Here too, they don't do things to make it **plain** right away. It's like this, once you say that it is yours, and you go to see them, they will agree on the spot. They can't say, "This place is not good for it." Then if you who are selling garden eggs say you will sell cloth, you [should] have to go and find a cloth seller, yes, for the one also selling garden eggs among the cloth sellers to come to your section. Then we would have arranged the market properly. If you are going to market, then you know that you are going to the cloth market. If you go, then you know that you are going to what? To buy matches or whatever. Before, you would have known, but they all have been mixed up. Here are the onions, but also pomade and dress materials are mixed in.

Now they have built up on each side of our shed. It means we have to get out. The thing we sell, if you just come, you will understand right away. The place where we are, even when you fall sick and go to the hospital, they tell you that the place you stay is bad. There is no air. When you are there, you sweat and you feel hot. That could have been different, but it is Ghana. When the person builds the shed, she doesn't even make it short, to allow a little air to pass through. She builds it up to the roof, and you sit there dying. You also have nowhere else to go, so you will stay there like that. If death takes you, then you will go away, *wahu?*

All these things, if Ghanaians would see them and correct them, it would be good. If we see to correct them, it would be good, but *agya!* They even see it clearly then, but they won't do it. We don't let a person take the lead, so he will tell them that no, at that place perhaps they don't allow those goods to be put there. These things are what we sell here, so because of this, if you intend to sell that, go on and sell it elsewhere. We say, whatever you want to do, do it. That's how we have made the market so disorganized [*basabasa*], and we just pile into it. As for me, I have become an old lady already, *agya!* In a little while, if I haven't died, and if I can't get up, I mean, I will just stay in the house.

But by God's grace, when Kwame Nkrumah first came, do you know, Saaboa Zongo, behind the palace as far as Aboabo, was a terrible place. Nkrumah planned some housing quarters, which were built there in Asawasi. At that time, I had only one child, my child who is with my sister. Today, her children are also having children. But then my sister made her husband, whose brother was a policeman, obtain one house there for me, and I went to live in it. At that time, the houses were there in Asawasi and nobody liked them. When you lived in one, you paid four shillings when the month ended. We came to pay it where the clinic was—today they have built a hospital there. When the month ended, we came to pay it where the clinic is today, where today they have built a hospital. There was a red building over there, in the clinic grounds. It was there that we paid our house rent, and we were living in it.

At last, the government said that we should buy it. We were not even charged a large amount. Because the money comes in thousands now, you cannot even know how much it was. It was less than ten thousand cedis. The thousands had not come yet; we counted money as ten pounds or a hundred pounds. It may be that it was a hundred pounds, more or less, that the government charged. They said, "You should pay in installments," and we paid the installments. When we paid, they said we could go live in it, and we did; now it is mine. I have even built onto it; ours were like those at the army barracks. Some other people had three bedrooms. The one we got was by the roadside, where the school for bad children is. Yes, I am near to that place. When you leave there, you are going toward Aboabo Junction. Little by little, I have built four more bedrooms. It has become a small courtyard, and I live there with my children. There is no problem.

So, if not for that, really, if I had to hire a room, I would have gone home to my village. Now, if you go live in a room, in a few days, [the landlord] says that if you don't pay this, if you don't bring **one million** cedis, we will take it back. If you had that **one million**, would you be living in that place? You would be going away. As for that, that [house] that I earned, it is how I know that I will always be a Kumasi person.

Even if I sleep in water flowing through a gutter when it rains, I am sleeping in a room along with my only son. I gave birth to seven, but two died; five are left: four women and one man. The son, right now, he has built a store just in the front of the building. He has opened up one room to make the store, and he has another one to sleep in. Then my eldest daughter sleeps in one. I was just talking about my third-born, the daughter who went to secondary school and says she is afraid of the doctor. I also gave her one room, but she married. She lives with her husband somewhere else, so she gave this one to my last-born, Ataa, the one who was with me at the market and her child was on my lap. Yes, she lives in that one. *Agya,* I live with them there, and if it hadn't been so, in today's Ghana, I myself would not have been able to stay here. With the work I am doing here, could I go hire someone's room by the month? It may get to the point that they say to pay thousands like that, and if you don't have it, they say, "My child is coming to live here."

[The houses] Kwame Nkrumah decided to build, many people got one but didn't like it. At that time people were afraid. We wouldn't cross the railroad tracks. Thieves would take your things, so only people who owned nothing would go and stay there. Today, now that the place has done well, people like it, but it is all spoken for. There are even some people who didn't even sell theirs, they just abandoned [the house] as worthless. Here? In front of the thieves' place? In that time, a cloth pattern came in that they called "A prostitute will go to Asawasi." You may not know the cloth, but maybe you haven't seen any. The design has squares like a checkerboard, with white and red alternating. We said its name was "A prostitute will go to Asawasi." So that is why people left, because they didn't like the place. Now, by the grace of God, the place has become nice enough to let anyone live there. So that is why I got that place to live.

It was only because of my sister, also; I'm sorry to say it, but she never had a child. So I had my first child, and she took her and she lived with her until today, until she had ten children. If you go there, her grandchildren are all over. Yes, look at my sister, my sister, forget it! The way she is treating those children! Now, those that are living with her, they don't even know me. She is in there with them. She has really struggled hard. Her husband took her to live in Tafo before then, but she fought with her husband. Then someone kindly gave her a small plot of land there and she accepted it. And at that time, because she used to travel to the countryside in addition to selling here, she could not build a proper house. She built six bedrooms that she also lived in herself.

Recently, our grandchild that came back from Europe even said that he would pull down what she built, but she said no. "Now, if you pull it down, am I going back to my home village? So you should have patience. Even if you have the money, get some land for yourself. This one I have managed to acquire for all of you. If I die, you can level the land and build on it just what you all want. But right now, you want to demolish it to build on." He has built his own, with eight bedrooms. It is left with the back side that has not been built. Where is she going to stay? So my grandchild said that he has heard. So then the big **gutter** that you saw when you went there, he is repairing it now. Her grandson has repaired it well, using stones and other things to rebuild it. Yes, he has built a wall around the little that he has built, and they are living in it.

About my sister, well, my mother had ten children, and I was the ninth-born, so this sister took me. I mean, since our mother had ten, she was already grown up.[9] When she was going into marriage, she used to take me along, all through my childhood. Also, she only had one miscarriage, very small, at five months, a boy. She never had another. But in raising children, how she treats my child, the oldest that I gave birth to! I was saying that me and my husband, the policeman, that man, when I left him he died. I hadn't even left him, and that daughter had started walking.[10] I went on a trip. They sent us to Wenchi. My sister had received her. We moved again to Borɔfoyeduru. My sister had received her. She was with her, so she did not know me until she had grown up. She went to school. They transferred her father to Accra; he didn't come to see her, and I had also divorced him. My sister was the one that sent her to school, at Nnuma Day School.

She looked after her herself, until there was one year left before she finished, and she got pregnant. The father of the child was abroad. She got pregnant and had a son. My sister said, "I will take this child, and you can go back." But that child of mine, really, she didn't like school. She said that she wouldn't go back, she would just sit at home like that. Then the same young man said that he would marry her again. Then they had the daughter that has just returned from overseas in addition. Later, the young man was not acting well and she left him. He hadn't looked after the children.[11] This same sister of mine took that child, too, and sent him to school. That boy, he finished school, and continued at Asokore Mampon Academy, and finished that, too.

Later, his father went overseas. When he came back and saw his children, he was very happy about them. He got passports for them and went back with them. Now they say the boy is continuing in school over there. But the girl did not go. Her story is that when she reached about form four, someone seduced her and she got pregnant. Even the baby didn't do well, and died. And this daughter didn't know her books. Every day she placed last in the class. If you went to talk to her, she would say, "If I am last, then I am last." The end of the year came, and they took exams; when her results came, she was always, "Josephine, you are the last." She would say, "If I am last, I am last." Today, she is more serious and regrets it. A few days ago, when she came here, she said, "Eh, if I had only gone to that school." She says, "Over there, if you go on and don't get educated, you won't get any decent work to do."

I mean, my sister and her grandchildren, they are having lots of children and leaving them with her, while I myself live somewhere else. I am with my two or three children, only the one son and two daughters, and we live in Asawasi and they also live there. My sister, how she has raised them, I couldn't say, only God will judge. She has looked after me very, very well, along with my children. If it hadn't been for her, I wouldn't have come here. I live in a village, what would I be coming to this town to look for? At that time, for Kumasi, you go and go to get to Kumasi. You would say it was overseas. Yes, if you lived in a village and you go to Kumasi, they say you are going there to lead a bad life. Yes, they will not let you come.

When I first married, my father gave me to his nephew, and he performed the *bragoɔ* for me. It was even said that I was still a child. My father said, "On this subject, well, my nephew Kwasdiyia, this is his wife, this is his wife." So he performed the *bragoɔ* for me. I did not have a child with him, and finally I did not want him, so I divorced him. I divorced him before I came to Kumasi here. Meanwhile, my sister was selling oranges, so she lived here. When I divorced him, she let me buy oranges to bring them to her. After a while, I also came to live here, and I got the policeman and I married him.

Our mother became very old and she died; our father was also dead. So, God help me, I had no one but this sister. If not for her, in the village she had built a full compound house, and when we all go there we stay in it. I mean, as for her, although she hadn't had a child, God blessed her, if only she worked, in these onions that she took up. If she had quit to go make a farm in the forest, or if she had even lived in that house, so that she could go to the forest, she would have been poor. For Ghana is good, but at the same time we don't let the truth do its work. If the truth ruled, Ghana would be really good. Everyone would do a little work, and earn some money.

Long ago, when my father and mother were alive, we had chickens in the village. Three chicken eggs cost threepence. You would not be allowed to take any. When Tuesday came, my father's town was about one mile from ours, and it was behind ours on the Kumawu road. It is called Akotohuu, and ours is called Dadease. On Tuesday, when we were coming to the market, we collected eggs. At that time, our father would not even pay money. When the hen has laid eggs, you go and pick them up, and they wrap them up as three for threepence. You might get ninepence or one shilling. One hundred herring might cost ninepence, or sometimes even eightpence. You count out fifty and you take them to your village.

At first, there was no work in the village. Now, some people there do work for money. Nowadays, some people there, even if they don't sell things, they can grow cassava. If you plant it and it grows well, people come to buy it. Today, even in our town there, some people can buy crops in the field. Someone says, "I am going to buy a cassava farm to harvest." So you go measure out land to give to her for about twenty or thirty thousand [cedis]. The farmer can divide it like that to give to about three or four people, and still leave some for her to eat, *wahu?* In the past, also, who would be buying cassava? That is why, today, people live there to do that. There are even some men living there that burn charcoal, and they put it in bags and people buy them.

In our own hometown, nowadays we buy firewood. Villagers can go around looking for it, and bring it back to pile here. I mean, the way things were, a short time ago, we who were strong could go way out behind the farms, and we would go bundle up the wood and we would go around putting them down. But not now, because there is school; even a **college** has come there. So in the village, teachers live there and they will buy things. Some people also have built big kiosks, with all kinds of goods, and a **fridge**. Today also, if we are eating, no one wants water that is not very cold. When we are eating, we buy some and we are drinking it and everything. For today, if someone lives there, and he can work, he earns money to go buy things for himself.

In the past, because there was no work, even if you had something no one would buy it from you. Everyone had some already. If you have cocoyam, everyone has some. Who is going to buy? Today, even in our hometown, there is no food. Only cassava is plentiful there. Today, if it gets to Tuesday, it is market day over there. So then this day, they are trading; so that today, this cassava, it is in the street and they take it to pile up in the market itself, and people are buying it. People from the Efiduase Zongo come to buy kola [nuts], and buy some of the cassava itself. We who live there do too. There may be someone who even comes from that town, but because she has no land to farm, she has been able to [trade]. Those of us who came to live in Kumasi, for example. If I had been there, I would buy cassava. You don't have a farm to make, so you have to buy cassava to eat. Even with plantain, you won't get any at the market, except for at Efiduase; when Sunday comes, they bring it from the Efiduase villages, Nkwankwannua and others. Then, in the past you would go with four hundred cedis to bring cassava.

But today, eh, there are lots of people living in our town. Today, the place is overflowing. There are hairdressers who do various things; there are people who have really studied hairdressing. There are big kiosks where people can sell things all night. Now electricity has also come there. All night people sit and are cooking rice and frying meat. *Agya!* Everywhere has turned into a little town for us.

But in the past, oh my. Was I happy? Yes, when we first lived there, we didn't know anywhere else; that's why it felt good to me. When I was a child, and I became a young girl, I was very happy; I was just happy for no reason. We didn't know what progress [*nkɔsoɔ*] was. When you get up, and you are a young girl of the age that you don't have a young man, you weed the farm. When the cocoa season comes, at night when you are sleeping, they are picking the cocoa and the young men are laughing at you. You get up at night and you go quietly to pick some, and you are awake. When Christmas time comes, he brings you one biscuit, because you have done well for him. He is thanking you with it, and that is all. If you get a biscuit, you are happy to receive it. He doesn't give you anything else, but there in the village, we didn't know anything else. So we were happy and stayed there. When we would get up, we went to our farm.

The firewood I was talking about, well, when Christmas is coming, you don't even realize that you don't have enough money for a chicken. We didn't even buy chickens. My father had chickens, and he had two wives. Even when he killed one at Christmas, he divided it into two and gave half to the other wife. He didn't allow two chickens to be killed for food. He went to give half to one wife before he gave my mother her share; only one chicken, but I am happy.

When Christmas is drawing near, you go for firewood several times. We all build a bonfire when Christmas comes. Even what you get, at last, will not be this much, but *wahu?* Because we had not yet seen the world, we were happy. When that time comes, if you are not yet grown, your mother will buy cloth and Christmas things for you.

Besides, when our children grow up a bit and they realize that they can, they go in to weed as laborers. They weed in cocoa farms. When Christmas comes, maybe you will buy cloth with the money. So when we were young girls, we came together and when we made four, we would go to take somebody's farm and weed it. The farm may stretch from here to the road that we came on, and the charge for weeding it is five shillings. Those of you intending to weed, then weed it. Then you may go to another place and work for two shillings. As it goes on, perhaps, if you even get ten shillings, it is real money; it can buy cloth. You buy one with it, and you put it on, and there you are. When you get two cloths, as a young girl, you are happy. Eh! when I married my husband at the village, I even had about four cloths.

About my mother, when she was alive she lived in the village. My mother worked hard; my mother was a hardworking person. In the past, she even bought a car for her son. At that time, cars were not common like today. I remember a certain car (what was its name?) that had a bell hanging on it. As it was going along, the bell would ring loudly. Her eldest child was named Yaw Owusu. My mother bought a car for him. She used to make soap, too, at that time. They say that at that time, regular soap had not come yet. She made *amonkye* [local soap] from cocoa pods. My mother knew how to make *amonkye* and made it into balls for a penny or threepence each, at that time. As we were saying, this car would cost today about how much? It was a thousand cedis then. He bought it, a small car, and a certain man came to drive it, and he was driving it.

My mother was hardworking, but even when I was a child, I was the ninth-born child, so my mother spoiled me. As for cloth, when I grew up I had about four cloths. I bought *yaadonko* and I bought *watapa* [cloth names]. I bought about four cloths before I got my period. My husband, the one I was saying that my father gave me to him, had already betrothed me. At the *bragɔrɔ,* he also brought me two cloths and other things: eggs, sponge, a bowl, and a stool. At that time, we said he was preparing you to sit down. Your husband's stool is included. When you are going to join your husband, you bring it with you. Then he buys towels and some additional things, with chickens. They are brought before you and they have been brought by your husband.

So you stayed in your house where you live, in the old days. If it belongs to a god, then you don't stay there. They let you go and stay in a house they have borrowed for you. You will spend six days there, and the young girls who are your friends all come to care for you. Perhaps your husband gave you two chickens, and your father will give you some, and your mother will give you some, with eggs. There might be someone who will bring you some eggs, even though she has nothing at all. You sit at the roadside, and you will receive lots of those eggs. So the girls will care for you like that for six days. They will eat your own food and look after you. When day breaks then they kill a chicken to cook for food. In the morning, they prepare *etɔ,* and they put eggs on it and give it to you, the *bragorɔ* girl.

As for you, you just sit in a room. All your hair has been shaved from your head with a razor or a razor blade. They apply shea butter all over your body for six days, while you stay indoors. When they give you some of the mashed yam, then they kill a chicken for when they prepare *fufu* for you in the afternoon. They give some to you, and they also give some to the children and take some for themselves. They eat and play and go to fetch water, and some come there and some go away. There might be some girl whose mother is a farmer. When her mother goes to the farm and comes back, look, she selects two bunches of plantains and calls her child to say, "Take it to your home, where the *bragorɔ* is taking place, so that (pardon me) you should cook it and eat it." In the old days, the father's share would also be brought. At noon, they would again cook boiled yam. Palm oil was abundant, so they would pour some on the stew and give you some. You would remain there like that for six days; then they would say you have come out from the *bragorɔ,* and you would put on cloth.

You know that we Asante knew how to dress with uncut cloth, until the Fanti and others came so that we knew how to dress with sewn cloth. When you reach your *bragorɔ,* you put on your mother's handwoven white cloth. You wear one underneath and you wear the white one on top. Your hair has been shaved six days ago, so it has begun to grow nicely, and the ends are trimmed nicely. Perhaps you may come out on a Tuesday. They fix six days for the puberty rites; so maybe they begin on Thursday, with Friday, Saturday, Sunday, Monday, and you come out on Tuesday. Tuesday is also the market day in our town.

Your husband will bring you sandals, the ones from tires. At that time, it was *ahenemma* [leather court sandals]. Kwahu people were making them at that time, but they were not as nice as the beautiful kind we see today. It might be that the Kwahu used a special kind of skin to make them, sheepskin for sandals. Your husband put some on top of the other things to bring to you.

So, when you came out, you wear them and you put on the cloth, and you go to thank those who gave you gifts. You thank them like that, and when you finish thanking the people in the market, a day will be fixed about two weeks after your coming out, and then you will go to your husband and thank him. They dress you with a cloth like the one they use when someone dies who is a foreigner. They cover him with red cloth. But for this they use good cloth, maybe *kente.* They dress you up like that, and they used to make a big pad with cloths at your buttocks. In the past, too, when you were going to thank people, your breasts were exposed. They say that if you were pregnant, they would know. They would also apply a cream made from the seeds of a tree, mixed with liquid from kola nuts, carefully over some parts of your body. The one who knows how to apply it comes to do it for you nicely.

You are going to thank your husband, and you find people to fol-low you. They say, "She is going to thank her husband," and they walk with you. It is not far; in my town it is about one mile; we don't go in a car. To even find a car at that time was something. It came once from Dadease, and the fare was ninepence. It didn't make another trip. Once it came to Kumasi, when it went back in the evening, it went to rest. It is not like today, when there are about ten of them. We used to travel by walking. Someone who was going might carry a drum called *donno;* when someone important was going along, they would play that drum. When they finished giving thanks, they would play the drums like that and bring you back home.

After the thanksgiving, you would pick a day and buy food, includ-ing meat. That's when you would be going into marriage. The day that you go, if it was today that you were going, you would go in the evening. They prepare you completely; they find food, meat and other things for you. About two of your neighbors who are your friends go with you in the evening and spend the night. At dawn, they prepare palm soup, with wild game, dried snails, and other things used to make the soup. They find a big bowl and put in the *fufu,* about twelve balls of it, and then bring the soup. They put some soup into another container, and put a little soup on the *fufu* and put some of the meat on it. The dried snails, they may cut some like this and not even wash them, and they will be in the soup like that. When the soup is cooked, they remove it from the fire and put it on the *fufu,* and take it to the husband in his house. He then gives them to other people. They will say, "Yes, that person's wife has joined him in marriage today." She has come to prepare *kuntunku,* as we call it. It is the husband's food, as we say, the Big Meal, and he gives some away.

Someone might be there who, after preparing *fufu,* will make stew. In those days, stew was not popular and we did not know how to make it. We would look for a sophisticated person, and call her to come and make it for you. Maybe she had traveled a bit. My older sister married educated people all the time, so she would be able to kill a chicken, for example, and make stew. She might be invited, and she would come and make a nice stew. Yams would be cooked in addition, and taken to the husband's house. He would also take some and distribute it to his relatives and all those he knows.

In the evening, when the bowl was being returned, money would be put into it, *wahu?* This was in the old days, and in that time it might even be two pounds and ten shillings. In those days, that was a big amount, too. Two pounds ten would be in the bowl for the husband's food. She came to prepare it, and it is brought back. After that meal, you would be cooking your own food, little by little. When you and your husband get up, you go to the farm; you don't have any other work to do. Myself, I did this for a while, but then I said, "I won't marry," and I stopped marrying and came to follow my sister.

There in my hometown, it is up to God. When a child was born, you don't know how far God says he will get. At that time, I lived in a village and I was happy over there. When I married, my father who put me into the marriage later died. I stayed there with the man for some time, and my aunts were also there. No, I got up suddenly and I came back. I said, "I will not marry." They asked, "Why?" "I will not marry." Besides, I had married him like that for about a year, but I hadn't got pregnant. Then I said I wouldn't marry him and I came back. Meanwhile my older sister, as I was saying, she was buying oranges to bring to town here, so when I had quit marrying, my sister said I should also buy oranges to bring here. With God, wherever he says you should go, you will arrive there. If my father were alive, he would not let me divorce. Yes, it was his nephew that I married; he would never have allowed me to divorce. But then my father was dead, and I divorced. Then God said that was not the place for me to live.

You see, when we sold oranges, they could be out of season. It is not like today, when at Christmas you still sell. Today, they pick oranges about nine times a year. When they are all gone, some of us even sell bargains. Some days, we can go buy something like beans, and sell them at the bargain market at less than the normal price, until the oranges come in again. When the oranges run out, then we go to buy this good maize. I go on foot to Adwaase. We get up in the morning to go cut the green corn, in order to boil it and bring it to hawk around. We can do it like this for a short time, just until our real work comes back. When people come into the world, there are many kinds of work, as God himself may teach you. I did it with my sister just like that, and later I stopped.

With this sister of mine, it was only in the onion shed that when we came, we stayed, and we never left. A friend of hers, yes, from Kwahu, sold onions, called Madam Afua Fofie. At the house we lived in, the landlord's wife, from Nsuta, also sold onions. She told my sister that she should come sell onions, for it was good. She came to see her friend from Kwahu. At that time, only Kwahu people were bringing most of the onions, the Asante kind. I was saying that the stalls were there and the Yorubas, well, they would say, "Come in here, the Yoruba it belongs to has gone away."[12] Then she gave the stall to us.

As for myself, what I was just saying was, I had married the police-man and I wasn't trading then. At that time, I lived at the police sta-tion. Maybe then they transfer us, and we go there, maybe then they transfer us and we go somewhere else, so I wasn't selling anything, *wahu?* But then [my sister] was selling by herself, until it happened that my husband, well, although I married him, he liked too many women. So when you went somewhere with him, after a little while he said, "Go back home." He had seen another woman. I went to live with him in Borɔfoyeduru just like that. He went and married a woman there and even had a child. That's why he looks at you, and if you are doing some-thing, he says go, he will take back his room. Even when we were living at Freebar here, he said, "Go back to your hometown," but I said, "It was in this town that you married me." He said, "Then go to your sister, because I am taking back my room." When he told me that, I came to stay with my sister.

Then I thought perhaps I could join her in the work she was doing, and I might earn enough money to buy about two cloths. At that time, whether you earn thirteen shillings, or even seven shillings, you can take it to buy some cloth. Then I stayed on like that, and he came back and said, "I apologize." I told him, "I bought cloth for this much, pay me back." That's how I treated him. He wasn't buying things for me. Well, when he wanted me, to take me with him, then he paid and I went with him. Later, I looked at the way we really were living, and it wasn't good, so then I left him, *wahu?*

Meanwhile this sister was still selling onions, and she said, "These onions that I got involved with are all right, you should come in." The way I am, I have even sold plantain before. Then I went to sell earrings, where they sit over there; I was in with them. So we took them around to villages, at Boase, Kiriki, here and there I was doing it. I was the young girl [assistant]. I did that, but later this sister of mine said that I should come and let us sell the onions together.

For the onions, at that time, there were rules. There were the Kwahu kind, so it was all right, *wahu?* Then we ourselves who were selling, we arranged ourselves so that the Kwahus who were bringing it were able to wait two weeks before they brought any more, which meant that the group was filled up. I sold those onions, and later, this husband of mine, I left him. I left to remain with the onions, *agya,* and if it went well, then we earned a little. My sister stayed in these same onions and built her house with them. Finally, we are tired. We have become old women, we aren't going anywhere any more, so then we stay put. If it hadn't been for that . . .

When I came to town here, we worked really hard. I went to market to carry maize from Adwaase to Zongo market. At that time, at Zongo market, when you arrived there, you had become like cotton [exhausted]. You tied a bundle of firewood on top, to cook [the maize cobs] with. When you finish cooking it, you load it on your head. Long ago, we from the Gold Coast, we even worked like crazy people once. That maize, too, sold for a penny or two, or a halfpenny. If you bought a shilling's worth, they said hey! With maize, the profit was all right. If it cost two shillings, and you earned one shilling, it was all right like that. You who were able to buy about two shillings' worth, you would get two shillings in profit out of it. Also, at that time, if you had two shillings on you, it was real money. When I had reached maturity in the village and came here, I brought one pound and one shilling into this town.

At that time, this sister of mine was marrying a husband, a driver, and living in Ashanti New Town, where the Salvation Army building is today, toward Mbrom. Beside their building was a house; the man was from Kumawu and his name was Akwasi Aniakyire. His house was where my sister lived, so I used to come to visit her there. She was mar-

ried to her husband, the driver. I had got a lot of money. When I had
the *bragɔrɔ* as a child, I got a hundred pounds and what? Two shillings.
At that time, when I was coming here, the car fare had gone up to one
shilling, for the car I took to come.

The cloth that I had set my eye on buying then was called *fie-mmosea*
[house gravel]. And then, when I came, my sister said, "Child, eh! Bring
it here, bring it here, this is what we call cloth." When I finished, my
husband was going on the road. "You and I are going to the store." I had
got three cloths. I bought one cloth, they say the name is *abe-tia-kube*
[the oil palm opposes the coconut palm]. It was really heavy. The half
piece was five shillings and sixpence. We went to buy some material called
maderɛɛsse [my address], with straight lines like that, for six shillings.
Then we went to buy a cloth called *adwuma-biara-yɛ-adwuma* [every
work is work]. That is the name of the cloth, so there are things on it that
look like the scales used to weigh gold. That also cost four shillings and
sixpence. We sewed them up, and got a spare yard out of each. At that
time, when they sewed up the blouse they gave me a yard. It is not like
blouses we sew today—to make them even a yard would not be enough.
Even two yards will not be enough. Then right there, I had got those
three cloths. And at that time, too, [my husband] said the *fie-mmosea* was
too expensive. You want to buy this for twelve shillings, and you go buy
that one, and the money is finished. But as for that, this other half piece
was five shillings and that one was four shillings and sixpence. I mean, I
got three cloths and had four shillings left with me. At our hometown, I
went to buy two yards of cloth for two shillings, and added what I had
kept from the other cloths. Then I made a patchwork cloth from it and
had four cloths. Stop it!

So in the past, we got tired. We did any kind of work, useless work.
If you don't push yourself, you won't get the two shillings we were talking
about, so you push yourself on like that. While we are talking about this,
I was saying that my husband was a policeman. He was not educated, so
his monthly salary was three pounds. If he gives me two shillings a day,
by the end of the month the whole three pounds will be gone. How does
he get money? I mean, the policemen have been cheating drivers for a
long time. He used to collect little by little from them.

My oldest child was born at the village, and when he came to give
me presents, he gave me three pounds. What did it mean? But with
those three pounds, I got something. I bought a pan to bathe the baby

in for one and a half shillings, yet it was big. My dress I bought from my sister; when I came here, he bought me a dress. There was a woman called Madame Owuo, from Efiduase, who died a long time ago. I took it to her and she sewed it. A dress then cost one shilling and sixpence, for a good-quality one. Even today dresses are expensive, but you don't know whether they are any good. Madame Owuo sewed it for me. I also bought some material called *maderɛɛse,* and I wore it to go and thank my husband at the police station, *wahu?*

Today, too, they give another hundred thousand [cedis]. When one person dresses today, like these young girls, just the little thing they wear around their necks costs a lot of money.

The change that has come today is with these onions. Those of us who first came to trade here, we traveled by train with bags of onions. Even when these people were bringing them, the cost was one pound and two shillings. A big kerosene tin which has been enlarged, like they use to sell groundnuts, it sold for four shillings. The onions that came from the Northerners, those ones the Asante didn't like much. So the day that they arrived, a whole bag might be six pounds and you buy it. The change that has come today is that even the Asante onions are sold by the bucket. It is not a matter of a kerosene tin. Today what we trade with is the plastic bucket, and it costs twenty-five thousand for the Asante onions, you see? The kind from Anloga sells by the hand [*saka*].[13] When they are brought here, the hand will be bought for what? I have bought a hand for five shillings before. The whole hand was sold for fourpence once. Today, when a hand comes in, it may be sold for fifty thousand, just one hand. So today, there are a few being sold recently at 1,500 cedis a bunch. Now things are going up [*kɔ so*].

But even when we bought it for five shillings, we could sell it at a loss, for at that time, a buyer might not come. When you buy, after a week that [the seller] may go to trade and come back, your goods may still be sitting there. Maybe you then reduce the price from the four-pence or sixpence that you need to sell it at to get your money back. Today, too, one hand cost five hundred cedis, a thousand cedis, or two thousand cedis, and we had to agree. Look at these onions, the Northern kind, they are just starting to come in, and cost twenty-eight thousand, but even then if you sell them, you do all right. I mean, that small rubber bucketful they used to sell for four thousand, it went up to five. Just today, they have reduced the price a bit, and it is now coming in. They are selling it for forty-five thousand, but when you sell it, you make that. So we will accept that, though it is expensive, but for today it is good.

Some of the difficulties I was talking about were in going to buy maize. If you struggle to go and buy this maize, maybe when you come to sell it, you may earn two shillings or one shilling from it. When you go to the market with that money, it can buy you something to come cook and eat. The onions that I was saying were cheap, that also, when you buy it that day . . . This sister of mine, for example, when we were first coming in, when someone had brought onions, we could not buy a whole bag. We were just then starting out. The big kerosene can, when you fill it, at that time they would press it down when they filled it. When it was full, it cost four shillings and she took it off behind the market. At that time, the inside of the market was not like it is now, and she went and arranged them on a sack for ten cedis. At that time, it was not even a hundred cedis. How do we say it? Five pounds, and people bought them. When she sold it, she made a profit: on one she bought for four shillings, she got sixpence profit. In the olden days, she shouted, "Eh, it is good." She would go back to buy more. That day she was able to sell two, and she made one shilling. She said, "Mm, this work is good, so I will get into it," and she has been in it all along. Then when someone comes, she gives them a bag, saying, "You are a smart one, you can sell, so you sell it too." So she gives some to her and she sells it.

With her husband and me, she lived at Zongo; her uncle had a house there and we lived there. Her husband's two children and me besides, and herself. Her husband gave her one shilling and sixpence, and it was enough for our meals. In that time there was "four o'clock meat." When it was that time, the meat was sold at two pennies. When you buy two, it makes thick soup. So when we pushed hard like that and earned like that, we were happy; then we didn't know what was coming. We exhausted ourselves like that up to today.

When today the price is so high, we can still take some. I also sell it at a little higher price so I can also make a profit. Even if it is not enough, for an old woman like me, it will be enough for me. I bought this bag of today's goods, but it won't be today that it gets finished. I will sit here a while with it. And now that I am so old, maybe I have a little money on me and I am using it to buy something to eat. By the time the bag is finished, I might get two or three thousand, and then I will say, "Eh, this is the profit on the onions." Then if I have a thousand or two thousand, I take one thousand and add it to my money.

Later, when I am selling this, then we are making a savings group. Maybe we give five hundred cedis to one person from what we have saved. In about a week we get ten thousand, then we give it to one person, and you get enough to pay your stall rent. If it wasn't for that, in this shed we have two [stalls] here, for five thousand and two hundred cedis. Then every month, they collect it. Because of this, and also because of God, whatever happens, the Lord stands behind it. So we do it like that, and we get money for the stall and for ourselves.

Now my sister has become an old woman; she doesn't sell any more, but she comes to sit beside us a lot. She picks out the bad ones from what I have bought. What I earn, I give some to her, and she takes it to go and buy food to eat. That's how it is.

With this world, whatever happens, you cannot say that it is no good; it is actually good. For we all live in it, and if we can even understand something, then a change has come. Today, look at these young girls with different cloths, expensive ones, but they are able to buy them and still buy shoes. When a person passes by, and you look at how she is dressed, it might cost even a hundred thousand cedis, and yet there she goes. So it is good. We will stay alive and take it like that.

The buying of goods by some people depends on who knows you. In the past, my elder sister went to farm in the forest, and I got to know about four or five people out there. Then, when she is coming here, she passes by some people and says, "I am going to buy some from Madame Nkrumah." There might be someone who is coming to buy goods on credit. When she goes and finishes selling them, then she brings the money to me. Otherwise, those who pass by, no, nobody passes here for you to call her to come and buy. They say it is cheaper behind the gate, behind the rail line, where they call it Allabar.[14] If you have someone who sells onions, she won't come to you. But if she is a very old friend of yours, if she comes and has taken the trouble to get through, she will pass through to buy some, along with groundnuts. It may be two or three weeks later that they come to pay and buy more. Now, that is what we are living on, because the one who is actually passing through, well, if I don't know her already and call "come and see," she will not pass here.

When someone goes and they reach the shed, they say, "This place is so dark!" If the goods are there, they don't even see them. It is dark there. If the government would just help us to shorten [the walls] a little, to let the air pass over them to get a little light over there. When they first came, Akua Nsiah spoke about this to the KMC people;[15] they own the land. It finally came to this: when you have yours, and the other person has theirs, if they are building on it, can you tell them that you will not allow them to build it? So they went on building there and, after some time, Kwasi Agyeman went and pulled them all down. That was it, and we were there nicely. Everyone who passed by, she came back here, and you saw that, long ago, they knew that this was the real onion market. *Wahu?* If someone was far away, she would see it. If she was walking in front here, she would see it and they would come in.

Today, though, it is not like that. Today if you tell someone, "I am sending you to the onion market," she doesn't know it. She could go to Allabar; if she doesn't go to Allabar, she goes to Bode.[16] You have to explain it well to her, that [behind] the shed where they sell tomatoes there are the onion sellers, before she will enter through there. Even me, sitting here, as I am going now, when I reach there and I enter, I don't see the way, and everything there goes black.

If you do know someone, when you say, "Go and show her the place they call *Ewiam*,"[17] on her part, she may not even have money, so she can't go to that place. So then when she comes, you fill some for her. Through that, they take away our money. She goes and comes to pay, she goes and comes to pay, and finally she does not come to pay. Before the stalls were built in front, those we are talking about, I didn't even know them. Then, when someone came they said, "How much are these onions?" This much. If she was buying a kerosene tin (at that time the plastic bucket was not around), then she says, "Fill it, the kerosene tin," and you talk about the price and you pour it out for her, and she pays you. "I am buying what has been set out in piles. How much?" Ten cedis, eh, a hundred pounds, like this and she buys.

And besides, when the market became like this, you couldn't get a person to be your customer and trade with her. In our stall over there, nobody will buy your things unless they know they have no money. You see? When she goes to the Malians at their place [Allabar] they will not give her any [on credit], because they do not know her. When she comes, and you do know her, you will give her some on credit and she goes off with it. That's why those of us here, when we buy some onions, a burlap bag will last for a week before it is finished. The Malians over there, they say that they sell two or three bags a day. The Kumasi people who go round to buy onions to sell, maybe one who lives at Aboabo, Ahensan, or wherever, they will not come here. They say that the Malians sell cheaper.

Trading in the past was good, but it all depends. At that time, there was very little money. But today, if someone helps you and buys even one plastic bucket full, it brings in a lot of money. It is hot over there now, and they can spoil. When there are some left there and you buy them, you have to pick out the bad ones. When they are left in a basket for some time and they are not bought, then when someone is buying some, you have to pick out the rotten ones and throw them away, and sell her the good ones. As for picking them over, we can do that whenever we are selling; you pick out the rotten ones and throw them away.

Poverty, too, in Ghana, I was saying that it is not like the Gold Coast; no one is any good. It was the white man that was the government that built the shed. He didn't make it for them to come and attach things to it to make it like this. He knew it as a big shed. Even when we came into it, sometimes when it was raining and the cloth sellers had problems, they would start a rumor that they were coming to take over this one. We too fought hard so we would not let them take it. If we had only known, we could have gone to stay behind the gate also, but we did not know. We didn't know that, so it came to be like this. You know, we have already gone to stay there.

You too, I'm sorry to say, you cannot go and remove someone's food from their mouth to eat it. When you said so, and the laws were working, we would show them that, maybe, this is the law, we don't do it like this, we don't do it like this. But you, the very one occupying that place, you cannot say that you will not allow someone to build behind your stall, and say it does not belong to him.

Have you seen now where Amma is staying? Someone has come to build one up. Even there, the person who is building is a young woman. Your grandmother was the one we were working with there. Your grandmother died long ago. You didn't even come into the market; your mother was the one that grew up here. If you want to build, come and see the one you share a boundary with, so we know, and then build yours, because you know everyone has built. When she came, when we came back on Monday, she had removed all of Amma's goods that were there. The beans and groundnuts had been mixed up, and she had built a huge stall.

We went to see the sanitary officers last Sunday, so Amma didn't even go to church. They have come to pull it down; she has come to break apart the blocks that she used and has taken them away. What remains is those boards standing there; she says that she will get a carpenter to come and cut the boards and take them away, so that Amma will also have a place to put her things. The back part which belongs to all of us; she has taken it all. The rumor I was telling you about, they say they took money for that stall; but I don't know for sure, or whether they said to build it on Sunday and finish it completely. Then it stands there; you have nothing to say about it, but that's what she says.

Little by Little

Listening to life stories, one realizes that their supposed weaknesses are really their strengths. Placing individual stories at the analytic center enables the analyst to take advantage of their strengths rather than apologize for their limitations. To learn most effectively from a collection of life stories, I advocate deliberately turning away from the familiar process of compare and contrast, of mapping their differences and sifting out what they have in common. Privileging their individuality instead focuses on the interpretive insights for which in-depth interviewing has the most advantages. The intensity of such interviews sustains their interpretive weight, even though their corresponding length limits their numbers and precludes recruiting a random sample of narrators.

Focusing on these complicated networks of idiosyncratic meanings allows them to create broader and deeper resonances instead of annoying static. They are rooted in multiple contradictory connections, meaning that while they do illuminate additional social cleavages, they do so by also partly bridging them. Like bridges, they define differences by constituting connections, making them an ideal place from which to examine the socially constructed foundations of both ends.

Identifying Divergences

The varying priorities of these traders are reflected most simply in the relative space they devote to various aspects of life. Maame Kesewaa and Abenaa Adiiya put their emphasis on trading activities and capital gains and losses, which reflects their professional attitudes and their identification with their trading expertise. Madame Ataa and Maame Nkrumah pay more attention to family relationships, with Maame Nkrumah discussing her own family relations at length and Madame Ataa emphasizing the effect of changing family patterns in general on the quality of life and the economy.

In the same way, the prominence of religious themes in the narratives varies dramatically, suggesting that some consider spirituality more central to their lives or to local life in general. Auntie Afriyie devoted a significant proportion of her session to Bible stories. She and Maame Nkrumah both featured detailed descriptions of the *bragorɔ* ceremony from the indigenous religious repertoire. Auntie Afriyie also discusses being accused of witchcraft by a relative at some length. Other women refer to God's power to open and close their stories, or as a final resort when secular explanations fail. Abenaa Adiiya is devout and diligent in her religious practice but rarely mentions religion when describing the course of her life. Maame Nkrumah also attended church very faithfully. Did they focus on trade here because they knew of my prior interest in trading practices, or because they saw religion as a separate sphere of life?

Life events provide another kind of indication of the relative priority of issues and problems for individual narrators. Like those of people anywhere, their assessments of community-wide trends sometimes contradict their own life choices and options. Their comments on how they set goals and made important decisions at critical points in their lives show how each woman weighs various issues against the others. For example, Auntie Afriyie and Maame Kesewaa both say they prefer "things of the Lord" to "things of the world" and both refuse the chance to be queen of their commodity groups, but only Auntie Afriyie seems seriously tempted. She speaks relatively little of her children in the description of her early life, other than counting them. She even disparages the one who works with her in the market as either fearful or lazy. Still, she takes for granted that her children's needs come first when she takes considerable capital from her business to give them better life chances through emigration.

Comments the narrators make about their own aspirations and fears also complement their explicit statements about values and virtues. In discussions of the relative merits of village and city life, for instance, village life sometimes comes out ahead. Yet when Amma Pokuaa, Maame Kesewaa, and Maame Nkrumah discuss suffering poverty in their old age, having to return to their home village consistently appears as the archetype of failure and destitution. Fear of this dire fate motivates their enormous efforts to build houses, while stories of abusive landlords further underline the need for home ownership. The adventures they and their relatives have experienced pursuing this goal only confirm its cultural desirability, although the best means of achieving it may change over time. More subtle goals emerge from what traders name as their accomplishments, frustrations, and regrets. When Maame Kesewaa jokes about her lost stalls, or Amma Pokuaa and Sister Buronya say they would go back on the road tomorrow if they could, they endorse those assets and strategies as bringing income and opportunity beyond their present situations.

Hopes and fears refract through a slightly different lens in relation to their children and grandchildren. Maame Nkrumah and Auntie Afriyie describe their children's problems in life rather more sympathetically than they portray more general societal problems. The children's successes and failures also differ from what they report as their own at the same stage of life, but neither generation has more than a small chance of reversing the effects of past events. Amma Pokuaa and Abenaa Adiiya express the most poignant aspirations and fears for their grandchildren. Their desperation and determination respond to a more abstract sense of the future, not yet restrained by the realities of individual ability and character.

Home and Market

Most of the speakers at some point mention that strong family relationships could be the most important factor helping some traders accumulate capital faster than others. Husbands and kin contributed both directly and indirectly to business success. Prosperous brothers, sisters, uncles, mothers, children, husbands, and neighbors are all reported as sources of working capital. They could provide it through credit guarantees, direct loans, inheritance, remittances from abroad, supplier credit, or employment in their enterprises. Access to goods on credit through family or neighbors was what enabled several narrators to start trading, and determined their commodity choice. Even the less prosperous networks introduce novice traders to suppliers, find them stall space, or let them learn by helping out. Blood relatives also indirectly subsidized the trading activities of Maame Nkrumah and Amma Pokuaa by providing access to free housing in family homes or by sharing the burden of caring for an elderly relative or child. In some instances full-time carers claimed a share of the trading profits or a room in the house for themselves and their children.

Family wealth plays several important roles in trading success. Beginning traders benefit especially from starting with access to more working capital, which gives them a broader range of more lucrative trading options. Family support continues to multiply these advantages through inheritances and loans, which make it possible to expand or seize new opportunities. Madame Ataa, for example, received goods on credit through her mother, a passbook through her husband, and a sewing machine from her older sister. Still, she and Maame Kesewaa also took up opportunities for manual labor to earn their own money as unmarried girls.

Wealthy families were also more likely to have members in lucrative business and professional positions, where they could provide not only investment loans, but skills training, free advice, and connections to potential customers among their wealthy peers. Richer families were also more likely to live in Kumasi, and growing up in Kumasi emerged as a significant independent factor making it more likely for women to be found trading in the desirable Central Market location (Clark 1994). Maame Kesewaa grew up with a rich aunt in her home village, and Amma Pokuaa with a wealthy village father, but both got established in Kumasi by moving in with relatives already there. So did Maame Nkrumah, who also got her house through the good offices of a policeman in-law.

The negative connection between family troubles and business collapse is equally strong, because sudden expenses from a family crisis can and do destroy many a trading enterprise. Traders generally try to segregate their working capital from the everyday demands of family consumption, though Maame Kesewaa notes varying levels of self-discipline on this. Legal trouble, serious illness, bereavement, and many other unpredictable family situations beyond the trader's control can create large debts rapidly, whether they affect her closest kin or collateral relatives. Abenaa Adiiya accepts that, in such circumstances, her own debtors must divert the money they had put aside to repay her. Prosperous and cooperative family members who contribute their share to both ordinary and emergency family expenses help insulate the trading capital from these crisis demands. Kin even help by covering expenses for their own parents and children, who might otherwise turn to the trader for assistance.

Husbands and fathers who pay a generous share of living expenses and children who stay out of trouble enable the more fortunate women traders to accumulate by insulating their working capital from domestic emergencies and the rising cost of living. Abenaa Adiiya and Sister Buronya used a widely accepted definition of the reliable husband to frame both positive and negative comparisons. Such a husband paid adequate chop money on a regular schedule, and took responsibility besides for rent, school fees, and medical bills. When Abenaa Adiiya first married, in the mid-1960s, steady male employment and the lower cost of living meant that she could save from her chop money for the proverbial headscarf or to expand her business, rather than draining her trading capital to fill the cooking pot. It was now widely accepted that many husbands could not or would not behave like this. Poor economic performance might justify divorce but was not surprising, as it had been in the golden past; now it was the reliable few who were surprising.

Traders need good interpersonal skills to build and maintain relationships with their husbands, children, and kin. Madame Ataa and Auntie Afriyie agree that careful adherence to cultural norms oneself is the best way to encourage others to contribute reliably to the household, though it doesn't guarantee that they will. For example, cooking carefully and promptly may cost trading time and income today, but make the business grow in the longer run by satisfying a husband, who will then provide generous child support or capital assistance.

The line between unable and unwilling is always a subjective one, especially in Asante culture, which places multiple conflicting claims upon everyone. The acknowledged tug-of-war that pits a man's matrilineal brothers and nephews against his wives and children was apparently not eliminated by the growing acceptance of wills and the 1989 Intestate Succession Act, which addressed it directly (Mikell 1997) Maame Nkrumah and Amma Pokuaa describe bitter disputes over inheritances, in which sisters, brothers, and lineal cousins contest each others' claims on various grounds of law and equity. They mention reevaluating or regretting their investment decisions as these inheritance patterns change. Women's property, such as market stalls and capital, once would have gone automatically to daughters, but is now diverted to sons, both before and after the women's death. Uncles now also divert property to their sons at the expense of their nephews.

The contemporary goal of sending at least one child overseas appears so many times in these narratives that it may have become an integral part of parental responsibilities. Abenaa Adiiya's son demands such a trip as his right, allowing him a fair chance in life, since there seems to be money available. Auntie Afriyie had the money and agreed with her son's claims of priority. Parents fear an open break with their child if they cannot fulfill their responsibility to establish him as an adult, in this or some other acceptable way. Bitter family tensions were reported by Abenaa Adiiya and Amma Pokuaa over who needs and deserves to go next, since money is inevitably limited. On the other hand, Abenaa Adiiya and Sister Buronya frankly discuss the significant risks that the emigrant will be deported, get ill, or just not find a job.

Amma Pokuaa, Sister Buronya, and Madame Ataa defend quite divergent positions in a more general debate about whether emigration is a good investment. Is it more likely to pay off than investing in business or education within Ghana? Does the U.S. or the Netherlands offer better chances than Ghana to someone without much capital or education? A high rate of return also depends upon the emigrant's emotional loyalty to his birth family to motivate him to send remittances, sponsor other relatives to join him, and perhaps later to build a house in Kumasi or the hometown. Abenaa Adiiya seems quite confident that her own children have bonded firmly to her, but tells of her husband's brothers, who were never heard from again.

Building a house not only allows an elderly trader to save rent or even charge it, but also reinforces her family ties. The lineage members who live there are continually grateful for housing allocated to them cheaply or rent-free. Once buildings have been inherited, the heir is under higher pressure to allow other descendants to live in them rent-free, but by doing so retains some of the prestige of the original builder. The careful division of single rooms among children and grandchildren Amma Pokuaa describes testifies to the high value placed on Kumasi accommodation, otherwise very expensive and difficult to locate.

Kumasi housing is one of the safer long-term investments, with demand rising steadily. Several traders in other interviews expected to rent out rooms for income when they could no longer work. One of the wealthier traders, not included here, built two multistory apartment buildings, only partly occupied by her kin. For past generations, mature cocoa farms played the same roles of retirement nest egg and notable legacy. The ideal is to build one house in town and one in the home village, as Maame Nkrumah's sister and Amma Pokuaa's mother had done. Auntie Afriyie had managed to complete her village house, but she also claimed her Kumasi house despite having completed only the foundation. The house in the home village costs much less, and the builder earns respect and domestic assistance there by offering housing to less fortunate relatives.

Retiring to the home village figured in several of these stories as a last resort, but also as a powerful symbol of failure and destitution in old age. Traders such as Madame Ataa, who spoke approvingly or nostalgically of rural farmers in general, still showed stricken faces when asked about the prospect for themselves. Even owning one room can make the difference between a retired trader's staying in Kumasi or retiring to her home village. The material benefits of better urban health care and easier living conditions, such as piped water, are particularly relevant to the elderly. Lifelong Kumasi residents like Abenaa Adiiya's mother could parlay their personal connections and local knowledge into a part-time business in old age, with lighter physical demands than their previous career. Except for the destitute, the prestige, excitement, and opportunity associated with city life hold their appeal well into old age.

Another Meaning for the Open Economy

When evaluating times and places as good or bad, traders most often judged them by the range of viable work options they offered. The availability of occupations that enable people with little capital to support a family or build a house seems widely accepted as a key indicator of a good local economy. The theme of local opportunity structures provided a unifying framework for traders to compare different time periods or different towns they had lived in, and to debate whether one policy or another was good or bad. Information on the subject was also widely shared. Traders closely monitored the entry requirements for various market positions, as well as other factors which might facilitate or obstruct entry for themselves or their children.

The women in this volume assessed these entry points in order to make immediate career decisions, not to evaluate the success of development policies. Despite their age, these women were open to changing their commodity or their position in the supply chain when doing so seemed to promise improvement, although the effort was not always successful. Maame Kesewaa, Maame Nkrumah, and Auntie Afriyie had tried several different lines of work in their youth, before settling into one that suited them. Sister Buronya had changed quite recently, and would have liked to change again. Women evidently did not automatically enter their mothers' occupations for lack of imagination or experience. Even Amma Pokuaa and Abenaa Adiiya, who worked closely with their mothers for many years, had sisters in other occupations and did not expect or want their children to follow them into the market.

Abenaa Adiiya and Amma Pokuaa expressed grave concern about the work options available to their maturing children. Amma Pokuaa and Madame Ataa discussed fluctuating earnings in the cocoa industry, the civil service, and education, and they worried about the higher capital now required in every type of business, as a result of higher prices and shrinking credit. Traders often had hoped to set their children on an upward path into professional jobs, and a few had succeeded. But often, after they had sacrificed to educate their children and grandchildren, the rewards they had expected their descendants to reap were now monopolized by more privileged graduates, whose parents had networks of elite connections and additional money for business capital. Other work associated with women, such as nursing or teaching, was as unreliable as marriage had become. Although well aware of the risks of emigration, these mothers suspected that the accessible occupations within the local economy were a sure dead end.

Even more chilling for traders was the realization that they could no longer assume that their daughters or granddaughters could at least become traders like themselves. Limited credit and consumer demand made it harder to establish an independent trading business now than when Amma Pokuaa and Madame Ataa had started. Credit from suppliers had eased their generation's entry into business, but credit was drying up for many commodities. As the capital squeeze tightens, more cash is required even to stay in the same position and retain economies of scale, such as renting a whole truck. The growing polarization between rich and poor has reduced the number of traders who have adequate capital for full-time work, and these few can collect a rising premium from those who do not. Squeezed between higher capital demands and the capital losses they had suffered during price raids and other political upheavals, many older women like Amma Pokuaa had been forced to reduce the scope of their own businesses. They could not afford to employ younger relatives or even extend them credit, and there might be few assets left to inherit when they died. Abenaa Adiiya was not sure that trading was even a viable option now for supporting a young family. Without more than minimal capital, even the market stall itself could not be put to very profitable use by a successor.

All but the most successful traders experienced this as a crisis of reproduction; biological reproduction had little meaning without social reproduction. They felt impotent, because they could not finish raising their children into properly functional adulthood. According to Asante ideals, both sons and daughters should have stable, independent incomes (however modest) before they start raising children themselves, but this was coming to seem unrealistic. Amma Pokuaa remarked poignantly that her younger daughters did not even know what the satisfaction of feeding a family was like, and so they didn't miss it. Tension over these changes in the expected life cycle affected more relationships than simply those of mothers with daughters. As a mother of sons, Amma Pokuaa sympathized with the young men who saw no prospects of marriage or a steady job, even while criticizing those who impregnated her grand-daughters. Maame Nkrumah noted that younger men unable to fulfill their proper responsibilities failed not only as husbands and fathers, but also as uncles and sons within the matrilineal system.

The rising tides of underemployed and unemployed workers enter-ing the informal sector, including market trading, also intensified a longstanding trend. The massive public-sector "redeployment exercise" layoffs that came with the SAP were dramatic and painful, but public-sector salaries had fallen so low in real terms by the late 1970s that it was common to see civil servants trading part-time to supplement their incomes. Occupations associated with women paid especially little, so many clerks, nurses, teachers, and secretaries quit altogether to trade full time. Their experience in white-collar work sometimes gave them advan-tages over career traders in literacy, numeracy, supportive networks, and saved capital. Civil servants and school leavers who might otherwise have aspired to formal-sector work, including more young men, also became a notable presence in market trading and small business before the 1980s, although their numbers multiplied in the 1990s.

The predicted economic expansion under the SAP partly failed to materialize and partly failed to trickle down into the marketplace sector.

Multilateral loans went mainly into the three established leading export sectors (cocoa, gold, and timber), which had relatively little linkage or multiplication through the marketplace system (Clark and Manuh 1991). Foreign direct investment was very slow to appear, because of continuing problems with infrastructure—electricity, water, and roads. These same problems already kept many local factories and offices operating at a fraction of their capacity, so private formal-sector employers were not able to absorb the "redeployed" labor, which flooded into the marketplaces.

Abenaa Adiiya and Maame Nkrumah are among many traders who understood very clearly how the influx of new competitors lowered their own incomes. They also recognized the dearth of other employment options for educated youth, from the experiences of their own siblings and children, which kept most traders from organizing to exclude them. Inequality did not outrage them; many had sacrificed to educate their own children and get them out of the market. Abenaa Adiiya and Maame Nkrumah called it unfair that educated people were forced to come and compete for market share with "professional" career traders. The advantages of education should open so many other upward paths to them that they should be able to leave the market for illiterates, who had only this one. As things stood, neither literate nor illiterate children could expect an appropriate job that would allow them to meet their needs, an indication of the truly deplorable state of the national economy.

Price control was one issue widely acknowledged as nationally and locally significant. The dramatic price control enforcement campaigns of the AFRC in 1979 and the PNDC in 1982 were historic events that affected every part of the country in highly memorable ways. Still, they played a much more conspicuous role in some traders' stories than others, depending on how much the vendors in their commodity were targeted. Auntie Afriyie and Maame Kesewaa reported changing what goods they sold in order to avoid unwelcome attention from the authorities, even if that meant less income. Roadside and itinerant traders still periodically face arrest and confiscation of their goods, as part of street clearances or civic beautification campaigns in Kumasi and other major cities that also affect fringe areas of their markets. The SAP devalued the national currency abruptly, but the new official rates were not so different from what traders had already been paying on the black market. Very few had had access to foreign exchange or imported goods at the official price when there was one. Price controls had been enforced off and on throughout the 1960s and '70s, so lifting them in 1983 was not unprecedented. Traders did not begin to trust that the change was permanent for many years, and so only gradually adjusted their commercial strategies.

Traders' commitment to mutual survival and dignity had a strong moral charge for them, as the definitive expression of mutual respect and loyalty in the market or the lineage. Neoliberal technocratic policies denied any responsibility for community welfare, so they seemed immoral and corrupt to Ghanaians, not just unfortunate (Clark 2001a). According to the World Bank, their and their neighbors' low income and inadequate diet were not a problem to be solved. In fact, in 1989 Ghana was celebrated as a success story and promoted as a global model by the UN and other multilateral agencies (World Bank and UNDP 1989). Although traders could accept a lack of success in addressing underemployment, they could not accept the evident disavowal of any obligation to respond to it.

Good Times and Hard Times

Each of these women had experienced the dramatic boom and bust cycles of the later twentieth century in particular ways linked to her social position as a market trader with her own level of capital and connections. While Maame Nkrumah and Madame Ataa idealized the past to some extent, most speakers were quite ambivalent about both the past and the present. Fortunately, this led them to give considerable detail about specific aspects of life that had improved and deteriorated in the interval. The dizzying inflation that peaked during the 1980s could not be ignored; real incomes dropped to 10 percent of their 1960 levels, according to international estimates. Memories of youth sparked a litany of the former prices of consumer items or trade goods in every narrative at some point, and several returned to the theme over and over.

Prices of food and housing had risen so precipitously that comparing real incomes and standards of living over the life span became too confusing for Maame Nkrumah to even try. Since I was most interested in their perceptions of economic change, I found that using subjective measures such as suffering or hard work elicited the most thoughtful comparisons, such as between the present and the years when someone had entered trading or moved to a new town. Maame Nkrumah, Maame Kesewaa, and Auntie Afriyie are about the same age, but they stressed different aspects of the economic situation in their comments. The interpretative form of the answers makes larger-scale cohort effects more complicated to trace, but it leaves more dimensions open for individual construction.

Economic considerations do not divide cleanly from moral and emotional considerations at the community level, just as they did not at the family or individual levels. A chief was expected to stimulate the economy of his town, including its commerce, or his citizens would move away. He did this partly by promoting and enforcing moral behavior through his court decisions. Maame Nkrumah provides a bleak example of the kind of protracted dispute that wastes money and creates moral confusion. The Kumasi city government drew criticism from Sister Buronya for not providing "real jobs," because its pay scales were too low to live on. Amma Pokuaa and Abenaa Adiiya remind us that creating this independence is also a primary obligation parents and elders have to the next generation. Respect and honesty figured first as moral values for Maame Nkrumah, but when she elaborated on their community benefit she shifted to their economic results: they create a social context in which the ordinary citizen can make a decent living.

Likewise, these traders debate the merits of urban life and modernization in moral terms, but the moral judgments are based in large part on their economic impact. In the more favorable assessments by Amma Pokuaa and Maame Nkrumah, these social changes expand opportunities for employment and material comfort. Skeptics like Madame Ataa question their value because they seem to undermine economic stability and community autonomy. They make the country poor by making its people envious, lazy, and greedy for quick profit. These are morally bad character traits, but they are also stupid as personal strategies to get ahead, because they do not work for long. Madame Ataa recommends slow but steady progress, *kakrakakra* (literally, little by little) over the lure of "easy come, easy go." Many other speakers also use that phrase for moments of emphasis, so some degree of consensus may exist that incremental betterment fits better with how change normally comes about, making it likely to last longer.

These Asante elders use the considerable Twi vocabulary available to invoke and critique different concepts about processes of social change. Which words each chooses to describe processes that policymakers would usually gloss as economic development reveals subtle analytic variations. The word *anibue* (literally, eye-opening) appears the most frequently and refers more to personal qualities than to community growth. Children acquire *anibue* at a certain age, some earlier and more thoroughly than others, as Auntie Afriyie notes. As a stage of maturation it represents something like good judgment or common sense, but it can also mean awareness and intelligence more generally. When Amma Pokuaa or Maame Kesewaa speak of a village, ethnic group, or history period as having more or less *anibue,* they mean more experience of the outside world and wider aspirations. It is one of the most positive terms, and yet it easily reflects social prejudice and lends itself to sarcasm.

My transcribing assistants most often chose the word "civilization" to translate *anibue,* but they also expressed serious reservations about using it. Like the word "culture," it is heard widely enough in Ghana to qualify as a glocalized appropriation, but much of its colonial baggage remains attached. Not all who use it do so naively; Madame Ataa's irony would do any postmodernist proud. The defining attributes of a "civilized" person include Western education, white-collar employment, Christianity, and access to Europeanized material culture, while those without these markers are stigmatized as "backward" and "ignorant." In the narratives by Maame Nkrumah and Auntie Afriyie and in wider local practice, those so stigmatized are often Northerners or villagers for good measure, replicating the negative racial and class connotations of the nineteenth-century use of the terms. Market traders themselves count as "backward" compared to more educated Asantes, and they know it.

In many contexts here I have translated *anibue* as "modernity," because this English word is commonly used and has a similar potential for irony or ambivalence. In the 1950s, development experts spoke of modernization with the same confident inclusiveness with which missionaries and colonial authorities spoke of civilization. Both words continue to be used this way in many circles. Where the narrative context here emphasizes exposure to new fashions in goods and new values, I have sometimes translated *anibue* as "sophistication" or "enlightenment."

Harder to translate, but perhaps more typical of Akan modes of expression, are two verb phrases indicating a direction of movement.

Twi often uses verbs where English uses a noun; marriage and child-birth are considered activities rather than events, for example. The origin of *anibue* as a verb phrase shows clearly in its negative form, *n'ani mmuɛ*, although one could argue that opening the eyes involves at least minimal activity. The two phrases, which are used more sparingly, mark the conceptual boundaries of *anibue*. A community, a series of events, or an individual can be said to "go ahead" (*kɔ w'anim*) or "go forward" (*kɔ so*) only if the change is considered positive, as definitely as with the English idioms "get ahead" or "upward mobility." These ongoing processes provoke ambivalence only when they move too fast, creating danger or damage. The phrases "to go fast" (*kɔ ntemtem*) or even "to run" (*de mmirika*) can evoke such out-of-control movement, but just as often they too have a positive connotation of amazing progress.

The word "development" is most often translated in policy and educational documents as *nkɔsoɔ* (literally, going up), another verb phrase turned noun. This one rarely appeared in oral discussions of community- or national-level socioeconomic changes, in which Ghanaians speaking English or Twi more often used the English word "progress." The aspect of the economy most obviously going up was prices, which discouraged the use of *nkɔsoɔ* with the more positive connotations of development or progress. When I asked traders and translators about the word, they connected it specifically to increases in individual wealth, which might or might not spark a change in values or behavior. This usage parallels the one-sided emphasis on capital accumulation or GNP in neoliberal development models.

A different conceptual boundary of *anibue* is marked by wisdom (*nyansa*), which can either complement or contrast to it. *Nyansa* is always attributed to an individual person, although it has an abstract existence as knowledge. Wisdom can be learned from Asante traditions, but also from experience of modern life, such as education. A person can gain wisdom in relation to modern institutions and things, in conjunction with *anibue,* or completely outside them. The *fiɛ-nyansa* (house wisdom) that Auntie Afriyie claims for herself derives primarily from indigenous traditions. It is based on deep knowledge and understanding of family history and relationships, and so it is better learned by staying home with the elders than by attending school. Auntie Afriyie sees her life as a perfect example of this learning process, which links knowledge so intimately with the holder that she and her sister have each become "a house wisdom."

Whatever the source of wisdom, it enables the wise person to navigate the dangers and opportunities of life safely and productively. Others benefit from this success both materially and by receiving useful advice on their own problems and choices. While wisdom can exist at any level of development, Auntie Afriyie argues through her examples of technical innovation that individual wisdom is what makes material progress happen. Wisdom does not become outdated, like technical skills or book knowledge, but enables the holder to actively adapt it to changing conditions through continual observation and deduction.

Good Girls and Bad Mothers

Close attention to the discussions of teen pregnancy in the stories here shows how the issue serves as a counterpoint or opposite to the concepts of wisdom and getting ahead. Examining these discussions reveals a very intimate intertwining of moral and economic issues. The traders condemn premature mothers for inevitably shirking their responsibility to support their children and respect their elders. Whether or not an individual narrator was traditionally inclined enough to blame the frequency of early birth today on the decline of the *bragoro* ceremony seemed to have little effect on her discussions of the disastrous consequences of early childbirth.

Maame Nkrumah, Madame Ataa, and Auntie Afriyie had been through the ceremony themselves in its more public form, and sang its praises. For them, the *bragoro* symbolized proper family values and responsible behavior, not simply sexual purity. Their longer passages pounded home the point that early sexuality demonstrated a lack of respect for mothers and for elders in general. Disobedience in refusing to run errands or help out at home was also condemned by Madame Ataa in this context. Proper respect and general helpfulness to elders were likewise rewarded in the subsequent *bragoro*. When the ceremony was held, a good girl was rewarded with enough gifts to get her started in trade, from relatives and neighbors she had helped. Notably defiant girls, even if they were not pregnant, suffered the humiliation of a skimpy ceremony with their meager gifts on public display.

The arch-traditionalists, Auntie Afriyie and Maame Nkrumah, held men to share some responsibility for sexual restraint to avoid early pregnancy, invoking the same principles of economic incapacity and disrespect. A man who stood by his pregnant young lover would be exiled with her when the ritual of *kyiribra* was enforced. A lecherous neighbor could be publicly insulted for not respecting an underage girl's parents, and taken to court. Men who spent too much time seducing women or who fathered more children than they could support found derision rather than admiration in the faces of their neighbors.

Even outright promiscuity drew censure from Madame Ataa mainly for enabling men to deny paternity. The baby's father had little incentive to accept responsibility for his child when his family was not involved, as it would be in a marriage. He might be equally young, incapable of earning much now without ruining his long-term prospects at school or in a career. A child born with such disadvantages would turn to theft and other irresponsible behavior, because more respectable options required normal parental support. The "virgin clubs" recently imported from the U.S. tend to emphasize current abstinence more consistently than physical virginity, and require similar discipline of boys. They also expand their nominal agenda to address issues of economic maturity by arranging vocational and business training (Bratton 2004).

Asante teen mothers are not just ruining their own future, they are also being bad mothers. To fulfill her duty to "replace herself," an Asante woman must not only give birth but keep her children alive and establish them as functional Asante adults. Raising children requires a steady supply of money for food, medical expenses, and school fees. Expanding and stabilizing her own business is an obvious way for a mother to ensure she will have the resources to protect her children from the hazards of daily life and to sponsor their long-term advancement. Mainstream U.S. discourse on motherhood takes for granted that children compete directly with paid work for a woman's time and commitment (Coontz 1992). These Asante traders take for granted a relationship more like mutual constitution between motherhood and work. In conversation, women frequently wrapped up their description of a past trading strategy and dated it by saying that it was how they had had one or more specific children.

Immediate conflicts over the allocation of money and time can still be acute, whether the business was expanding like Auntie Afriyie's or contracting like Amma Pokuaa's. Trying to maintain adequate invest-ment levels in both trade and consumption with inadequate incomes can pose some hard choices. Maame Kesewaa gives a grim example of halving the food budget to reinvest more in the business. This might easily risk a child's health through undernutrition, yet enable the same child to attend school without interruption if he stays well. Most of these dilemmas involve balancing short- and long-term returns rather than trade-offs between family and work. Neither arena offers much chance of long-term achievement unless the other is built up as well. Mothers sacrifice for their children not only because they love them, but because children remain their major avenue to long-term economic security.

Market Partnerships

In their trading relationships, these market women maintain a similarly delicate balance between long- and short-term considerations. Respecting their commitments to the leaders and members of their com-modity groups immediately reduces transaction costs by preserving the smooth flow of goods and limiting negotiations and monitoring to fewer issues. Amma Pokuaa and Abenaa Adiiya cooperated closely with their fellow travelers, exchanging price information and respecting bargained deals in rural supply areas where breaches of trust could easily pass unre-ported. The services the commodity group provides, by settling disputes and representing the traders in external contexts, are essential for the long-term survival of their businesses. Without them, credit could not be given or received as easily to balance supplies and demand, and hostile policies could not be moderated.

Traders generate ideological reinforcement for this strong loyalty to their erstwhile competitors by drawing explicit parallels to kinship. In these stories, traders often refer to their peers (and main competitors) as their sisters. One as hard-nosed as Auntie Afriyie spoke of the com-modity group leader as a mother taking care of her family, looking after their welfare and settling their disputes. Leaders also spoke of their love for their market "children," and even poured libations to their prede-cessors in office, as one does to ancestors. I heard subordinates working for wages or on credit or commission referring to the senior trader as "mama," though there was no blood relationship. Even without the fictive kin terms, the bonding over many years of working side by side can be intense and create an "off-duty" friendship that includes visiting each other's homes and attending family occasions.

Building up committed relationships with suppliers and buyers (whether inside or outside the commodity group structure) is the most common strategy traders use to expand their businesses. Steady clients, called "customers" in Ghanaian usage, include those who always buy from a given trader and those who always sell to her. In return, the trader must always be willing to buy when a supplier arrives with goods, at least on credit, regardless of her immediate need for supplies. Likewise, she must always find some goods for a loyal buyer when they are scarce, even if this means buying them from a competitor and reselling at cost. Abenaa Adiiya sees balancing the demands of her numerous customers as her biggest business challenge.

Customers assure a reliable minimum volume of trade that helps buffer fluctuations in supply and demand, securing access to economies of scale and reducing risk for both partners by moving goods even during unfavorable market conditions. Maame Nkrumah now depends almost entirely on her long-term customers, who seek her out despite congestion around her stall. Their loyalty is partly due to their need for revolving credit from her. Buyers who intend to retail almost always count on receiving increased credit over time, so that they can expand their own businesses. They lay the groundwork for this increase by buying regularly from one trader for some time, to establish the relationship.

Both large- and small-scale traders structure their trading practices to foster and take advantage of these relationships. Small-scale retailers develop a customer base among the low-income householders who patronize them. Sister Buronya's suburban customers will even bypass closer neighborhood markets to come to her in the Central Market. The strongest mandate for wholesale traders is simply to be present and available during all normal working hours, so that their customers will not need to turn to one of their neighbors. As Madame Ataa relates, this can force traders to drop profitable sidelines with incompatible schedules or locations.

Both partners nurture the emotional side of their relationship with friendly comments and personal services beyond their actual purchases. Stallholders, for example, can offer their customers a place to store purchases and rest before leaving the market, or arrange for delivery to the minibus loading area. Travelers buying in farm villages bring along city treats like fresh bread and good soap for their old friends.

Lower transaction costs due to trust benefit both the small-scale and larger-scale traders. Because of their special relationship, both partners expect honest behavior and fair pricing without hard bargaining or constant checking of quantity and quality. Price concessions requested should be moderate, and are often obscured from onlookers in the form of quality upgrades or gifts, as Sister Buronya mentions. Hard-pressed working mothers can safely send their younger children to buy from familiar traders they have visited many times. Wholesalers can invest their capital more fully, keeping less in reserve as a cushion against the risk of credit going bad. For those facing increasing capital demands, like Amma Pokuaa, this can make the difference between keeping and losing economies of scale such as renting a whole truck.

This trust, based on ordinary transactions, builds confidence that customers will extend help when it is needed in extraordinary times, which come all too often. Credit can be extended in either direction to accommodate excess supply, reduced buying power, or an unexpected misfortune like the vehicle breakdowns and theft that Abenaa Adiiya suffered. Just accepting delayed payment quietly, as Sister Buronya did, avoids a public scene that would damage the reputation of the customer. Those who have helped each other weather myriad minor crises for years will feel angry and betrayed if the relationship is severed or abused.

Supplier credit is extremely common throughout the marketplace system in West Africa, though traders sometimes qualify as loyal group members rather than as loyal individual customers. This credit cycle might turn over several times a day for retailers in the same market, or last several weeks for village peddlers. When credit is expected at a certain stage in the distribution chain, simply refusing to give it is not a viable option. Abenaa Adiiya asserts that her coastal tomato buyers would not and could not pay cash, so without enough capital to extend credit she might as well stay home. And if she stayed home she could not recover her debts, because the debtor could not earn enough to repay her unless she gave out more supplies on credit. If she did not, the delinquent buyer could often switch her allegiance to another seller and get credit from her as a familiar member of the local group.

Extending cash advances to reputable farmers to enable them to hire help with weeding and harvesting was another common practice. The farmers could expand production and become better customers, while the trader smoothed out the volatility of her supply. The farmer could not sell to someone else, and the trader normally had considerable leverage over the date of delivery. For yams, palm nuts, and tomatoes, represented by Amma Pokuaa, Auntie Afriyie, and Abenaa Adiiya, the direction of credit changed seasonally. Traders gave cash advances to traveling buyers and farmers in times of shortage, such as the pre-harvest months, and farmers advanced goods on credit to traders when there was a glut. With this in mind, neither side wanted to alienate the other by insisting on steep price concessions or other abuses.

Managing credit relations successfully takes skills not every trader can muster. Several traders mentioned changing commodities or changing their position in the distribution chain specifically to avoid having to extend credit. Whether arising from bad luck or bad management, bad debts can drain trading capital rapidly, until it falls below a critical level. Bad lending experiences also figure prominently in the tales of bankruptcy or other setbacks, in which they serve to deflect blame.

In a successful customer relationship, both partners should be committed to increasing the other's viability and prosperity. The opportunistic drive for profit should be moderated by a longer-term accumulation strategy that depends on having many big trading partners with financial stability. Negotiating a balance between short-term profits and longer-term savings through risk reduction is a delicate process precisely because it triggers very sensitive evaluations of moral intentions and trading competence.

Intended Purposes

All of the speakers' statements about their needs, accomplishments, and virtues need to be interpreted in light of their purpose in telling their tale. Most narrators intended at least parts of their stories to convey moral instruction, which I had not expected. Madame Ataa's especially lengthy moralistic passages reflected not only her relatively judgmental attitude but also her greater experience with explicitly moral discourse in church meetings and *bragoro* homilies. Very active in a church women's society with her friend Mrs. Appiah, she was used to advising other women on their moral choices.

Maame Nkrumah was equally judgmental but focused more on her individual problems. She and Amma Pokuaa seemed particularly interested in vindicating themselves, while certainly willing to censure others. This intent makes their comments particularly revealing about what motives they consider justifiable and what arguments plausible, regardless of their accuracy in portraying specific events. Auntie Afriyie and Abenaa Adiiya seem the most pragmatic, making a virtue out of practices that others might consider selfish or imprudent and sometimes explicitly rejecting abstract models of behavior. As Auntie Afriyie says, everything has its season as God has planned.

The sections aimed at teaching also adopted several different formats, and not only because they were aimed at different learners. As already mentioned, several passages seemed designed to instruct teenage girls, whose sexual behavior or other life choices were still at issue, rather than the middle-aged women in the room at the time. Madame Ataa tailored another of her early sections to a broader population of ordinary citizens, in Ghana or overseas, when she drew attention to the social and economic problems created by rural-urban migration and emigration overseas. Auntie Afriyie aimed some of her advice at the government— take people like her more seriously.

The way I introduced the project also made teaching me a plausible goal. Abenaa Adiiya took pleasure in explaining the tricks of her trade, which I appreciated for their subtlety, whether or not she really thought I could use them. Auntie Afriyie focused more on teaching me how to learn, communicating the value and process of traditional learning by explaining the concept of *fiɛ-nyansa,* and also by modeling it when she told me stories and riddles of various kinds. She praised her granddaughter for "always watching everything," thus showing some of her grandmother's potential for wisdom. She and Maame Kesewaa also referred often to their own ability to learn by themselves, through careful observation, patient listening, and thoughtful deduction.

One common intention was to solicit aid, financial or otherwise, as Kumasi residents did with their *nkwansu* and the cassette tapes they sent to relatives living abroad. A few appealed to me for gifts, either directly, after the voice recorder stopped, or indirectly, by using my Twi name, Akua, for a hypothetical helpful friend in the stories they told. The most politically minded asked me to relay their demands and needs to those controlling international assistance, for example, my president and senators. Although I tried to deflate unfounded beliefs about my political influence, I had already admitted that affecting public policy was one of the goals of the project. These requests were sometimes unsettling, but did serve as a healthy reminder to try to publish my work in formats that could be read locally and influence policy.

Moral Directions

The moral values inscribed in these narratives create some basic positive mandates that apply to the market and home alike. Hard work and reliability, wisdom and intelligence are needed to do well in both contexts. The use of kin terms in the market signals that traders see structural and emotional parallels between them. Patience, love, generosity, and unselfishness were concepts highly relevant to trading contexts for Abenaa Adiiya, Sister Buronya, and Auntie Afriyie. They do not restrict these virtues to home life or situations of self-sacrifice, but freely associate them also with aggressive leadership and with toughness in the public sphere. Sister Buronya related in detail how her polite manners, based on respect for others and for herself, helped her pass more smoothly and quickly through border posts. She and Maame Kesewaa also remarked that determination, or "having a purpose in mind," makes an essential contribution to success. All these personal qualities work toward one's own benefit and the benefit of one's fellows.

Loyalty to family and loyalty to market colleagues are seen as the foundations of both these important social institutions. Asante consider the lineage and house the root of good character and good sense, treating coming from a good family as a valued personal attribute rather than an arbitrary stroke of luck. Inheritance, child support, and credit sponsorship all can be expected to result from dutiful attachment to a well-ordered family, along with the reputation its members share and safeguard. If treated with respect, elders also provide the relationships within which one can learn and demonstrate individual virtues. Individual ambition is normally seen as consistent with group affiliation, not in contradiction to it.

Competition is expected and rewarded, but within a framework of mutual benefit that gives each person a responsibility to contribute to the common good. Material wealth and progress toward modernity are viewed as positive for their own sake, but not when they undermine the commitment to mutual survival. One's personal reputation and the prosperity of one's associates are closely linked. Personal accountability means answering for individual misdeeds and mistakes and helping solve the problems they may have created. It also means consulting elders and peers before making an important final decision, and taking their advice seriously.

Early pregnancy and various kinds of laziness are criticized with very similar vocabulary and analysis in the moralistic passages. For example, Madame Ataa condemns "today's" people for refusing to farm and leaving the village behind. This urban migration leaves elders alone in the village, deprived of proper attention, and floods the urban informal sector with excess labor. Thus "too many people in the market" means that "there is no money." Some of the less qualified villagers and Kumasi-born workers will then be unemployed, leading to crime and street children just as teen pregnancy does. This enables Madame Ataa to draw an explicit connection between teen pregnancy and general overpopulation. In the abstract, the trend toward greater polarization of incomes has a similar cause and effect. Rising selfishness makes people lose sight of the need to keep their peers economically viable, and this loss of mutual respect leads to less buying power among the lower-income groups who most consistently patronize public markets.

A theme that resonates through many instructive explanations is that of orderliness—the opposite of *basabasa*. That dismissive term can be used to condemn bad behavior in nearly any context as wild, disrespectful, senseless, and useless. There is a beauty to the process of doing something *kamakama*[1] or *fɛfɛɛfɛ* that goes beyond obedience to social convention, though Ghanaian English speakers often gloss either word with the pedestrian translation "proper." It incorporates the intention or dedication to make sure a worthwhile task is admirably accomplished, yielding a sense of completion that satisfies oneself and others. Going about things *basabasa* is both a moral failing and a practical disaster; the two cannot really be separated. Behaving so carelessly cannot be innocent, because such people must not care about the consequences of their actions. Their lack of concern is wicked in itself, apart from the actual deviant deeds that it may generate. It demonstrates lack of respect for oneself, for others, and for the way the world works.

Why Things Happen

The concrete discussions in these interviews about what helped individuals survive and prosper also address larger questions of causation and agency, both directly and indirectly. Which factors a speaker holds responsible for past or current conditions, at either the personal or the community level, indicate which causative principles she accepts as most powerful. Such hints are especially valuable from those who cautiously hesitate to attribute responsibility or blame for current conditions in ways that might constitute an explicit ideology. When describing specific problems or events, however, they often let comments slip out that have certain causal implications.

Specific narrators locate causation of the general course of events at both the most general and the most personal levels. Individual wisdom, cleverness, hard work, honesty, and obedience each have their reward in some anecdotes, or else good and bad luck trump them. In very different ways, both Auntie Afriyie and Abenaa Adiiya hold God and Satan responsible for much, while the government ranks as a popular third choice. The intermediate-level causes also vary widely, from moral decline to the price of gasoline. Rural-urban migration, reduced food production, and the collapse of state industries all take their share of the blame.

These traders emphasized a wide variety of specific social and economic changes in their narratives, tacitly identifying them as significant causes of national decline or revival. Despite this variety, whether a change was considered positive or negative was almost always determined primarily by its impact on the range of viable work options. A good local economy enabled people with little capital to support a family (in cooperation with other earners, if necessary) and hope to build a house. Traders were most distressed when their economic situation did not allow their children and grandchildren to get started on this road to adulthood. Moral concerns derive from this issue because lack of opportunity destabilizes family relationships. Poverty prevents young people from undertaking respectable marriages and prevents people in every generation from fulfilling the responsibilities they already have.

Spiritual conceptualizations of change were very obviously dominant for Auntie Afriyie, but appeared more subtly in Abenaa Adiiya's narrative and a number of the others. Christian and indigenous cosmological beliefs informed their understanding of past and current events and their choices of appropriate or effective behavior in response. Sister Buronya implied that her recalcitrant debtor would receive divine punishment; Auntie Afriyie presented evidence that she is not a witch, instead of dismissing the whole idea. Portrayals of the "good old days" by Madame Ataa and Maame Nkrumah also carry an unspoken spiritual aspect in their focus on respect for elders and for their cultural norms and practices. This respect is informed by Akan belief in the power of ancestors to demand and reward loyalty. Even Maame Kesewaa, who did not feature ritual practices such as the *bragorɔ,* praises the authenticity and virtue of rural life, a presumption rooted as much in Christian as in traditionalist discourses.

Both Christian and secular causal frameworks acknowledge personal agency and its limits. Stories about Adam and Eve and other characters derive their credibility from their biblical origins, but do not always replicate the biblical accounts precisely. The apocalyptic rhetoric of the Book of Revelation inverts the "golden age" aura of Genesis and the gospels. Afriyie's choice of story and modifications to the plot leave room for her to express her own intentions and messages, much as the *Anansesɛm* stories do. Maame Kesewaa and Maame Nkrumah, more secularly oriented, rate the virtues of honesty, hard work, and self-discipline as a firm foundation for long-term success, but they would not claim that good character is always rewarded. Even Auntie Afriyie stresses that her intelligence or wisdom was what enabled her to pull ahead of her colleagues, and that a similar capacity for ideas is responsible for most human progress. Although she labels this complex set of intellectual skills a gift from God, she notes that some intelligent but lazy people never use their gift properly.

Individual misfortunes, whether attributed to malevolent witchcraft, God's wrath, bad luck, or human weakness, can always be contested or reinterpreted. For example, infertility carries enormous stigma and can be attributed to witchcraft, promiscuity, or pure accident. Yet Maame Nkrumah inverts all this and declares her childless older sister a saint and a success in life. Clearly bad luck is no more absolute than good luck, and both leave considerable room for negotiation and accommodation.

Conversely, by invoking the authority of God even briefly, Amma Pokuaa, Abenaa Adiiya, and Sister Buronya lay claim to a powerfully comforting means of explaining the upheaval of their world and disavowing responsibility for it. The idea that their recent suffering and the rapid and disorienting changes they see in political and economic conditions are part of some larger divine plan has a growing appeal. According to the popular slogan, "God is in charge," so his loyal followers will eventually make it through. Getting on God's side makes absolute sense for the long run, though it does not prevent immediate suffering. Such beliefs also provide certainty about what to do—-prohibitions and priorities labeled as "things of the Lord" or "not of this world" even by Maame Kesewaa. Auntie Afriyie shows it is quite possible to reconcile such renunciation with aggressive and profitable trading, both intellectually and in practice.

Final Examination

The deepest lessons embedded in this collection arise directly from the diversity of the narratives selected. Their divergence challenges common assumptions about the relation of social positionality to analytic perspective, because their authors broadly share categories of ethnicity, gender, occupational status, nationality, and age. Identity analysis tends to map variation as if society were a mosaic of single-color chips. The meaningful sociocultural unit is identified or assessed by searching for a homogenous response, initially within the boundaries of expected social cleavages. Residual variations are then explained away by sufficiently multiplying subcategories to identify smaller homogenous units, for example class fractions or personal status categories—-relative success, historical cohort, or other life experiences.

Postmodern modes of analysis have been highly productive in generating awareness of the complexity of difference, yet they can still privilege homogeneity indirectly or unconsciously. When they sensationalize its absence within widely accepted identities, they imply that this absence undermines the validity of those identities. Arguing this point from deconstruction analyses still tacitly presumes that truly valid social categories would indeed speak with unanimous voices, even while denouncing such categories as an unattainable mirage. This argument discredits the legitimacy of organizing principles based on non-homogenous identifications, the only ones that actually exist and have social effectiveness. It may glorify them as play, when many practitioners are deadly serious, even struggling for their lives.

Insights that arise from personal intellectual invention and emotional subjectivity, no longer tied to the measuring stick of representativeness manqué, unleash their potential to generate broader meanings and deeper resonances by means of uncommon juxtapositions. The irreducible multiplicity of voices then becomes a rich resource with the potential to widen analytic perspectives and deepen understanding of the equally complex currents of social change and development. Those currents are so contradictory themselves, always and everywhere, that following a path defined by contradictions paradoxically offers more direct access to their core generative processes.

Walking away from the dream of homogeneity makes room for taking contingent and situational identifications seriously on their own terms. A more radically relational analysis seems particularly appropriate to these Asante market women, whose moral and economic understandings place such emphasis on relationality. Their ambitions for upward mobility are achieved through strengthening relationships, not shucking them off. They debate the right and wrong of specific actions in terms of their effects on others, not only their conformity to abstract principles of equality or entitlement. They evaluate the economy in terms not just of its fairness or benefit to themselves, but of the opportunities for engagement it presents to others in the community.

Leaving behind the urge to categorize opens a way to move beyond learning *about* diversity to learning *from* diversity itself. The unique characteristics of each of these stories will also find distinct resonances within each reader. By awakening multiple cross-cutting identifications, these subjective contradictions establish a virtual analog to the dialogic relationship negotiated during fieldwork between the narrator and the recorder. Since such a relationship generated the stories in the first place, allowing it to be replicated in the reading experience marks a particularly direct path to learning from them.

Relational analysis stimulates a critical appraisal of every relationship, close or distant. It validates incorporating diverse perspectives into local discussions as well as into international policy debates. Even local audiences that share many of a speaker's social identities and experiences will not therefore already know most of what she may have to say. Conversely, global audiences also can expect to find at least some accessible bridges among the many possible connections. These situational commonalities enable new understandings to take root and grow within a framework of active, two-way relationships that include the concrete and the imaginary. The beauty and inspiring character of these stories need not be discounted for them to inform economic and social processes, with substantial material consequences.

APPENDIX

Parallel Passages in the Stages of Transcription, Translation, and Editing

FIRST EXAMPLE

1a: Twi transcript by Mr. Yeboah

Nhoo, ampa deɛ, tetehɔ asetena no deɛ, ene ɛnnɛ Ghana deɛ yi, ɛbɔ abira nanso deɛ anya aba no, yɛse, ɛno na ɛyɛ. Anka tetehɔ no na yɛte hɔ no, woyɛ aketeesia, wosi so a, wonnyiniie no, yɛn maamenom koraa, wonnyiniie no, mmɔwerɛ koraa, wommubu, yɛse, wonkyimae; wobubu wo mmɔwerɛ a, woahunu amane. Wokyima a, ansa na yɛbɛbubuo. Ennɛ yɛnkyima. Akɔdaa te hɔ ara a, wobɛhwɛ ara na ɔnyem. Sɛ ɔnyem a, waru kwan, wonhunu. Akane no nso, yɛn, yɛma yɛn Kyima a, wo papa na ɛde wo bɛma awadeɛ. Sɛ oyi na yɛpɛ, ware no. Ɔfiri efie yei mu. Efie hɔ yɛ enti wokɔ awadeɛ no a, papa bɛba, na wokɔ. Ampa ara nso, enti na tetehɔ no, yɛnwowo nnipa basabasa wɔ fie. Wohwɛ efie bi mua, na ɛhɔ nnipa no, sɛnee yɛsi teɛ no na yɛhwɛ.

1b: English translation by Mr. Asiedu

Yes, it is true that life in the past and that of Ghana today are quite opposite but what has come is what we say is good. In the ancient days, when we were sitting there, when you are an adolescent, in your prime of life, you are not yet fully grown, even our mothers at all, when you are not fully grown, you don't cut your finger and toe nails; it is said that you have not reached puberty age; when you trim your nails, you are in trouble. You reach puberty age before they are trimmed. Today, they don't reach puberty age. Suddenly, you find a child pregnant. When she is pregnant, she travels so you don't see it. Formerly too, when they perform the puberty rites for us, your father will give you to someone for marriage. "This man is the one we like, marry him. He comes from this house. That house is good so if you are married into it, goodness will come" and you go. Really true too; in the ancient times, rough people were not born at home. If you go into some homes, you would like to observe how the people in the house are like.

1c: Published version by Dr. Clark

Yes, it is true that life in the past and life in Ghana today are quite opposite, but what has arrived now is what we say is good. What it was like long ago, when we were young, was this: if you were a young girl, you had grown but you were not mature. Our mothers insisted, if you were not grown up, you didn't even trim your nails. They would say, you haven't grown up yet. If you trimmed your nails, you would be in trouble. You would start your periods before they trimmed your nails. Today, they don't wait to grow up. A girl is just standing there, and you will see that she is pregnant. If she gets pregnant, she even travels away so you won't see it. In the old days, we let the girl mature.

Then your father would give you in marriage. "If this is the one we like, marry him. He is from that house. That house is good, so if you go to marry him, good will come of it," and you went. It was really true, too, that in the old days they didn't have children every which way [*basabasa*] at home. You observed a house closely then, and the people there, you watched how they lived.

SECOND EXAMPLE

2a: Twi transcript by Mr. Yeboah

Mako, seesei, abu. Abosome enum mu ni, abu. Woba a, mɛkyerɛ wo. Mabubu, mabubu ne tiri no, na mede bɛsi gya so. Meremfa nsuo ngu mu, na mafa rɔba na mede akara dadesɛn no so, na egya no, ɛrebɔ ɛtoɔ, dadesɛn no so, na egya no, ɛrebɔ ɛtoɔ, dadesɛn no to. Nkakrankakra nkakrankakra nkakrankakra nkakrankakra; na tuto aba mu. Afei, mɛbue rɔba no a, na ɛkyerɛ sɛ kaa no, yɛwuraa mu, woahu sɛ na emu yɛ heɛ? (Hoo) Eti yɛhinihinii nhwehwɛ no na mframa baa mu. Enti mekɔbue rɔba no a, na ani deɛ no nyinaa abene; na abene na masesa na mede kɔ nkyɛnsee no akyi na mede akɔgu hɔ. Ebedi three days na awia no abɔ no na awo, na masesa agu bɔtɔ mu. Meyɛ saa ara, ebia mesesa agu bɔtɔ mu. Meyɛ saa ara, ebia mesisa bɔtɔ bɛyɛ dumienu. Nnansa yi a mako heraeɛ no, na meretɔn. Sɛ woahu? Eyɛ nyansa. Obi nnim, obi deɛ bɛtumi abere saa ara, na wakɔto agu bɔɔla. Obi deɛ bɛbere saa ara, na

wakɔto agu bɔɔla. Ɔnni nyansa te sɛ me. Enti, nnansa yi, barima baeɛ
a, ɔse ɔde me bekɔ FM so. (Adɛn?) Mayɛ dɛn. Ɔse, wohata mako, ɛbɔn.
Mese a, owura, woayɛ mfom soɔ. Ghana, wonya nyansani baako ka me
ho a, anka ɛyɛ. Adɛn? Me, Ghana, adeɛ a ɛresɛe no, mereboaboa ano,
na ɛyera a, mayi no adi ama me nuanom anya bi adi. Sɛ obiara tumi de
bi sie a, anka adeɛ no year a, obiara yi ne deɛ ara na abu. (Anka ne bɔɔ
nyɛ den) Ne bɔɔ nyɛ den.

2b: English translation by Mr. Yeboah

Pepper, now, is plentiful. It was plentiful in five months ago. When
you come, I will show you. I have broken off the heads and I will put
it on fire. I will not put in water and I will take polythene paper and
it means that when we entered the car, did you notice that, inside was
hot? (Yes) So when we rolled down the windows, air came into it. So
when I go to remove the polythene paper, the top ones were all cooked;
they were cooked and I pick them and take them behind the roofing
sheets and put them there. About three days time, they will become dry.
If it doesn't rain to wet them, after three days, the sun will make them
become dry and I will pick them and put them in a sack. I do like that;
maybe I will gather about twelve bags. Recently when pepper became
scarce, I was selling them. Do you see? It is wisdom. Nobody knows;
that for somebody's can ripen like that and she goes to throw them away
in the rubbish dump. She has no wisdom like me. So, recently a man
came and said he will take me to FM (i.e. on the radio) (Why?) I have
done what? He said when I dry pepper it produces bad scent. I said, Sir,
you have made a mistake. If you get one wise person in addition to me
in Ghana, it would be a blessing. Why? I, in Ghana, what is spoiling, I
am gathering them together and when it becomes scarce, I may bring it
out for my sisters and brothers to get some to eat. If everyone can store
some, and the thing becomes scarce, as soon as everyone produces his/
hers, it will become abundant. (The price won't be expensive) Its price
will not be expensive.

2c: Published version by Dr. Clark

Now, pepper is plentiful. It has been plentiful for the past five
months. When you come to market, I will show you. I have broken off

the heads and I will put them on the fire. I will not put in water, but I will take a sheet of **polythene** to cover the pot. The fire heats the bottom of the pot gradually, and makes steam. Then I will remove the **polythene**. I mean, when we entered the car, did you notice that the inside was hot? When we rolled down the windows, air came into it. So when I go to remove the **polythene** sheet, even the top ones are all cooked. They are cooked and I pick them out and take them behind the roofing sheets and put them down there. In about three days' time, they will become dry. If it doesn't rain, to wet them, after three days the sun has made them dry, and I will collect them and put them in a sack. I keep doing that, and maybe I will gather about twelve bags. Recently, when pepper became scarce, I was selling them. *Wahu?* It is wisdom. Someone else doesn't know; hers can ripen like that and she goes to throw it away on the garbage dump. She has no wisdom like me.

Recently a man came, and said he will take me to the FM radio station. What have I done? He said that when I dry pepper it smells bad. I said, "Sir, you have made a mistake. If you get one wise person in Ghana in addition to me, it would be a blessing. Why? In Ghana, I am gathering together what is spoiling, and when it becomes scarce, I can bring it out for my sisters and brothers to get some to eat. If everyone could store some, and it later becomes scarce, as soon as everyone brings out theirs, it will become abundant. Its price will not be expensive."

GLOSSARY

AFRC. Armed Forces Revolutionary Council.

Agya! Literally, father! Has some of the same spectrum of usages as "God help me!" or the Italian "mamma mia!" It expresses dismay, helplessness, amazement, even censure.

Akua. Literally, a female born on Wednesday. It can be used as a nickname.

Akwasidae. A festival celebrated on a set Sunday (*Kwasiɛda*) every six weeks, by the *Asantehene* and other leading Asante chiefs. Part of the ceremony is public and part takes place very privately in the ancestral shrine.

Ampesie. A popular breakfast and lunch dish made of yams, plantains, cocoyams, or cassava that have been peeled, cut up, and boiled. It is served with stew.

Anansesɛm. A famous genre of Akan folk tales featuring Ananse the spider and other animal characters in anthropomorphic situations that are both entertaining and instructive. They often include musical interludes and explain well-known proverbs.

Anibue. Literally, eye-opening. Awareness or sophistication.

Asantehemma. See *ɔhemma.*

Asantehene. See *ɔhene.*

Basabasa. Disorderly or sloppy, as adjective or adverb. The word describes actions done at random or every which way, always with a negative connotation, and can also describe thoughtless or careless people. It is sometimes translated as "rough," but "rough" can have connotations different from those of *basabasa.*

Bragorɔ. Literally, it-has-come ceremony. The ceremony held for an Asante girl at puberty, after her first menstruation. It initiates her into adult life and introduces her and her newly legitimate fertility to her ancestors and the wider community.

Calico. An inexpensive checked cotton material often used in school uniforms. It originated in India, at Calcutta or Calicut.

Cedi. The Ghanaian unit of currency. One cedi is equal to one hundred pesewas.

Chop money. A transnational English colonial phrase meaning an amount of money paid regularly, usually daily or weekly, and intended for buying food.

Cloth. In Ghanaian usage, the word "cloth" refers only to *ntama,* the cotton "African prints" which now constitute traditional dress. Cloth can be worn uncut, by men in one large, roughly square sheet and by women in two smaller sheets. It can also be cut and sewn into the familiar "up-and-down" outfit of skirt, blouse, and cover cloth, or a variety of newer styles for men and women. Funeral cloths can be plain or with hand embroidery or Adinkra printing, instead of "African prints."

Compagnie. La Compagnie Française d'Afrique de l'Ouest (CFAO). Literally, the French West African Company. The largest French import-export firm operating in Ghana.

Collar. A style of tying a single cloth around the neck, worn by children and young people, and some royal attendants. Small children can tie a small scrap of cloth this way, and it will not fall off as they run around.

College. Used as in England for good secondary schools, but also for teacher training colleges and for technical schools that substitute for an academic secondary school or rank below university level.

De mmirika. Literally, to run. Can mean getting ahead very fast, or getting carried away.

Etɔ. The food most commonly used in rituals, but also popular for lunch. Yams or plantains are boiled and then mashed, usually with palm oil.

Ɛna. Mother.

Fufu. The signature dish of Asante, which can include yams, cocoyam (taro), plantains, or cassava. These are peeled, boiled, and then pounded in a large wooden mortar to make an elastic ball, which is served with soup poured over it.

G. A hospital in Kumasi, now named the Komfo Anokye Teaching Hospital. Before independence it was called simply Government Hospital, to distinguish it from mission hospitals, so local residents still use the abbreviation "G." It is the largest hospital in the Ashanti Region.

Garden eggs. A type of small eggplant.

Kakrakakra. Literally, little by little. Can be repeated many times to emphasize slow continuation.

Kama. Proper, nice, appropriate, complete, or satisfactory, as adjective or adverb. Often translated as "proper" or "fine."

Kenkey. A dumpling made from fermented cornmeal.

Kɔ so. Literally, to go forward. To move ahead or progress.

Kɔ w'anim. Literally, to go where your eyes are. The phrase is often used in directions to mean "go straight ahead," hence, getting ahead. It is also roughly equivalent to "progress."

Kyiribra. Literally, before it comes. Premature pregnancy, when intercourse takes place before a girl has had her *bragorɔ,* and supposedly before she has menstruated. It also means the ritual punishing such pregnancy.

Material. Yard goods, or textiles sold by the yard to be sewn into various kinds of clothing and household items. Does not include *ntama*.

Nkɔsoɔ. Literally, going up. Improvement, roughly equivalent to the English word "progress." It is often used to translate the English word "development."

Ntama. The familiar cotton cloth used in traditional dress and so-called "African prints." In Ghana the English word "cloth" is used only for this type of cloth. Twelve-yard lengths are sewed at the factory into bundles called a piece, so a half piece is six yards.

Ɔhemma. The female chief at each level of the Akan political hierarchy. In Asante, the highest ranking *ɔhemma* is the *Asantehemma.* In the market, the title is used for leaders of predominantly Akan female commodity groups, prefixed by their commodity. For example, the yam queen is called the *Bayerehemma.*

Ɔhene. The male chief at each level of the Akan political hierarchy. In Asante, the highest ranking *ɔhene* is the *Asantehene.* In the market, the title is used for some leaders of predominantly Akan male craft groups. For example, the chief shoemaker is called the *Mpaboahene.*

Ɔkwansu, *plural* nkwansu. Literally, on the road. The story told by a newly arrived guest to explain the reason for the visit.

Papa. The English word may be used in Twi for any adult man.

PNDC. People's National Defence Council.

SAP. Structural Adjustment Programme.

Sister. The English word may be used affectionately in Twi for any woman of about one's own age.

Trotro. A passenger vehicle for urban public transport, originally a modified Bedford truck. Trotros now include minivans, small buses, and other motor vehicles. The original fare was threepence; *trɔ trɔ* means "three three."

UAC. The United Africa Company, the largest British import-export firm in Ghana, created during the colonial period by the merger of several smaller firms.

Wahu? Literally, have you seen? Seeing is a metaphor for understanding, learning, figuring out, and experiencing the consequences.

Woate? Literally, have you heard? Hearing is a metaphor for paying attention and obeying a request or command from a senior person.

Woate aseɛ? Literally, have you heard the underneath? Asks if the listener has understood both a stated fact and its meaning, causes, and consequences.

NOTES

INTRODUCTION

1. In 1979, the ruling Armed Forces Revolutionary Council ordered the demolition of markets in all of Ghana's regional capitals (Robertson 1983). Kumasi Central Market was spared the complete leveling seen elsewhere, but only the section within the original market walls remained standing.

2. They used the English word, see p.18.

1. ABENAA ADIIYA

1. A huge car and truck repair area in Kumasi was built up on the site of a World War II ammunition depot, called in British usage a magazine.

2. In this passage she uses the English words "civilized" and "civilization." They have been given here as "modern" and "modernization."

3. A "nursing mother" is one whose efforts are dedicated to her children's daily subsistence. See Clark 2001b.

4. Older traders still speak of prices in pounds and pence, using the exchange rate that was standard when cedis were first introduced: two cedis to one British pound.

5. These are all tomato-producing villages.

6. The Fantis are an Akan ethnic group on the Atlantic coast.

7. Nursing-mother work earns only enough for subsistence; see Clark 2001b.

8. There are two chiefs of the whole Asante people, a man and a woman from the same royal family. The woman, the *Asantehemma,* is formally senior to the *Asantehene.* In Ghanaian English, the title *ɔhemma* is conventionally translated as "queen mother."

9. The *Akwasidae* is celebrated every six weeks, or forty-two days.

10. Men from the town of Gao in Mali nearly monopolize the role of carrying goods in this market.

11. Kuro foforɔ mu is a Kumasi suburb.

12. The gates of Kumasi Central Market close at 6 PM and reopen at 6 AM. Cars that arrive overnight often wait just outside the gates on the streets leading in, so they can unload first in the morning.

13. These are all Kumasi suburban neighborhoods.

2. MAAME KESEWAA

1. Passbook accounts were the standard form of secured credit at European firms in West Africa. The store manager recorded the initial deposit, the goods taken out, the payments made, and the commissions in a small account book that the customer carried with her, like a savings account passbook.

2. The United Africa Company is one of the largest British import/export firms. It was created by the merger of several older firms.

3. The "African prints" called cloth come in twelve-yard lengths, so a half piece is six yards.

4. The district commissioner (DC) was the lowest-ranking colonial administrator. After independence, the title was retained for officials at the same level of local government.

5. In the 1979 currency exchange enterprise, all existing banknotes had to be exchanged for new ones at a ratio of 10:7 within a month, after which they became worthless.

6. Women traders might carry large sums tied into waist sashes.

7. To "weed the house" means to cut the grass and weeds in the yard.

8. ATL, TTL, and GTP are major textile companies in Ghana.

9. Paterson Zochonis (PZ) is another old, large import firm.

10. Hawkers sell from a head tray while walking around a neighborhood or market.

3. MADAME ATAA

1. G. P. Ollivant and the Compagnie Française d'Afrique Orientale (CFAO) were old, large import firms.

2. The "boys' quarters" style is a row of single rooms with a separate bath and kitchen attached. In the colonial period, servants' quarters were built in this style, behind the main house.

3. Kwame Nkrumah was prime minister of the Gold Coast from 1952 to 1957, and prime minister and then president of independent Ghana from 1957 to 1966.

4. The naming or "outdooring" ceremony generally takes place on the seventh day after the child's birth.

5. For a long time, City Hotel was the most glamorous hotel in Kumasi.

6. Theft, alcoholism, asthma, and certain other problems were considered hereditary.

7. Passbook holders were only allowed to withdraw their accumulated commission and deposit for a few approved purposes, including marriage and building a house. They could not use the money to buy from another firm.

8. "France" here means the former French colonies bordering Ghana.

9. The dash or *tosu* is an extra amount of goods added to a purchase as a gift.

10. Some varieties of cassava contain enough cyanide to be toxic, if not prepared very carefully.

11. Anwona Patuo owned the first commercial minibus in Kumasi.

12. G is the common name for the main government teaching hospital in Kumasi.

13. She is contrasting two-piece outfits sewn from printed cotton "cloth" in a distinctive local style, called "up and down," to European-style clothing bought ready-made or sewn from "material," especially one-piece dresses.

14. Rawlings's second coup, in 1981, was called the December 31st Revolution. For details, see Clark 1988.

15. Seamstresses, like traders, usually call their apprentices their children, their "boys" or their "girls."

16. She means Moslems, who fast each year during the month of Ramadan.

17. Christians hold a thanksgiving service after a child is born, when the mother first returns to church. The father should give the mother a new cloth for the occasion.

18. Ewe people live in southern Togo and Ghana's Volta Region.

19. Tema is an artificial harbor and planned town just east of Accra.

4. AMMA POKUAA

1. Akua Konadu is my Asante name.

2. She uses a bag of two hundred cowries, a unit of shell currency used before British rule, to mean two hundred cedis, the current national currency.

3. This is a polite way of referring to a slave who has been integrated into the family in a subordinate position. When a matrilineage has no child-bearing women left, the children of these domestic slaves are its only next generation. Lineages in this demographic crisis sometimes bought women to become slave wives for the purpose of bearing heirs.

4. Since a mother's sister is also called "mother," her children are called "my mother's children." The same word for "sister" or "brother" applies, but this is a way of politely distinguishing maternal cousins from siblings. Paternal cousins would never be called siblings, either in Twi or English, but are sometimes called "my father's children" if they are children of the father's brother. All of a woman's children are siblings, even if they have different fathers; one has to note that fact explicitly.

5. AUNTIE AFRIYIE

1. She refers to a variety provided by the Ghana Department of Agriculture.

2. A standard black plastic or rubber bucket is used to measure many commodities, as is an empty kerosene tin.

3. Many northern communities have distinctive patterns of facial scarification, which Asante do not.

4. These are large statues at traffic circles and other major intersections.

5. Dunkirk is a Kumasi road junction.

6. "Ashtown" is short for Ashanti New Town, or Kuro fofoɔ mu.

7. Kejetia is the central loading yard for passenger buses and trucks, across from the market.

6. SISTER BURONYA

1. The Aliens Compliance Order of 1969 forced many foreign merchants to return home abruptly.

2. Ghana borders several former French colonies.

3. There are legends about magic money that always returns to the original owner somehow.

4. This was a truck with wooden benches fitted in the back, that carried freight and passengers between villages. Salt was scarce in the forest zone, so travelers returning from the city would usually bring some back as gifts.

7. MAAME NKRUMAH

1. *Kyiribra* literally means "before it comes."

2. A euphemism for menstruation, first sex, and childbirth, all involving a show of blood.

3. Most Asante look down on ethnic groups from the Northern and Upper Regions of Ghana.

4. A baton or billy club.

5. *Fufu,* especially boiled and pounded yam, is more expensive and time-consuming to make than other dishes.

6. The chief commissioner of Ashanti (CCA) was the governing British colonial official for the region.

7. The Yorubas live in southwestern Nigeria.

8. Kwasi Agyeman is a former chairman of the Kumasi City Council, notoriously corrupt.

9. This older sister was the sixth-born.

10. This means that she was old enough to be weaned.

11. That is, he had not taken care of their financial needs.

12. Nigerian Yorubas were expelled in large numbers in 1969, along with other non-Ghanaian traders, under the Aliens Compliance Order.

13. Shallots harvested in Anloga, on the east coast of Ghana, have their green stems braided together to dry. The dry hands are woven together into huge round stacks.

14. A street outside the east edge of the market named for the Muslim prayer "Allah Akhbar."

15. Akua Nsiah is her sister, the onion queen; the KMC is the Kumasi Metropolitan Council.

16. The line of wholesale yards on the west edge of the market.

17. *Ewiam* literally means "out in the sun." It is an area where no permanent stalls have been built.

CONCLUSION

1. The word is actually *kama;* reduplication is used to intensify the meaning of many common words.

REFERENCES

Abu, Katherine. 1983. "The Separateness of Spouses: Conjugal Resources in an Ashanti Town." In *Female and Male in West Africa,* ed. Christine Oppong, 156–68. London: Allen and Unwin.

Afonja, Simi. 1986. "Land Control: A Critical Factor in Yoruba Gender Subordination." In *Women and Class in Africa,* ed. Claire Robertson and Iris Berger, 78–91. New York: Africana.

Amadiume, Ifi. 1987. *Male Daughters, Female Husbands: Gender and Sex in an African Society.* London: Zed Books.

Appiah, Joseph. 1990. *Joe Appiah: The Autobiography of an African Patriot.* New York: Praeger.

Appiah, Peggy. 2001. *Bu me be: Akan Proverbs.* Accra, Ghana: The Centre for Intellectual Renewal.

Arhin, Kwame. 1979. *West African Traders in the Nineteenth and Twentieth Centuries.* London: Longman.

Barnes, Sandra. 1986. *Patrons and Power: Creating a Political Community in Metropolitan Lagos.* Bloomington: Indiana University Press.

Behar, Ruth. 1993. *Translated Woman: Crossing the Border with Esperanza's Story.* Boston: Beacon Press.

Bratton, Angela R. 2004. "Teenage Pregnancy, Education, and the Construction of Sexuality in Ghana." Ph.D. diss., Indiana University.

Brown, Karen McCarthy. 1991. *Mama Lola: A Vodou Priestess in Brooklyn.* Berkeley: University of California Press.

Chernoff, John. 2004. *Hustling Is Not Stealing: Stories of an African Bar Girl.* Chicago: University of Chicago Press.

Clark, Gracia, ed. 1988. *Traders versus the State: Anthropological Approaches to Unofficial Economies.* Boulder, Colo.: Westview.

———. 1990. "Class Alliances and Class Fractions in Ghanaian Trading and State Formation." *Review of African Political Economy* 17(49) (winter 1990): 73–82.

———. 1991. "Food Traders and Food Security." In *The Political Economy of African Famine: The Class and Gender Basis of Hunger,* ed. R. E. Downs, Donna O. Kerner, and Stephen P. Reyna, 227–56. London: Gordon and Breach.

———. 1994. *Onions Are My Husband: Survival and Accumulation by West African Market Women.* Chicago: University of Chicago Press.

———. 1999. "Mothering, Work, and Gender in Urban Asante Ideology and Practice." *American Anthropologist* 101(4): 2–28.

———. 2001a. "Gender and Profiteering: Ghana's Market Women as Devoted Mothers and 'Human Vampire Bats.'" In *"Wicked" Women and the Reconfiguration of Gender in Africa,* ed. Dorothy Hodgson and Sheryl McCurdy, 293–311. New York: Heinemann.

———. 2001b. "Nursing-Mother Work: Power and Frustration in Asante Women's Lives." In *Women Traders in Cross-Cultural Perspective: Mediating Identities, Marketing Wares,* ed. Linda Seligman, 103–26. Stanford, Calif.: Stanford University Press.

————. 2002. "Market Association Leaders' Strategic Use of Language and Narrative in Market Disputes and Negotiations in Kumasi, Ghana." *Africa Today* 49(1–2): 43–59.

Clark, Gracia, and Takyiwaa Manuh. 1991. "Women Traders in Ghana and the Structural Adjustment Programme." In *Structural Adjustment and African Women Farmers,* ed. Christina H. Gladwin, 217–38. Gainesville: University of Florida Press.

Cole, Catherine. 2001. *Ghana's Concert Party Theater.* Bloomington: Indiana University Press.

Coontz, Stephanie. 1992. *The Way We Never Were.* New York: Basic Books.

Cornia, Giovanni, Richard Jolly, and Frances Stewart, eds. 1987. *Adjustment with a Human Face.* Oxford: Clarendon.

Daily Graphic (Accra). 1979. Letter to the editor, June 23.

Eades, Jeremy S. 1979. "Kinship and Entrepreneurship among Yoruba in Northern Ghana." In *Strangers in African Societies,* ed. William A. Shack and Elliott P. Skinner, 169–82. Berkeley: University of California Press.

Eames, Elizabeth. 1988. "Why Women Went to War: Women and Wealth in Ondo Town, Southern Nigeria." In *Traders versus the State,* ed. Gracia Clark, 81–98. Boulder, Colo.: Westview.

Escobar, Arturo. 1994. *Encountering Development: The Making and Unmaking of the Third World.* Princeton, N.J.: Princeton University Press.

Fortes, Meyer. 1970. *Time and Social Structure and Other Essays.* London: Athlone.

Geiger, Susan. 1986. "Women's Life Histories—Method and Content." *Signs* 11(2): 334–51.

————. 1997. *TANU Women: Gender and Culture in the Making of Tanganyikan Nationalism, 1955–1965.* Portsmouth, N.H.: Heinemann.

Granada Television. 1983. *Asante Market Women.* Video. London: Granada Television International.

Haraway, Donna. 1988. "Situated Knowledges: The Science Question in Feminism and the Privilege of the Partial Perspective." *Feminist Studies* 14(3): 573–99.

Hill, Polly. 1966. "Landlords and Brokers." *Cahiers d'Etudes Africaines* 6:349–66.

————. 1969. "Hidden Trade in Hausaland." *Man* 4(3): 392–409.

Hopkins, A. G. 1973. *An Economic History of West Africa.* New York: Columbia University Press.

Huxley, Elspeth. 1954. *Four Guineas.* London: Chatto and Windus.

Kendall, Laurel. 1988. *The Life and Hard Times of a Korean Shaman: Of Tales and the Telling of Tales.* Honolulu: University of Hawaii Press.

King, Rudith. 1999. "The Role of Urban Market Women in Local Development Processes and Its Implications for Policy: A Case Study of Kumasi Central Market, Ghana." Ph.D. diss., University of Sussex.

Kwanteng, Nana Yaw, Omantihene. 1946. *Palaver Held at the Central Market, Kumasi on Sunday the 13th October, 1946.* Kumasi: Asantehene's Record Office.

Kyei, T. E. 2001. *Our Days Dwindle: Memories of My Childhood Days in Asante.* Portsmouth, N.H.: Heinemann.

Little, Kenneth. 1973. *African Women in Towns.* Cambridge: Cambridge University Press.

Lurie, Nancy Oestreich. 1961. *Mountain Wolf Woman, Sister of Crashing Thunder: The Autobiography of a Winnebago Indian.* Ann Arbor: University of Michigan Press.

MacGaffey, Janet. 1991. *The Real Economy of Zaire.* Philadelphia: University of Pennsylvania Press.

Manuh, Takyiwaa. 1999. "Migrants and Citizens: Economic Crisis in Ghana and the Search for Opportunity." Ph.D. diss., Indiana University.

Marees, Pieter de. [1602] 1987. *Description and Historical Account of the Gold Kingdom of Guinea.* Ed. and trans. Albert van Dantzig and Adam Jones. Oxford: Oxford University Press.

Maynard, Mary, and June Purvis. 1994. "Doing Feminist Research." In *Researching Women's Lives from a Feminist Perspective,* ed. Mary Maynard and June Purvis, 1–9. London: Taylor and Francis.

Mbilinyi, Marjorie. 1989. "'I'd have been a man': Politics and the Labor Process in Producing Personal Narratives." In *Interpreting Women's Lives: Feminist Theory and Personal Narratives,* ed. The Personal Narratives Group, 204–22. Bloomington: Indiana University Press.

McCaskie, T. C. 2000. *Asante Identities: History and Modernity in an African Village, 1850–1950.* London: Edinburgh University Press for the International African Institute.

Menchú, Rigoberta. 1984. *I, Rigoberta Menchú: An Indian Woman in Guatemala.* London: Verso.

Meyer, Birgit. 1999. *Translating the Devil.* Trenton, N.J.: Africa World Press.

Mikell, Gwendolyn. 1989. *Cocoa and Chaos in Ghana.* New York: Paragon Press.

———. 1997. *African Feminism: The Politics of Survival in Sub-Saharan Africa.* Philadelphia: University of Pennsylvania Press.

Mintz, Sidney. 1960. *Worker in the Cane: A Puerto Rican Life History.* Westport, Conn.: Greenwood Press.

Moran, Mary H. 1990. *Civilized Women: Gender and Prestige in Southeastern Liberia.* Ithaca, N.Y.: Cornell University Press.

Nkrumah, Kwame. 1957. *The Autobiography of Kwame Nkrumah.* New York: Thomas Nelson.

Obeng, Samuel. 1997. "Language and Politics: Indirectness in Political Discourse." *Discourse & Society* 8(1): 49–83.

Obeng, Samuel, and Beverly Stoeltje. 2002. "Women's Voices in Akan Juridical Discourse." *Africa Today* 49(1–2): 21–42.

Okali, Christine. 1983. *Cocoa and Kinship in Ghana: The Matrilineal Akan of Ghana.* London: Kegan Paul for the International African Institute.

Okonjo, Kamene. 1981. "Women's Political Participation in Nigeria." In *The Black Woman Cross-Culturally,* ed. Filomina Chioma Steady, 79–106. Cambridge, Mass.: Schenkman.

Ong, Aihwa. 1988. "Colonialism and Modernity: Feminist Representations of Women in Non-Western Societies." *Inscriptions* 3–4: 125–49.

Oppong, Christine. 1974. *Marriage among a Matrilineal Elite.* Cambridge: Cambridge University Press.

———, ed. 1983. *Female and Male in West Africa.* London: Allen and Unwin.

Overå, Ragnhild. 2007. "When Men Do Women's Work: Structural Adjustment, Unemployment, and Changing Gender Relations in the Informal Economy of Accra, Ghana." *Journal of Modern African Studies* 45(4): 539–63.

Patai, Daphne. 1991. "U.S. Academics and Third World Women: Is Ethical Research Possible?" In *Women's Words: The Feminist Practice of Oral History,* ed. Sherna Berger Gluck and Daphne Patai, 137–53. New York: Routledge.

Personal Narratives Group, ed. 1989. *Interpreting Women's Lives: Feminist Theory and Personal Narratives.* Bloomington: Indiana University Press.

Rattray, R. S. 1923. *Ashanti.* Oxford: Clarendon.

Robertson, C. 1983. "The Death of Makola and Other Tragedies: Male Strategies against a Female-Dominated System." *Canadian Journal of African Studies* 17(3): 469–95.

Sarpong, Peter. 1977. *Girls' Nubility Rites in Ashanti.* Tema, Ghana: Ghana Publishing Corp.

Schildkrout, Enid. 1978a. *People of the Zongo.* Cambridge: Cambridge University Press.

———. 1978b. "Roles of Children in Urban Kano." In *Sex and Age as Principles of Social Differentiation,* ed. J. S. La Fontaine, 108–37. London: Academic Press.

Seligmann, Linda J. 1989. "To Be in Between: The Cholas as Market Women." *Comparative Studies in Society and History* 31: 694–721.

Sen, Amartya. 1981. *Poverty and Famines: An Essay on Entitlement and Deprivation.* Oxford: Clarendon.

Sen, Gita. 1985. *Development, Crisis and Alternative Visions: Third World Women's Perspective.* New Delhi: Development Alternatives with Women for a New Era.

Stoeltje, Beverly. 2000. "Gender Ideologies and Discursive Practices in Asante." *Political and Legal Anthropology Review* 23(2): 77–88.

Sudarkasa, Niara. 1973. *Where Women Work: A Study of Yoruba Women in the Marketplace and in the Home.* Ann Arbor: University of Michigan Press.

———. 1979. "From Stranger to 'Alien': The Sociopolitical History of the Nigerian Yoruba in Ghana, 1900 to 1970." In *Strangers in African Societies,* ed. William A. Shack and Elliott P. Skinner, 167–72. Berkeley: University of California Press.

Trager, Lillian. 1985. "From Yams to Beer in a Nigerian City: Expansion and Change in Informal Sector Trade Activity." In *Markets and Marketing: Proceedings of the 1984 Meeting of the Society for Economic Anthropology,* ed. Stuart Plattner, 259–85. Monographs in Economic Anthropology. Lanham, Md.: University Press of America.

Van Allen, Judith. 1972. "'Sitting on a Man': Colonialism and the Lost Political Institutions of Igbo Women." *Canadian Journal of African Studies* 6(2): 165–81.

van Dantzig, Albert. 1980. *Forts and Castles of Ghana.* Accra: Sedco.

White, E. Frances. 1982. "Women, Work and Ethnicity: The Sierra Leone Case." In *Women and Work in Africa,* ed. Edna G. Bay, 19–34. Boulder, Colo.: Westview.

———. 1987. *Sierra Leone's Settler Women Traders: Women on the Afro-European Frontier.* Ann Arbor: University of Michigan Press.

Wilks, Ivor. 1975. *Asante in the Nineteenth Century: The Structure and Evolution of a Political Order.* London: Cambridge University Press.

Wolf, Diane L. 1996. "Situating Feminist Dilemmas in Fieldwork." In *Feminist Dilemmas in Fieldwork,* ed. Diane L. Wolf, 1–55. Boulder, Colo.: Westview.

World Bank. 1981. *Accelerated Development in Sub-Saharan Africa: An Agenda for Action.* Washington, D.C.: World Bank.

World Bank and United Nations Development Programme. 1989. *Africa's Adjustment and Growth in the 1980s.* Washington, D.C.: World Bank.

Yankah, Kwesi. 1995. *Speaking for the Chief: Okyeame and the Politics of Akan Royal Oratory.* Bloomington: Indiana University Press.

INDEX

Italicized page numbers indicate illustrations.

Anibue, 22, 52, 230
  (used), 78, 91, 93, 101, 118, 192

Bargaining, 37, 91, 118–119, 177, 191,
  203, 207, 212, 214–215
Basabasa (used), 22, 74, 95, 116–117,
  131, 142, 188–189, 198
Bible stories, 132–133, 149–150, 153,
  242
Bolgatanga, 44–45
Bragɔrɔ. See Puberty ceremony

Capital, 15, 17, 30, 32, 36, 40–41,
  46–49, 64, 66–68, 74, 80, 90, 97,
  113–118, 120–122, 125, 130,
  165, 182, 220–221, 224–225,
  236, 241
Carriers, *110,* 169
Chiefs, 23–24, 44–43, 133, 147, 152,
  229
Childbearing, 25, 34, 48, 52, 86, 89,
  93–94, 115–116, 123, 128, 142,
  200, 233, 241–242
Children, 15, 25, 48, 64, 67, 76,
  80–81, 83, 89–90, 92, 94–95,
  100, 104, *107, 111,* 113–116,
  120–122, 159, 180, 184, 191,
  195, 200, 225–226, 233–234
Chop money, 25, 34, 47, 49, 51, 65,
  68–69, 84, 90–91, 103, 115,
  122, 124–125, 178, 180–181,
  190–191, 222, 234
Christianity, 30, 47, 54–55, 83, 86,
  101, 116–117, 136, 167, 186,
  204, 207, 209, 214, 219, 237–
  238, 241–243
  end times, 17, 32
Cloth, *62,* 63–64, 66, 67–69, 73, 80,
  89–90, 93, 95–98, 101–102, *105,*
  124, 143, 173, 178, 191, 193,
  205, 211

Cocoa, 26, 33
  farms, 25, 27, 123–125, 127,
    195, 204
  picking at UAC shed, 64, 83, 91
Commodity groups, 6–7, 16, 37,
  43–44, 53, *62,* 234, 239
Cooked foods, 115–117, 120
Cooking, 67, 92, 103–104, 190–191,
  204, 206–207
Cosmetics, *59–61*
Credit, 7, 37–38, 70, 73, 178, 182–
  186, 217, 220, 236
  lending money, 36, 40, 70, 75,
    80, 152, 183, 221, 237
  to/from suppliers, 38, 40–41,
    64, 66, 73, 77, 99, 115,
    121, 172, 215–216
Customers, 16, 38–40, 66, 73, 174,
  180, 214, 235–236

Drains, 153–155, 158, 200

Economic cycles, 1–2, 6, 17, 52, 70, 83,
  90, 91, 112, 120, 168, 193, 207,
  214, 216, 227–228, 241
Editing, 18–21, 65, 89, 93, 95, 116,
  120, 131, 135, 188, 235, 247–250
Education, 25, 30, 34, 45–46, 48, 85,
  89, 93, 95, 116, 120, 135, 165,
  167, 173–175, 180, 201, 203,
  211, 221–227, 231, 238
Emigration, 17, 30, 47–48, 50, 54, 68,
  90, 115, 117, 120, 125, 137, 142,
  150–151, 167, 169–170, 176, 219
English, use of, 21–22, 40, 93
Ethnicity, 41
  assignment of trading roles by,
    6, 27

Farm labor, 24, 64, 72, 103, 118, 166,
  202, 204

Father, 88, 95, 114–115, 117, 120–124,
    135, 188–189, 200–201, 205,
    221, 232
Food farming, 24, 67, 72, 75, 86, 119,
    127–128, 135, 147, 151, 166,
    191–192, 203
Food shortages, 10, 37, 42, 120
Fridge (refrigerator), 49, 79, 86, 203

Geiger, Susan, ix, 8
Gender, 6, 25
    assignment of trading roles, 6,
        26–27
    ideals, 6, 24–26, 28–29
    tensions, 6, 7, 27
Grandchildren, 30, 64, 116, 150, 187–
    188, 200–201, 220

Happiness, 165–168, 192, 204
Hard work, 102–103, 120, 166, 168–
    170, 181, 183, 205, 211, 219,
    223–234, 229, 239, 242
Hawking, 81, 121, 135, 144, *157,* 162
Hometown, 72, 74–75, 203, 209, 224
House-building, 16, 47–50, 52, *62,*
    64, 66, 69, 73–76, 83–84, 89–91,
    100, *112,* 124, 137, 167, 188,
    198, 200
Humor, 17–18, 64, 113
Husband, 66, 221

Illness, 119, 221
Inflation, 6, 65, 70, 116. *See also* Prices
Inheritance, 24–25, 45, 103, 114, 117,
    123–125, 151, 194–195, 222
International trade, 23, 102, 173–174,
    182, 215

Kejetia lorry park, 6, 152
Ko verb phrases, 2, 12, 118, 132–133,
    182, 231
        ko so (used), 85, 118, 204, 222

Landlord, 77–78, 185, 199, 219
Layout of market, *45*
Lineage kin, 15, 24–25, 124–125, 167,
    181, 187–188, 194–195, 202,
    220, 234, 239

Little by little, 15, 61, 69, 74–78, 80,
    84, 120, 151, 170–171, 176, 178,
    181, 183–184, 195, 207, 229

Market queen, 81–82, 131, 149–150,
    219, 234
Marriage, 16, 34–35, 47, 67, 85–86,
    103–104, 115–116, 180–181,
    200, 205, 207, 241
    age at, 14, 24, 85, 88, 94, 120
    arranged, 85, 87, 95, 125,
        134–135, 142, 188–189
    relationships, 25–26, 85–86,
        97, 103, 181, 209–210, 222
Matriliny, 6, 24–25, 194, 231
Methodology, ethnographic, 1, 7–9,
    11–15, 113, 116, 130, 165–166,
    187, 238, 244
    life history, 8–9, 11–14, 17–18,
        22–23, 29, 164, 218, 237
Modernization, 35, 53, 101, 118, 131,
    229
Mothers, 45, 71, 87, 97, *112,* 113–115,
    117, 233
    nursing, 4, 120
    training by, 45, 48, 90, 113,
        115, 118, 120, 135–136,
        148, 165, 172, 221, 225

Narrative, 9–15, 17–19, 23, 29, 114,
    117, 241, 243–244
Negotiation, 149
Neighborhood markets, 2, *3,* 54, 235
Nigeria, 46, 85, 114, 173, 196
Northerners, 152, 190, 193, 212

Onions, 58, 159–160
Oversupply, 140–141, 148

Palm oil, 64–66, 68, 70, *81, 107,* 130,
    136–137, 141, 151, 155
Passbooks, 64–66, 68, 70, 84, 89–90,
    95–99, 172, 221
Pawns, 71
Police, 94, 190, 198, 217
Political conditions, 3–4, 26–27
Population growth, 53, 203, 240
Pounds (sterling, UK currency), prices

cited in, 68–70, 84–85, 90, 117–120, 177–188, 196, 211
Price control, 7, 17, 27, 63, 79, 97, 225, 227
Prices, 32–33, 35–36, 86, 90–91, 96–97, 101–102, 118, 120–121, 129, 134, 188–190, 205, 219, 232, 242. *See also* Inflation
Proverbs, 10–11, 135, 151–153
Puberty ceremony, 24, 131, 134, 188–190, 205, 219, 232, 242

Regional role, 2, *3*, 102
Residence, 26, 117, 120, 124, 174, 194–195, 199–200, 220–221
Respect, 21, 94–95, 116, 134–136, 165, 175
Retail, 45, *56*, 59–62, 148, 157
Risks, 36, 41–42, 46, 169–170, 212, 223, 236

SAP (Structural Adjustment Programme), 2, 7, 16, 113, 226–227
Saving, 50, 74–75, 90, 97, 122, 159, 191, 214
Scarcity, 50, 91
Seasons, 101, 133–134, 140–141, 176–177, 209
Sewing, 83, 97, 100–101, *106*, 178, 211–212
Slavery, 114, 123
Soldiers, 6, 130
Spoilage, 37, 39, 140–141, 148, 216
Stalls, 78–79, 89, *105, 107,* 110, 130, 148, *157,* 187–188, 188, 195–

197, *201,* 215–216, 220, 222, 226, 235
Stereotypes, 23–24, 27, 206
Stores, 67–68, 80, 90, 93, 97–99, 177, 195
Streetcars, 92, 99–100, 132, 158, 191

Takoradi, 39–40
Taxes, 44, 70, 78, 102, 116, 149, 182
Teen pregnancy, 85, 93–94, 116, 135, 142, 144, 189–190, 232–233
Theft, 32, 125, 168
Tomatoes, 30–46, *56–58*
Training, 39, 52
Translation, 18–22, 231, 247–250
Travel, 30, 36, 38–39, 46, 115–117, 120, 124, 130, 172, 176, 220
Trucks, 33, 40, 42, *108,* 113, 116–117, 119, 143, 183–184, 191, 205

Urban life, 35, 86–87, 202, 224
Urban migration, 34, 64, 72, 75, 86, 124, 192, 202, 246

Villagers, 54, 86, 118, 122, 124, 129, 132, 186, 188, 191, 193, 199, 202, 209, 224, 236

Wholesale yards, *57, 108–110, 112,* 113, 157, *162–163*
Wisdom, 130, 136, 140–142, 148, 150, 157, 185, 231–232, 238, 242

Yams, 33, 72, 92, *108–110,* 113–118

Gracia Clark is Associate Professor of Anthropology at Indiana University Bloomington. She is author of *Onions Are My Husband: Survival and Accumulation by West African Market Women* and has edited several volumes dealing with gender and economic life.